Don't Call Me A Victim

Don't Call Me A Victim
Faith, Hope & Sexual Abuse in the Catholic Church
By Gary. M. Bergeron

COPYRIGHT © 2005 BY Gary M. Bergeron
Arc Angel Publishing
Printed in the United States of America

ALL RIGHTS RESERVED. No part of this work covered by the copyright hereon may be reproduced or used in any form or by any means-graphic, electronic, or mechanical, including by not limited to photocopying, recording, taping, Web distribution or information storage and retrieval systems– without the written permission of the publisher and author.

For permission to use material from this text or product please contact us
via email: information@arcangelpublishing.com
via written request :Arc Angel Publishing *P.O. Box 9134*Lowell*MA*01852

Or find us on the World Wide Web at:
www.ArcAngelPublishing.com

ISBN # 0975899341
LCCN # 2004110904

For additional copies please visit your local bookstore or order directly by visiting us on the world wide web

www.ArcAngelPublishing.com

Manufactured in Lowell, MA USA
By King Printing Company
Kingprinting.com

A portion from the proceeds of the sale of each book will go to help fund survivor support programs.

Don't Call Me A Victim

Faith, Hope & Sexual Abuse in the Catholic Church

By Gary Bergeron

Edited by Anne Driscoll

In the Archdiocese of Boston amid the evolving clergy sexual abuse scandal, a group of men from different backgrounds came together to form a unique bond. A bond, established from the common thread of being sexually abused by the same priest, and, a bond, strengthened because of their determination in preventing history from ever repeating itself. This story began over 30 years ago at the hands of a priest named Joseph Birmingham. Though they differ in ages, education, background and past histories, the horrific abuse would become a common thread that bound them in the beginning, and continued to bind them as they found out that their differences paled in comparison to the similarities they shared. Their story, which begins one Tuesday evening in the basement of a bar in Lowell, Massachusetts, would take them from that basement, to the brass doors of the Vatican one year later, and beyond.

Dedication

This book is dedicated to men like Jamie Hogan, the first man who had the courage to publicly say the name Birmingham in 30 years and to the incredible group of men who became known as the group Survivors of Joseph Birmingham.

To my parents, who, through their guidance and support taught me how to truly be a survivor.

To my sister Terry, who, through her 18 year struggle with cancer, challenged me to fight the good fight. I hope I haven't forgotten.

To my friends, Bernie and Olan. Winston Churchill once said, "It is no use saying, 'we're doing the best we can.' You've got to succeed in doing what is necessary." You have both succeeded in doing what was necessary.

For Julie

You are the wind beneath my wings.

Acknowledgments

There are many people that I would like to thank. I know that I'm going to miss some, I'm still going to give this a shot.

To brave survivors like Phil Saviano and Frank Fitzpatrick who have been at this for a lot longer than I have. Thanks for having the courage to speak up so many years ago, when it seemed like no one listened. To all those parents who tried to do the right thing decades ago, when it seemed like no one listened. To priests like father Tom Doyle, and nuns like Sister Mary LaBollita, it may have seemed like it didn't matter then and that no one was listening. Rest assured that because of your efforts, my journey and the journey of others like me has been easier. Believe me, they're listening now.

To the attorneys who have been my shield, sword and armor over the last two years at Greenburg Traurig: Bob Sherman, thanks for returning my call over two years ago and believing in me at a time when I didn't believe in myself; Eric MacLeish, for convincing me to take those 2 weeks off and motorcycle across the country, it recharged my batteries and kept me writing. I still have a scar on my thumb; Courtney Pillsbury, 2 years ago I wrote an email that said that "I'm placing my trust in you, don't let me down." Thanks, you never did ; Diane Nealon, not just a social worker, a Super Social Worker Hero. Thank you for helping us save lives, There's no other way to put it.

To Barbara and John, thank you for having the courage to see hope in us, when it was a rarity and for believing that "these might just be the guys who will get through to him."

There is not enough time for me to say thank you to the entire SOJB crew. For all the guys that went to our one hour meeting on Tuesday nights (that always lasted four hours), Paul, Tom,

Dave, Mike, Roger, Danny, Larry, Mark and Moe, thanks for arguing with me, crying with me, laughing with me, and listening to me. For a bunch of guys that "couldn't agree on what to put on a pizza", we did ok. You have truly changed my life.

Bernie and Olan, I don't know how I could have gone through the last two years without your support. For pushing me forward, and for holding me back, Thanks. Bern, the song "Lean on me" will never sound the same. Olan, thank you for our regular 2 hour conversations based on "Olanisim's."

To my Editor and friend, Anne Driscoll. Thank you for believing in what others said was not important. Thanks for picking up the phone one day and telling me that you couldn't do it my way, and thanks for telling me it was because I already did.

And finally, Thank You to the 26 publishers who said "Thanks but no thanks." You reminded me that there truly is no use in saying we did the best we could. You have to succeed in doing what is necessary. Thanks to Tom Campbell and King Printing for helping me do just that.

There may have been 26 publishers who were fearful of challenging such a powerful institution.

I think there are 65 million Catholics in this country who deserve to read a story about a few guys from Boston, who weren't .

Peace.

Gary

Introduction.

I believe that everyone in life has what some may call "a defining moment." I like to think of it in another way. In everyone's life there is one time when you have a decision to make. Its that moment in time when you can decide to do nothing, or do everything. It's that simple. Only you will know when that time is. It may be important to the world, or, more likely, important to your world. I believe that you are the only one who knows what you decide to do, because it only matters to you. Others may be affected by your decision, but only you will know what you decide to do.

For me, that moment came at the end of March of 2002. That was the day when I got the call from my mother. That was the day when a picture and a story about Fr. Joseph Birmingham, a Catholic priest who had molested me, as well as my brother (as I found out later) was front page news. That was the moment that I decided that silence was no longer an option. I wasn't sure what I was going to do, but I knew that I was going to do "something." I'm writing this during the middle of my "something." It started almost 30 years ago and I'm not sure where it is going to end. I do know that although I didn't start it, I am going to end it. And I'm going to end it on *my* terms. No one else's.

I have several reasons for writing this book. Hopefully some of the questions you have many of which I've been asked over and over again will be answered. What happened? Why did you come forward? Why did you wait so long? Isn't this all about money? Don't you think that this has been blown way out of proportion? These are some of the questions on people's minds.

This book has evolved over time. There was a time when I had attempted to sit with a writer to write this book. Over time though, it became painfully clear to me that the only way that I could tell my story, was for me to tell it this way, my way. I'm not a professional writer. I'm a carpenter, but to borrow a quote from someone else, the Ark was built by amateurs, the Titanic by professionals. The only advice I followed while I wrote this was advice given to me when I first came forward almost 3 years ago, *"Talk from the heart".*

Part of this is a healing journey for me. I know that this is the time for my story to be told. With knowledge comes power, and hopefully, with the public awareness of all of these stories, will come the power to change the future. Not my future, but the future of my children and the future of your children. Someone had once said, "Those who do not learn from history are doomed to repeat it." For our children's sake, this is one time in history that we absolutely cannot afford to repeat. By telling my story, and by others telling their stories, future parents will never have to say, "I didn't know." And future children will never have to write a letter to their family like I felt I had to write to mine.

I hope that in this story, you will find answers, healing, understanding and the realization that if you are one of the many that have suffered, or are a relative or a spouse of some one abused, and still suffering the effects of clergy abuse, you are not alone. There are many of us here and there is help.

Joseph Birmingham did not put me on the road that I am on, he took me from the road that I was once on. I'm off that detour now. I'm back on my own road. There's a difference now. I'm not a kid anymore and I'm not that child who had no choice. I'm not a victim. I'm a man, and unlike some of his victims, I survived. More than anything else, *I'm a Survivor*.

Prologue

The car door slammed shut. It was loud, too loud for this peaceful place. Did I slam it by accident, or was it because I was aggravated at myself for not being here sooner? Angry with myself because she deserved better from me?

It was late morning, the ground was still moist, the air was cool, and there wasn't a soul around. I knew that this was the first place I should have come before heading into Boston. It was only right, after all it had been a long, long time since I had visited her. I had thought about it often, but just couldn't bring myself to come back here. After Ricky had died, I visited this place often. After Terry left us, it was different. I knew why, but I didn't tell anyone. It was my secret, and up until today, I shared it with no one. Today would be different though, today it would all change. I knew that, and I knew that this is where I had to come this morning.

The slamming of the car door startled me, I was back in the present again. I walked over the grass and stared. It had been almost 10 years, but my sister's grave was exactly as I had remembered. I felt a chill, my eyes welled up. " I'm back. I'm sorry I haven't been here for so long. I've thought of you both all the time. I need you guys today." I knelt down, and kissed the stone. "Please give me the strength to do the right thing today. I promise you I'll make it right today. It's over."

I walked back to the car. Putting the car in gear, I drove out of the cemetery and headed to Boston. Whatever happens today, it's going to be different. If I do anything about this, I'm going to do the right thing. I knew that, and I knew that I had to start today. Here, on this ground where it had come back to me, hauntingly almost 10 years ago. It has stayed there in the back of my mind for almost 10 long years. Always there, never spoken of, but never having left.

It's over today. I'm going to make sure of that. I owe it to her, I made that promise a long time ago. Today I keep it.

*"If not recorded, history becomes legend...
...legend becomes myth."*

1.

My name is Gary Bergeron. I'm part of a large Catholic family in a suburb of Boston called Lowell. I have a grown daughter Katie, who is 23, and a son Evan who is 6. I've been both married and divorced twice.

My parents are Joseph and Catherine, or Kay and Eddie as everyone who knows them calls them. They've been married 52 years My mother came from a large Irish family and my dad was an only child of a French family. I was fortunate enough to have been part of a family that had a total of six boys and two girls. I'm fourth from the bottom. I also have a half brother and a half sister from my father's first marriage. My parents lost their oldest, my brother Rick, to an auto accident and their youngest, my sister Terry, to cancer.

Regardless of the endless trauma which life seems to have dealt our family, we survived it because above all else we were a family. Not the "one for all and all for one" kind of family, and definitely not the "Ozzie and Harriet" kind of family. It was actually more like "The Osborne's" meet "The Brady Bunch." I have the kind of family that no matter where I am, what I needed, or what kind of trouble I was in (and yes, I had my share), I could always pick up the phone and find support. Whenever there was any kind of crisis, no matter if it was a crisis of one, or a crisis of many, as a family, we rallied. We were, and continue to be, close. A pretty regular kind of family, probably not much different from yours.

Growing up with a family that large was fun. It was also hectic.

By the time the younger ones were born, the older ones were able to help take care. With three boys, a girl, another three boys and another girl, each of the older ones would be paired off with their younger match. It would work the same way with clothes. By the time someone had grown out of something, another was right behind ready to grow into something. That usually worked well until the younger set of boys grew into their teens. At that time it became, "Who took my new jeans?" We lived in a long ranch style home that my father designed and built in the late '60s. We each had our own bedroom. The kids had a bathroom and my parents had a bathroom. With two bathrooms at that time, you'd think we were well off. I can tell you that with eight kids fighting over bathroom time in the morning, there was nothing "well off" about it. Even as hectic as the mornings were, it was much better than where we had lived before. We used to live in a 3 bedroom house with one bath and eight kids. All the boys were in one room, complete with bunk beds that my father built. The two girls had their own room. The new house was a welcomed change. Our house also had two small apartments in it, as well. My grandmother lived in one and my aunt lived in the other.

We lived at the end of a dead end street in a small, regular neighborhood. The family next to us had 14 children. Between our two families we were large enough to have two separate sports teams. The sport that we'd play late into the night was kickball. At that time, living on a dead end street, we'd play in the middle of the road. Hot summer nights were spent playing kickball until the street lights went on, then it was time to come in. There were no worries about traffic and there were no worries about child abductions. It was a great time and a great place to grow up.

My parents were firm. Sometimes, according to my memory, probably too firm by today's standards. They were also fair and exceptionally supportive. I've often said lately that I wish that everyone who has been through what I'd been through had the parents and family that I had. I'm very fortunate. Some of the people I've met along the way have not been so fortunate. My father worked for the same floor covering company for over 30 years. When that company filed bankruptcy, he started his own business. That year was the same year that he turned 50. It was also the same year that Terry was diagnosed with cancer. My father was what most dads were in that era, he was the provider. My mother was a stay at home mom, although she usually had something going on the side:Bee-Line clothing, Tupperware, Avon. It was probably out of a necessity to make ends meet. At 79, my father still works two nights a week at my brother's flooring store and my mother, at 75, drives handicapped kids back and forth to school in a minivan.

My parents were not affluent, by any standards. Money was never around, but, I never remember money being missed. If my father was the provider, then my mother was definitely the glue that kept it all together. I'm still not sure how they ever were able to pay tuition for all of us to go to private schools. It wasn't free. I remember the envelopes that were sent home at the end of every month for tuition. I don't know how much it was but I know it was probably more that they could afford. I also know that regardless of how much it was, they found a way to make it possible. To them, a Catholic education was the only answer.

Religion had always played a large part in my family's life, usually at the insistence of my father. There was never a question about going to Church on Sunday. Sometimes, if there was something family oriented going on, my mother would have let us slide a bit. My father, forget it. Swearing was also a major deal with my father. In his mind, there was, and still is, a huge difference in swearing. There were certain swears that were okay but if he ever caught you saying he Lord's name in vain, watch out! My father was, and continues to be, a firm believer in the Catholic faith. There were many years during Lent when he would be at the 7:00 a.m. mass every day. There were Lenten offering boxes at the kitchen table and there was never meat on Fridays. I remember driving with him in the morning during Lent, or whenever he felt the need, when he would take out his prayer beads and say the rosary.

When my sister Terry was diagnosed with cancer, he started going to church daily again. "Just one more day." he would say. "I go to church and ask God for just one more day." He didn't stop going daily until the day she died 18 years later. He was, and still remains, a man of immense faith. I remember every Sunday there would be small piles of coins laid out on the kitchen table. Those coins were for the collection. Whoever was bringing us to Church that day had the responsibility of handing out the change right before each collection. Sometimes my mother or father would bring us. Sometimes it would be one of my older brothers. The church was Saint Michael's in Lowell. There was also never a question about that.

I went to Saint Michael's Grade School, as did all of my brothers and sisters. There was never a question about that either. It was eight years of Saint Michael's and then four years of Catholic high school. Get in trouble at St. Mike's, too bad, there was no other place, at least not for our family. Blue pants, blue shirts, plaid ties, that was the dress for eight years. I remember my mother ironing those blue shirts at nights, putting them all on hangers, and hanging them on the side of the ironing board. I remember eight brown bags for lunch in the morning. Each day a different sandwich, usually some kind of cold cut meat, and each day a different dessert, usually a store brand though, never a name brand. The only other thing we'd get was a dime for milk money. That was before there was ever a school lunch program. Saint Michael's was run by the Dominican nuns. At that time, there were very few lay teachers. All the kids in school had their favorite teacher. All the kids had their not so favorite, as well. My favorites were Sister Mary Leonard, a soft spoken nun who would play the piano and teach us to sing, Well try to teach us., and Sister Noberta, who taught everything else.

Like my father and my brothers before me, if I behaved well enough and if my grades were good enough, I could become an altar boy. I have fond memories of my early years both at St. Mike's school, as well as being an altar boy. Being an altar boy meant that you could leave school for the 9 a.m. mass. Of course, it also meant that you had to show up for the 7:00 a.m. mass. But there were always trade off's. Altar boys had field trips and lots of perks the other students didn't have.

The priest in charge of the altar boys at St. Mike's was Fr. Joseph Birmingham. "Fr. B", as everyone called him, was a powerful figure to any adult, let alone any child. He was over 6 feet tall, almost balding, with black strands of hair that he would use to do a comb over. Square chin, square glasses, and always a broad smile. He'd always say hello with a big wave of his hand and his famous, "Hi, how are ya?" He had been placed at St. Michael's in the winter of 1970, after leaving his former parish in Salem, Massachusetts. St. Michael's was actually his third assignment, his first being Sudbury, Massachusetts.

To everyone who knew him, he was a personable and friendly guy. To parents, he was the friendly, young priest who was always willing to help out with the kids. There were field trips, skiing trips, trips to the beach, trips to the amusement park, sporting trips and trips for ice cream. Fr. B. was a likeable guy. Not only did he take an interest in kids who attended St. Michael's school, he also was one of the leaders in St. Michael's C.Y.O. group. Shortly after his arrival he went to great lengths to turn the basement of the rectory into a drop in center. The drop in center was open after school and evenings to teenagers who had graduated from St. Michael's or neighborhood teenagers who were in the C.Y.O. There was a pool table, a dart board, as well as card tables and games. I can remember many nights when my older brothers were asked by my parents where they were going, they would reply, "I'm going to the drop in center." My parents believed the older kids were just as safe at the drop in center as the younger kids were playing kickball.

Fr. B. was friendly to everyone and most everyone was his friend. If you had a problem, you could talk to him because he understood. It was as if he was "one of us." To those of us that knew him well, he was much more. As I graduated from eighth grade of St. Michael's, the school year ended with a CYO trip to California with Father Birmingham. I left Saint Michael's that year and never looked back. It was 1976.

2.

Monday, March 25, 2002. The phone rang, it was my mother. "Fr. B. has made the paper," she said. All of a sudden I started to sweat and my stomach lurched. "What?" I asked. "Father Birmingham is in the paper." Fr.B. I hadn't heard the name Fr.B. in a long time. Not nearly long enough. But I knew exactly who she meant when she first said that name. I also knew what she had meant by when she said he "made the paper." I felt a sudden knot in my stomach. Since graduating St. Michael's more than 25 years ago, I had only seen the name of Father Birmingham once and that was 10 years before. Over the previous several months I had wondered if his name would ever come up. Never giving it much thought, his memory just sat in the dark past of my mind, lurking. It had moved forward every now and then as the occasional story about an abusive priest would come to light. The most recent name had been Fr. Paul Shanley. By all accounts, he was truly a menace. Like Fr. Porter of 1992, Cardinal Law had come out and denounced Shanley as "one bad apple which does not spoil the whole bushel." As one story after another came out, I watched and patiently waited. I also wondered if maybe Father Birmingham was different, maybe it really was only me.

After my mother's call, I went upstairs and grabbed our home town news paper, The Lowell Sun, came downstairs and sat on the couch. It was the picture. My God, after all these years, the picture. My palms were sweaty and that knot in my stomach was turning to nausea. I looked at that picture for a long time. Those dark glasses, the comb over hair-do, that square chin, and that grin. His face was exactly like I remembered, it was the face that I tried to forget for 30 years. The face that had been put on the shelf, avoided, and the face that I never wanted to see again. After all this time, I couldn't believe that the sight of his picture, just the sight of his face, could do this to me. Palms again sweaty and sick to my stomach. I started to read… "Former Lowell priest…. past allegations…. allegations of child molestation." Wait a minute, they weren't talking about Lowell. Someone had finally talked about Fr.B., but he was not from Lowell. The parish they were talking about wasn't Saint Michael's. It was Saint James in Salem, Massachusetts. Then it hit me. I wasn't the only one. There were others. Soon I would discover there were many others. I was anything but alone.

I had to do something, although I didn't know exactly what. In the instant my mother spoke that name, Birmingham, I was transported more than 25 years into my past. I was also transformed from a 39 year old man to a 12 year old boy. It only lasted a minute, but it felt like it lasted a lifetime. I couldn't deny it any longer. I had to do something. I wasn't sure if I had what it would take to go public. I was sure that someone needed to know that these guys in the paper were not lying. The first call I made was to my brother Edward. Through a brief conversation with him 10 years before, I found out that he "knew" Fr. Birmingham like I "knew" him. It was early in 1992 when I had visited Ed at his home for a week before I made my move to Florida. I vividly remembered him picking me up at the train station and Ed was not looking well, at all. Ed had been dealing with issues of drug abuse and alcohol for most of his life. I could never understand where it stemmed from. With two failed marriages and an ongoing battle with alcohol and relationships, my parents continued to wonder where it all stemmed from. I knew that he had had some trouble in his last year at St. Mike's, but it had never dawned on me that there was a connection. Even in 1992, I still believed that I was the only one who knew Fr. B. in the special way that I knew him.

During my visit that year, Ed talked emotionally about his alcohol problems, as well as his problem relationships. I was giving him my best version of "you just have to get your shit together" speech, when he said that it wasn't as easy for him as it was for me. He blurted out that Fr. B. had "gone after him." I was shocked, but I wasn't about to reveal much of something that I had never told anyone in my life. I said, "Yes, Ed, he grabbed me too, but he's dead. Get over it and get your shit together." That was the extent of it, we never talked openly about it again.

After reading and re-reading the article that afternoon, I called Ed, who usually wasn't home. He answered the phone. "Fr.B. made the paper," I said. "Are you shitting me?" was his reply. " No, I'm serious. What do you want to do?" I asked, and then read him the article. We talked for a half hour, finally both deciding that it was time to come forward. We both agreed that we had to somehow make a show of support for the guy who had put his life on the line. The guy we were talking about was Jamie Hogan who was from Salem, Massachusetts. The only other name in the paper was the attorney who was representing him. We decided that I would try to locate the attorney who was handling this case and find out as much information as possible regarding what they knew about Fr. B. I told Ed that I would try to make the call. I just didn't feel comfortable telling anyone else about what we were talking about until we decided where we were going with it. The last thing I wanted was to have the same label hung around my neck as this Jamie Hogan person, who the press was calling a "victim of sexual abuse at the hands of a priest." I wanted no part of that title. It definitely wasn't for me.

As I sat staring at the paper I was thinking about the fact that I was about to turn 40 and was wondering why the hell I was opening up this can of worms. I didn't need this in my life. I was finally settling back into what I called a normal life. With two years passing since my divorce, my life was slowly getting back to a comfort level. However, with the sick feeling still in the pit of my stomach, I knew I just had to do something. I must have read that article a dozen times that day. I found out that Jamie Hogan was being represented by a firm called Greenberg Traurig and by an attorney named Robert Sherman. I called another attorney friend of mine and asked him if he had ever heard of Robert Sherman. As he looked up the contact info in the lawyer's directory and gave me the phone number, he asked me what I needed it for. I replied, "It's for a friend of mine."

I looked at the clock. "It's after 6:00 p.m., he wont be there any way," I said to myself as I dialed the number and got his voice mail. "Mr. Sherman, this is Gary Bergeron. I read an article today in the local paper regarding a priest named Joseph Birmingham. I would like to talk to you when you have time. Please call me." And I left my phone number. After hanging up, I called my brother Ed back to let him know that I had left the attorney a message. I was in the middle of telling Ed this when the phone clicked, someone was on the other line.

"Hello," I said, "Could I speak to Gary Bergeron? This is Robert Sherman." My stomach was churning. "This is Gary, but I have to tell you that I didn't expect a call back this soon and I have no idea what I'm comfortable talking about," was my reply. "That's fine Mr. Bergeron, but I want you to know I realize that it took a lot just for you to make that call. And I wanted you to know that when you're ready to talk, I'm ready to listen." I explained that I was calling for my brother and myself and that we both had served as altar boys at St. Michael's in Lowell. Without giving any more details than I had to, I set up an appointment to meet and, at least, talk to him. The date was March 29, 2002. At some point I realized later that the appointment date was Good Friday.

From that day on, I didn't have a full night of sleep. I constantly checked the news, read the papers, looked for anything, any bit of information regarding news about Father Birmingham. I also stayed pretty much to myself, although Ed and I talked several times a day. We went back and forth about what we should do. With the almost daily articles in the paper and in the news I was worried about my name being associated with this kind of story. I told him that I didn't want anything to do with the news regarding whatever we did on this. Half jokingly, he said not to worry about it. "Hey Bro, don't worry, I'll handle the press." One thing I've learned and realized is that you don't find fate. Fate finds you. Looking back now, man, did that not go the way we planned.

3.

On Good Friday, I drove into Boston with my 6 year old son Evan and my girlfriend Julie. Evan lives with his mother in Virginia and was up visiting me that week. On top of the anxiety I was already feeling about what I was about to discuss, I was battling a huge sense of guilt for leaving Evan for a few hours. My time with him was limited, at best, and I was heading into Boston.

We decided that Julie and Evan could spend some time at Fanueil Hall while I was at my appointment. I knew the address and I knew the name of the person I was going to see. That was about it. I had never heard of Greenberg Traurig. Their address of One International Place sounded impressive. I ended up being dropped off in the general vicinity and asked for directions. I soon saw that One International Place was as impressive as it sounded. As I approached the building, I realized that I was not walking into some fly by night firm.

One International Place is a circular shaped marble façade building with a grand view overlooking Boston Harbor. Its main lobby is a beautiful circular shaped room at least 5 stories tall, complete with a waterfall. Taking the elevator to the third floor, I walked into the waiting room. Sitting in the rich, wood paneled waiting area looking around, I was thinking again that I was crazy to have gone there. I was actually a half hour late for the appointment and contemplated canceling for another time. No such luck. When I called to say I was running late, the response was, "Not a problem, Mr. Bergeron. We'll wait". Several minutes later, I was shown into a conference room with floor to ceiling windows overlooking the Boston skyline. Sipping a cup of coffee, I sat for the first time in a room which I would come to visit many times over the upcoming months. As I waited I looked at my watch. It was 1:00 in the afternoon. An eerie thought suddenly ran through my mind. As it did, I again grew nauseous. Here I was on Good Friday at 1:00 in the afternoon. It was the same time that Christ would have been hanging on the cross 2,000 years ago. Here I was about to tell people things that could hang the Catholic Church. I had never thought much about the timing of my appointment before. Now I couldn't get it out of my head. As the minutes, which seemed like hours, ticked by, only one thought was there. Was I doing the right thing?

Several minutes later, a slight knock on the door sounded as attorneys Courtney Pillsbury and Robert Sherman walked in and introduced themselves. It was there in that room that I would sit, gazing out those large windows, as I told part of my story for the first time to two people who were complete strangers. Yet they would ultimately grow to become two of my most trusted confidants. I would not tell them the whole story, though. There were many details that would take many months before I could reveal them. It would be months before I would trust them enough to tell them everything. One of the major issues that survivors of clergy sexual abuse have to deal with is the issue of trust. I trusted no one. At least up until that point, I had trusted no one. I finally decided that I had to entrust someone by telling my story. I chose them. I told them about deciding to trust them point blank that day.

I spent over two hours that day telling perfect strangers things that had happened in my life which I had not told anyone. Things that I had avoided telling anyone. Things that I had hidden and put away for almost 30 years. Up until that point I had avoided any conversation regarding the clergy abuse crisis that had been plaguing the Catholic Church. If it was in the paper, I would turn the page. If it were on the evening news, I would change the channel. I didn't want to deal with it. I'm not sure if it was the pain I was trying to hide from, or, if by watching it, I would connect the dots in my own life. In my mind, I refused to give Father Birmingham or the abuse that he inflicted on me, any credit for the events in my life. Reading all the accounts that had been in the paper would have forced me to make a connection. That was a connection that I didn't want. Anyway, I was okay, there was nothing wrong with me, and my life was normal. Or so I thought.

When I was finished telling them what I was comfortable with sharing, they started telling me their story. I was told what they knew about Joseph Birmingham. I was told about what parishes he had been assigned to. I was told about Jamie Hogan who had first come forward, about Bernie McDaid, whose parents had actually gone to complain about Birmingham in the 60's.

Shockingly I also found out that there were survivors coming forward from every parish that Father Joseph Birmingham had been, Sudbury, Salem, Lowell, Brighton and Gloucester. More shockingly, I had found out that there had been children who had told their parents about the abuse and that those parents had contacted the diocese on several occasions prior to his placement at Saint Michael's. ***Prior.***

"Oh my God, they knew," was the only thought that kept ringing in my head. They knew before and did nothing, they knew after and did nothing. They just let him continue. I couldn't believe it. There was no way possible that I could accept the fact that the church pastors, the personnel at the Chancery and even the Cardinal knew, and did nothing. Bob and Courtney didn't have proof of those meetings, yet, but they were working on getting written proof that those parents and many other parents complained about Fr. Birmingham's behavior. Proof that the archdiocese not only turned a blind eye, but continued to transfer him to other parishes with fresh new sets of victims. In time we would see that proof in writing. In time we would see written proof of much more.

Robert Sherman and Courtney Pillsbury spent a great deal of time telling me about the importance of seeking therapy. They both urged me to, at least, keep an open mind about it. "Whether you decide to become a plaintiff in a lawsuit or not, it is important for your own self that you consider seeing a therapist," he said. We then slowly began to discuss the painful effects that clergy sexual abuse has been known to have on people.

The list he started to read hit me like a ton of bricks. I could swear that this guy had known me for years. It was starting to sink in that maybe, just maybe, I didn't survive totally unscathed through all this. Maybe. When they started asking me basic questions like a history of where I had lived, it hit me even harder. "Gary, where do you live now? And if you've been there less than two years, where did you live before that?" was the first question. When I finished answering that very first question, I realized that I had moved 22 times in the last 21 years. It was that one question that was like a light bulb going off in my head. A very harsh light bulb at that. I had actually moved 22 times. Was I running away from something, or running to find something. One thing was for sure, I had been running my whole life. The irony of it was that after moving all those times, I was now actually living in the very same house that I had grown up in. I guess I was actually about to start back from the beginning. I wasn't sure if I was even ready to. Bob encouraged me to get into therapy, at least to have an initial visit. He also encouraged me to think about what exactly it was that I wanted to do. "It's important for you to decide what direction you want to take and where you want things headed in the future for yourself," They also told me that should I decide to use them for legal issues regarding this, that I will have to undergo a psychological evaluation first. I actually liked that thought. At least if I use them I know that they represent level-headed guys just like me. Right ?

As we spoke I found out that the Archdiocese of Boston was offering to cover 6 months of therapy for anyone who would meet with them for a pre-screening interview. They were agreeing to do this at their cost. It wasn't a lot, but it was, at least, something. Therapy? I didn't need therapy. There was nothing wrong with me. I was only there to help the other guys who had come forward. I didn't need it, there was no question in my mind. Not only didn't I need it, I didn't believe in it. People make their own problems and they can fix them. It was that simple to me. In my opinion therapy was over used, for the weak and for those who didn't or wouldn't own up to their own problems. That definitely wasn't me.

Before I left we talked about the article in the paper. They were talking about an article in the Boston Globe and I was talking about an article in the local paper. I had no idea that there was an article in the Globe about this. He suggested that I get a copy. He also gave me the name and phone number of the woman at the Chancery that I could get in touch with if I decided to get therapy. As I left the office, I felt better. I'm not sure why. Maybe it was the fact that I was finally telling someone at least part of my story. Just the fact that I was getting some of it off my chest and that I felt that they actually listened to me, and possibly believed me. I was impressed with the compassion that was shown me.

Driving home that day and realizing what I had just been talking about, I remembered that last time that I had ever mentioned any of it. The more I thought about it, the more I hoped that I had become a better judge of whom I could trust. Ten years before, the story about Father Porter went public. Porter was another Catholic priest from the area who had molested dozens and dozens of children. It was constantly on the television and I would constantly change the channel. One evening my wife (at the time) and I were watching the news. The reporter was talking about Fr. Porter and she was telling a story about a child that had been abused. The abuse that she was talking about was that Porter had touched the child on his buttocks. I turned to Tanya and said, "God, they think that that's abuse? They have no idea. Could I tell them a story?" She looked at me wide eyed and said, "What do you mean? What are you talking about?" I told her that a priest had gone after me when I was in school. End of story, that was it. She prodded me for more information but I wasn't budging. I told her that it was in the past, that it hadn't affected me and that I didn't want to talk about it.

That two minute conversation would come back to haunt me when I was served with divorce papers years later and she requested sole custody, with supervised visitation. She also requested that I be made to go to counseling. I fought counseling and avoided opening up that can of worms fiercely back then.

Now, several years later, I was opening it up on my own. My only hope was that this time, it would turn out better. I would still ask myself if I should have told them. I would still ask myself if I could actually trust them.

4.

When I got home I called Ed and told him about my meeting at Greenberg Traurig. Again Ed and I talked about where we were headed with this. He was astonished when I told him about all the other survivors from all the other parishes. He couldn't believe that the Archdiocese knew about Father Birmingham's past abuse in prior parishes long before he came to St Michael's. I told him that I was going to look up the Boston Globe article online and then I would forward it to him.

My first reaction after reading the Boston Globe article was, "They're going to think I was lying the whole time." I couldn't believe what I had just read. There was one part of the article that was almost word for word my story regarding one of the times I was abused. It was talking about a survivor abused during an outing at the beach, who had a stomach ache. That person ended up being molested in the back of Father Birmingham's car. It was unbelievable. The names and places had changed but the method of operation was almost exactly the same. I would learn that he had used this ploy on many other survivors over his 30 year reign of abuse.

Within the next few days, Ed and I were constantly on the phone and e-mailing each other. We both agreed that we wanted to make some type of public statement but neither of us knew exactly what we wanted to say. Within those few days, Ed also has a long phone interview with Bob and Courtney. He would tell me that he felt comfortable talking with them. Neither of us were sure yet about signing on to a lawsuit. I was worried about the reaction of my family. My parents still went to Saint Michaels Church every Sunday. At that point, I was very concerned about how they would be viewed in the midst of all this.

In between the hourly phone calls and emails, I decided to place a call to the Archdiocese of Boston. I made up my mind that I was going to attempt to talk with them and tell them a bit about my story. I also innocently believed that I would give them the opportunity to know me on a personal level. I wanted a chance to explain to them how I felt regarding the way that they were reacting to this issue. (Or should I say the way they were not reacting to it.) Ever hopeful, I felt as though maybe I would be able to get through to them and maybe I could make a difference. I called and awkwardly stumbled through my attempt to tell the woman who answered the phone the reason for my call.

After several minutes she finally asked, "Are you making an appointment because of sexual abuse by a priest?" "Yes," I answered. Again, I found myself saying those words. After a brief discussion, I made an appointment for later in the month. Though I had the option of having someone come to Lowell to meet with me, I opted to drive into Brighton to the Chancery to meet them there. I realized later that I did that so they would not think that I had any fear regarding seeing them "on their turf." I also did it to prove to myself that I was not afraid.

After many, many drafts, Ed and I agreed on making a public statement about our abuse. We finally agreed on what it was we wanted to say. The most difficult part for me was a paragraph that Ed wanted inserted into the statement which would say "and what of the men we could have become." I had a major issue with that kind of statement. I simply refused to admit that Birmingham had any affect on my life. There was no way I was going to give him that much credit for anything. I refused to believe that Birmingham's actions more than 25 years before had resulted in any lingering effects on my life. In the end, that line was left out. Ed and I agreed that for our statement to do any good and help anyone, we needed to make it formally, as well as publicly. We just weren't sure how yet.

As Ed and I grappled with how to present our statement an opportunity came into view. I found out that there was going to be a press conference regarding Fr. Birmingham held on Thursday, April 4. It just so happened that a group of friends and I had been planning a vacation right around the same day as that press conference. We were to be leaving on April 7th. on a 7 day cruise to the Caribbean. Ed and I agreed that there would probably be no better time to have our statement given out than that day. I knew that there were other abuse survivors who would be at that press conference that could use our support. We forwarded our statement to Bob and Courtney with the understanding that they had our permission to use it at the press conference. With that statement I also sent Courtney an email.

```
Courtney:

Here is the final draft, I'm placing a lot
of faith in you and Bob.  Please don't let
me down.
```

I was placing a lot of faith in them, faith that didn't come easy for me. I wanted to make sure they both knew that. I was trusting them to "do the right thing," not only by me, but by all the survivors of Birmingham, even though I didn't know them all.

With the date set for our public statement, I decided that I would leave ahead of my friends and spend a few days in Miami prior to the cruise. I'd be in Miami relaxing while all hell was breaking loose in Massachusetts. I changed my flights and I was to leave on Thursday morning, which would put me in Miami hours before the press conference.

With my vacation and the press conference approaching, there was only one problem left, my family. How was I going to tell them? I was about to tell the world something so deep and personal, up to that point I hadn't even told a single member of my family . I told Ed that I felt that we needed to tell them at least something before they read it in the papers. He suggested calling them. I lived in Lowell and he lived in South Carolina. That was easy for him to say, but I wasn't comfortable with that. His next suggestion was to tell them on Sunday. It hit me that he was talking about Sunday, March 31, which happened to be Easter Sunday. For a little while I had actually thought about that idea. Everyone would be there, it would be a perfect time. But it really wouldn't. I realized that the last thing I wanted everyone to equate the Easter holiday for years to come as the day that they learned that Gary was "sexually molested by a priest." I finally decided that I would write them a note and attach it to a copy of the statement that we were giving out at the press conference.

My memory of that Easter Sunday will forever be in my mind. My whole family was there sitting around my parents. Some of us were at the dinner table, some in the living room, but we were all there, which was normal for any family holiday. Like all family gatherings in our "Brady Bunch" meets "The Osborne's" style we were all ribbing each other. I was listening and watching everyone. All I could think about was the bombshell that I was about to drop on them. I was wondering what their thoughts about me would be in the next few days, as well as the next few months, to come. I watched my nieces and nephews around the house and wondered what they might go through because I had decided to come forward. They were just kids. This wasn't likely something they would have been following in the news. I was hopeful that they wouldn't suffer any consequences for the actions I was about to undertake.

On the following Tuesday, I finally sat down and wrote a letter to my family and friends. I had to tell them in writing. After all the time that had gone by, almost 30 years, I still did not have the courage to tell them face to face. On Wednesday morning, with the press conference just a day away, my parents, brothers, sisters, and my daughter received the following letter.

```
To my family:

Enclosed is a joint statement from Eddie and myself
concerning sexual abuse that was endured at the
hands of Father Birmingham at St. Michael's. This
statement will be made public on Thursday April 3.
For me, this is a situation that I have not spoken
of for almost 30 years, however, I have decided that
it is time.

Though I cannot speak for Eddie, I had previously
decided not to come forward regarding these issues.
I have not mentioned Father Birmingham's name in
many, many years. Several weeks ago when his name
came up, a wound was opened. Even at that time I was
not sure as to how I was going to handle it. Upon
finding out that the parish of St. Michael's was
warned about his behavior by the parents of the par-
ish that he was at prior to St. Michael's and that
nothing was done, sickened me.

The fact that someone did come forward regarding Fa-
ther Birmingham and his actions, and that that per-
son, as of yet, had not been taken seriously, infu-
riated me. These two facts as well as several oth-
ers, have been gnawing at me. I could have made
these remarks and remained anonymous, however as the
statement reads, I do not want to make anonymous al-
legations as a "John Doe."

Publicity is not my intention, however, with the at-
tention that this issue is getting, hopefully our
children and our children's children will never have
to write a letter like this.

I am not sure how the public is going to view some-
one that, in their eyes, is attacking a dead priest.
I personally don't care. However, should you or any-
one in your family feel the heat because of my deci-
sion to come forward, I apologize.

For me, it is time.
Gary
```

I didn't mail it, though. I decided to drop a copy off at everyone's house in that Wednesday morning before everyone left for work. I dropped them all off. I went home and I packed. I left next morning for Miami, timing is everything.

That night, like most nights since Birmingham's picture was in the paper, I didn't sleep. I was worried about my family's reaction, I was worried about the press conference. I was worried if I was making the right decision. I was worried about whether or not I should be taking a vacation at all. My adult daughter Katie talked to me about not going on vacation. She actually said that I should reconsider going to the press conference. "Dad, this is a big decision that you've made. Are you sure that you don't want to be there? I know you, I think you'll regret not being there. This is pretty important for everyone." I opted not to go. Seven days on a cruise ship, no phone, no newspapers, no television, and most importantly, seven days with no one knowing anything, that's was what I was looking forward to.

I arrived in Miami Thursday, grabbed my rental car and checked into the hotel. My cell phone was not ringing and that was a good sign. Maybe the press conference was put off for some reason. At that point I didn't care. I just wanted to relax. I was still worried about how my family was reacting to the letters I had dropped off. Other than my parents and my daughter, I hadn't heard from any of them. My parents and daughter, as well as my son's mother, were exceptionally supportive, as I knew they would be. I spent the afternoon relaxing and walking the shoreline.

Friday afternoon, as I was sitting on a balcony in my hotel overlooking the ocean, I found myself sipping a cocktail and gazing at the beach. The weather was beautiful and there was a mild balmy breeze blowing that I realized I missed since moving back to New England 10 years ago. My cell phone starts to ring startling me. For a few hours prior to my phone ringing, I had actually forgotten what was happening back home. I was suddenly back in reality. The first call was from Katie, my daughter. "Dad, it's in the paper," she said. "I figured it would be," I replied. She then went on, "No dad, you don't understand. It's really in the paper and it's on the front page and it's really big. When you said that something may be in the paper, I didn't think that it would be this big." That was my first call that day. For the rest of the day, my cell phone would constantly ring, one call after the next until I ended up shutting it off.

With that first phone call, my daughter got her first lesson in what the newspaper considers a newsworthy story. She started to read it to me

LOWELL SUN… Gary Bergeron, of Lowell, and Edward Bergeron, now of South Carolina…The Bergerons did not attend yesterday's news conference but in a statement that was made public…...

It was finally out. On Thursday, April 4, by issuing the following statement, for the first time in my life I told the world something that I hadn't told anyone else. A priest sexually molested me as a child. I suddenly became a "victim of sexual abuse."

It has been said recently that you should not speak ill of the dead. We believe that that statement should only refer to those deserving of it. To us, because of the actions that Father Birmingham took, that statement means that we shouldn't speak of our childhood, because for us, it was our childhood that died long before Father Birmingham did.

After years of self denial and silence, we have made a decision that it is time for us to heal, and for that to happen, we must come forward. We are not faceless names in the news making anonymous allegations. We are men with families, strong community ties, reputations, and have children of our own. When our pain began, we were innocent children. As children we became innocent victims. As men, we refuse to remain victims. We have learned over the years to become survivors.

No one can undo the damage that Father Birmingham has done to us. No one can make it right. The effects on our lives and the lives of our family have been tragic, and many. Yet it is time for us to stand up and say, "Yes, this happened." It is also time for the Archdiocese to admit that, "Yes it did happen" and to take responsibility for the wrongs that they have committed not only to us but also to all the children they delivered to the hands of Father Birmingham before us and continued to knowingly deliver to the hands of Father Birmingham after us.

Not only were our innocent lives stolen on those days spent with Father Birmingham, but also something just as precious was taken from us. Stolen from us was the very thing that we were sent to receive at Saint Michael's, a belief in, and trust of our Catholic faith, the very thing that we need to overcome our difficulties.

This is no longer just about what was done to us, but also to those around us. It is about admitting the truth and taking responsibility for what has been stolen from us, our innocence, our trust, our faith in our religion and at time our trust in ourselves.

The horrific truth that the Church refused to admit that they knowingly continued to give Father Birmingham a fresh set of victims over and over again, is shocking. The only word that can be used to describe it is "unbelievable." Recognizing these facts will help to prevent them from happening again, and only in doing this, can they ensure the present and future safety of our children and your children.

As a society we have always said, "The children are our future." We would like to know, what does that mean to the Archdiocese of Boston when they continued to supply Father Birmingham with a children to become his victims year, after year, after year. The fact that the Church continues to deny these facts only refreshes these wounds and makes the healing process for us and the Church itself take longer.

Some of us were delivered to Father Birmingham because of trouble we had gotten into at school. We now ask the Archdiocese of Boston, please tell us.... Is our punishment over yet? When will the wounds heal?

Gary M. & Edward W. Bergeron

It was finally out. Later during the day I was to learn that not only was it in the local paper, but it was also carried by newspapers and broadcast news both locally and nationally. I was also amazed that it was carried as front page news in the New York Times.

At least I was on vacation for a week though. No one knew about it that was going on vacation with me. Or so I thought. It wasn't until Sunday that I found out that at least one of my friends who was on vacation with me had seen the papers. Diane Taylor, who was the sister of Ron Taylor, who had been my best friend for 20 years, had seen it before she boarded her flight. I had just told Ron about it for the first time.

To say that he was shocked would be an understatement. He couldn't believe that after all the things we had talked about, not to mention all the things we had been through, that I had never talked to him about it. Over 20 years, he and I had talked about everything. Everything, but this. Like my family, Ron was very supportive. He knew that I had made up my mind. If I felt the time was right for me, then he was there for me. Like her brother, Diane was also kind, compassionate, supportive and respectful of my privacy. She never mentioned it again for the next seven days. Knowing them both the way I do, I should have expected nothing less.

True friends show true colors. They are both true friends. Aside from the private conversation that Diane and I had that first day, for the next seven days there was nothing to do but relax. I didn't realize how much that vacation was going to help me in the weeks and months ahead. Looking back, it was the best possible thing I could have done at the time. Nothing else could have better mentally prepared me for the long road that I had decided to take a jog down. With that public statement, my "something," had begun.

Returning to the airport for the flight home that Sunday, I could feel my mood change. In a matter of hours, it went from carefree to angst. I knew that by taking that vacation what I had really done was put off facing everyone and every question that would eventually have to be answered. I realized that the questions from everyone would still be there. In one way, I couldn't wait to get home and in another, I dreaded even the thought of it.

5.

Back from vacation, reality wasted no time in catching up with me. My phone was constantly ringing. Sometimes there were hang ups, sometimes there would be men from my past talking to me. Sometimes in whispers. I got several calls from men asking me questions, and looking for advice. They were men that had seen my name in the paper and were looking for answers. I had no idea what to tell them. There were no magic pills, no magic phone numbers. At least there were none that I knew of. All I could do was talk, and listen. If they were interested, I gave them the phone number to the Archdiocese and told them of the therapy that they were offering. Every one of them said "thanks but no thanks." The last thing they wanted was to talk to the Church. Like me, they probably remember the last time that they had placed their trust in the Church. There were more than several long phone conversations, and many, many cups of coffee during that time.

Soon after I got back my mother called to let me know that there was going to be an informational meeting at a local hall regarding Father Birmingham. She had received a call from the mother of another survivor who was also a neighbor of ours. I wasn't crazy about attending but I definitely wanted to go if there was going to be additional information about him. The meeting was being held in the basement of a Lowell club. Survivors, as well as parents and spouses, were invited. I decided to go.

The hall was pretty full when I got there. Being one of the last to show up, I stood for a while in the back when a man came up to me, shook my hand and said. "Thanks for having the courage to be out in the public." His name was Olan Horne. I didn't know who he was, I had never heard of him before. As the night progressed, I would find myself, at times, in awe of him. Here was a man talking openly about his abuse and letting the world know what he intended to do about it. He was talking about support groups, getting organized, making public statements, and much more. After meeting him and listening to him speak, my initial reaction was, "I want nothing to do with this guy." Olan was pretty outspoken that night. I wasn't sure I wanted to align myself with him. He seemed light years ahead of where I felt I was. I had heard enough of him to realize that although I may not want to be aligned with him, I didn't want to be an enemy of his either. Olan is one of those guys who sees an issue that he knows needs to be addressed and he goes after it with guns blazing, no fear in his eyes. I wasn't sure if I could ever speak as openly about the things that he was speaking of that night. The Olan that I have come to know and trust and call my friend is a person who took me months to get to know and trust, but I'm glad that I took the time to do both. With his friendship and his "balls to the wall" attitude we have been able to make strides where others have not. There have been times when we have definitely not agreed with the "how," but there has never been an instance where we have disagreed on the "why." During the many months since I first met him, Olan has pushed me to my personal bounds of comfort and ability. Olan has the continued courage to ask, "What are you willing to do about it?" and "How far are you willing to go?" Those are questions that are hard to ask, and are, more often than not, harder to answer. I remember those questions and I try and answer them everyday.

That evening I also saw familiar faces of my past. Many of the faces of the men I saw that evening surprised me. One of those faces was Roger Hamilton, who used to live around the corner of my street. As I walked into that room and found a seat, his mother came up to me and said, " Thank you for going in the paper. Because of you, my son is here." Roger said to me that when he saw my name and Ed's name in the paper he said, "Hey, I know those guys." That's when he came forward. I was overwhelmed with emotions. These people were thanking me. I knew at that moment that I really was doing the right thing.

Another person who came up to me was Bernie McDaid. What he said to me that night is something that, to me, truly put Bernie in a league of his own. I had seen Bernie in the paper a short time ago. He was one of the first to come forward and was from Salem, where Birmingham had been prior to coming to Lowell. Bernie walked over to me and said, "Hey, you're the guy in Lowell that came forward, aren't you?" "Yes," was all I said. "You've got a lot of guts. By you coming forward, there are a lot of guys that are here right now." He then did and said something that will stand out in my mind for a long time. He extended his hand and said, "I just want to tell you that I'm sorry. You shouldn't have to be here. Birmingham should never have been in Lowell. We tried to stop him in Salem and thought we had. He never should have gotten to Lowell and never should have gotten to you."

That night I would hear Bernie's story for the first time. I would begin to actually realize that I wasn't the only one, not by a long shot. Bernie, along with some of his schoolmates who were also there, went and told his parents what Birmingham was doing back in the late '60s. It was Bernie's parents that went to the Chancery and told them about Birmingham's activities. It was Bernie's parents that the Archdiocese had promised something would be done. Instead, they shipped him to Lowell, where he would find his next batch of innocent victims. Here was this man, Bernie McDaid, who had done the right thing so many years ago and he was apologizing to me.

There were many men and many parents there that night. There was also representatives from The Sexual Network of those Abused by Priests (SNAP). I couldn't believe that there was actually an organization named for this issue. There were also representatives from a group called Voice Of The Faithful (VOTF), a group of Catholics that I would learn much more about in the upcoming months. My horizons were getting broader and broader by the hour. I would hear stories from several men who were from several parishes where Birmingham was before Saint Michael's, stories which you could almost just interchange names and faces. I would learn that Birmingham had a method of operation that he used and groomed as he was moved from parish to parish. Many relationships were forged that night. I can remember leaving that meeting and thinking to myself, that's a great group of people. They have the great goals in mind but those meetings are not for me, I thought. Support groups? No way. That would be another instance of nothing being further from the truth. In time that meeting would evolve into a support group that would be called Survivors of Joe Birmingham. That group would grow to include men like Tom Blanchette.

Tom's an extraordinary man with an incredible story. Tom and three of his brothers were abused by Birmingham when he was at his first parish in Sudbury. As an adult Tom had actually sought out Birmingham. Tom publicly talked about how he had forgiven him for what he had done. Not only had Tom forgiven him but also he had actually asked Birmingham to forgive him for the hatred that he had carried in his heart for all those years. Tom would be one of the last persons to see Birmingham alive when he visited him in the hospital the day before he had died. As Tom puts it, "I believe that I was there the day before he died as a representative and a reminder of all the little boys he molested."

After hearing Tom tell his story, I admired him for his ability to forgive. I wasn't sure if I would ever be able to achieve this level of healing and forgiveness but it definitely was something that worked for Tom and I admired it. From that first meeting in the basement of that hall in Lowell that evening, SOJB would continue to grow. In the months that followed the Survivors of Joe Birmingham would initiate support groups in every parish where Birmingham had been. Each support group would help to facilitate healing for many, many survivors. In the weeks and months ahead this group would also be in a position to get help for those who need it. Help for not only the survivors, but for the loved ones and family members of the survivor. Those are the fallout survivors that are often lost and forgotten, but that are as important as any. S.O.J.B would continue to grow to include many more men and would accomplish much, much more. We still meet every week. Yes, I said we, because I haven't missed a meeting since the initial meeting that night. It's a group with which I'm proud and honored to be associated. Our group has been able to hold true to ourselves and true to our cause. We started as a support group and never wavered the line between support and advocate group. It has been a tough line to have drawn in the sand. Though we may disagree on the "how," and we have, we never ever disagree on the "why." Over the months since that first evening, I have developed a clearer sense of what a support group is about. I also have a deeper appreciation of them as well.

Several days following that meeting I received a call from Courtney. She was calling and asking if I would consider coming to the office to answer some questions from the local newspapers. "It's called press availability," she said. "We are adding a few names of men from Lowell to the lawsuit and press availability means that there may be some local newspapers here asking some questions. Because you and your brother were the first to come forward from Lowell, we thought it might be a good time for them to interview you." She went on to tell me the tremendous positive effects of the statement that Ed and I had submitted.

It sounded simple enough. She knew that I was not crazy about doing an interview. "I'm not interested if there are going to be TV cameras there Courtney, I'm in no way ready for any of that," I Said. "Gary, I know how you feel about this, that's why I called you. This is not going to be a press conference, it's only press availability. There aren't going to be cameras here" After convincing me of that, She told me that there was going to be one other person from Lowell there, and she told me that Bernie was going to be there. I decided that I liked Bernie immediately after meeting him in Lowell, for whatever reason, I felt better knowing that he was going to be there. I realized what it had meant for me to see and hear Bernie talk that evening. I also realized what it may mean for other survivors from my own town to know that I had come forward. I called my brother Ed and talked about it. Shortly after, I called Courtney back and told her that I would see her in the afternoon. It was Wednesday, May 1st.

I remember the same feeling in the pit of my stomach, driving into their office this second time. But I also knew that it was my choice to open the door and I'm not the type to turn back. Walking into the reception area I was surprised when the receptionist said "Hello Mr. Bergeron, I'll tell Mr. Sherman you're here." She knew who I was, yet I didn't know her. In the lobby there was what seemed to be a TV camera there, it was only one, but it definitely was a TV camera. As I sat, I was thinking about what they're doing there. In a few minutes I was brought into Bob's office and I was now sitting at a table with Bernie McDaid and Dave Lycos. I had seen Bernie in the newspapers before and had met him in Lowell. Though I didn't know Dave, he was another survivor from Lowell that had come forward.

"Bob, what's up with the camera out there? Courtney said that this was not going to be a press conference. I thought that meant no cameras," I said. "Well, there has been a slight change. When we sent out a fax about adding the names and that there would be press availability. our phone started ringing off the hook. We didn't think that there would be that much interest in it, but we were wrong," was his reply. Suddenly Bernie looked at me and said, "Don't worry, it's no big deal. It's only one camera and it's just this little round thing that you're looking into. No big deal, don't worry. I'm going in with you. If you're not ready to talk, then don't. It will be good for other guys in Lowell to see you out there. Even if you don't speak, you're showing support. If you decide that you want to say something, don't worry about not knowing what to say, it's all on tape and they can just delete it if you make a mistake."

At that moment, Courtney walked in. I think before she had even gotten one word out I said, "Courtney, I thought you had said no cameras?" I could tell that I had caught her off guard. Apparently even she had not yet learned that the setup had changed because of the interest. When Bob told her of the changes she looked at me, beet red, and apologized over and over again. Then Bob looked at her and said, "I can't believe that you lied to Gary about this just to get him in here." She looked up, not knowing if I had taken him serious. We all burst out laughing. At least we were able to laugh. Little did I know, that by the end of the day, my emotions would go from one extreme to the other, and in a very short time. Bob went on to tell me that by being there I was showing support for the survivors that have already come forward. He also said that by me being there, it may have the same effect on other survivors that it had on me when I had seen the article on Birmingham. He thought I may give them the courage to come forward and start to deal with the issues and possibly heal. I started feeling weight on my shoulders.

Walking out his office with sweaty palms, I followed in the rear as they walked down the hall. As we went around a corner, Bob said, again, "Don't worry. If you don't want to say anything, you don't have to. Just remember, if you want to speak, don't worry about what you're going to say. Just speak from your heart." Those words had no sooner come out of his mouth then we reached the end of the hall when I started to see people coming towards me. What had started out as "press availability" had turned into a press conference. At the time, it seemed to me like the biggest press conference since the Monica Lewinsky story.

The people walking towards me were news reporters and cameramen. They were not, however, walking towards me to interview me. They actually had to leave the room we were entering so there would be room for us. All the local affiliates of CBS, NBC, and ABC were there, as well as CNN, MSNBC, NECN, the Bloomberg Channel. There were also newspaper reporters from every local paper as well as reporters from some of the major papers outside the area. I had never seen so many cameras in my life. Cameras, reporters, flashing bulbs, microphones. My palms, which had been sweaty already, were drenched. It was the most intimidating site I had ever seen. Or was it ?

Bob sat the three of us down and then sat down, himself, and began to speak. He gave the chronology of Father Birmingham. He told them how he had been accused of molesting children at every parish he had been to, six in all. He went on to tell them that this priest had over a 30 year history of abusing children and that he had done this all under the knowing eyes of the Archdiocese of Boston. Immediately after Bob had finished, someone asked if the survivors that were with him would address the press.

Bernie spoke first. I wish I could tell you what he had to say, but I can't. As he finished, he looked at me and said, "Are you okay to talk? Remember, you don't have to." "Yes, I do have to," I told him. As I sat there watching the bulbs go off and watching the reporters moving around the room, squeezing against each other for the best angle, I remembered that almost 30 years ago a priest intimidated me. A priest named Joseph Birmingham. That thought burst in my head like a flash of light. Somehow I knew that I would get through this. I knew that I was going to address these people. I was going to tell my story. This was no longer a question in my mind. I had to. That day I would tell them all things that I had not even shared with Bob.

I sat down in front of all the microphones, all the cameras, and all the reporters. I gulped and looked at Bernie. Thank God for Bernie. If he hadn't been there, I never would have been able to speak that day. As I looked at him, he winked, and lowered his hand so that the reporters couldn't see it and gave me a thumbs up sign. As my emotions of over 30 years directed me, my eyes began to swell up, just as they are now, as I recall that day. I began to speak.

First I would like to say that I sit here today, not only for myself, but I also represent my brother Edward, who is also a survivor of Father Birmingham's, but is not here. On my way here today, I stopped at the cemetery. I went there to visit my sister Terry, who died of cancer in 1992. To me that is hallowed ground. Today was the first time in almost ten years that was able to visit her there. That reason is because of Father Birmingham who died in 1989. When my brother Ed and I, after burying my sister, who had more courage than anyone I know and who fought a battle with cancer for almost 18 years, walked around the cemetery the day she was buried, we found out that Father Birmingham is buried within 25 feet from my sister's grave. I have not been able to visit her for almost 10 years because of it. I went to the cemetery today and I asked her to give me strength. And she has.

As I made that statement, I fought back 30 years of tears and emotions, but as I said that last line and glanced at Bob and Bernie, I realized that I wasn't the only one who was emotional. As I watched the camera flashes continually go off, I also noticed that there were reporters wiping their eyes, as well. I tried to fight back tears and a peace and strength came over me that I had never felt. I knew that at that moment, my sister was there and I knew that she was giving me the strength and courage that she had shown during her entire life. The cameras continued to flash, and I went on.

The fact that the Archdiocese of Boston knew that Father Birmingham was molesting children from every parish that he attended and did nothing astonishes me. I can not believe that they knew and did nothing but give him a fresh set of victims, over, and over, and over again for over 30 years. They knew. They knew and did nothing. The fact that innocent children were molested over and over again in order to do nothing but protect the image of the Catholic Church is unbelievable. There has been proof that parents had come forward from Salem to complain about Father Birmingham and all they did was shift him to Saint Michael's and give him another fresh batch of victims…

Now, I'm going to make a remark that I know is unpopular. As far as Cardinal Law is concerned, I don't want him to leave. I am sitting here criticizing the Catholic Church for moving these priests that have molested children from parish to parish to parish. I want Cardinal Law here. This is his mess. I want him to stop hiding because, to me, that is exactly what he is doing. I want him to stay here and clean this mess up. I want him here because he is the only one that can begin to restore the faith of my parents who don't have another 40 years to heal like I do. I want him to stop hiding because, to me and to a lot of people, that's just what he's doing. I want him to admit that this has happened, I want him to apologize to me and to my parents. I want Cardinal Law to stay here, clean up his mess. I want him to work to restore my parent's faith, and I want him to restore my faith.

When I finished I got up and moved over. Dave Lyko got up and spoke next. I realized later the immense amount of strength and courage it took Dave just to be there. I found Dave a shy and kind person that day. More often than not he sits and observes quietly. Though he seems like a quiet soft spoken guy, he has been at every turn of events with all of us. He was definitely one of the most unlikely candidates for a press conference. It is definitely true that some people "rise to the occasion." Dave Lyko was definitely one. While Dave spoke, I sat and watched, but my mind was reeling. To me, I sounded like an emotional wreck, and I was. As the realization hit me that I was just on TV, telling the world that I was a survivor of sexual abuse at the hands of a priest, I was covered in sweat and my stomach was turning. After Dave spoke, there were a few questions by reporters regarding dates and times, etc., but it was just about over.

My initial worries regarding talking to the reporters were not realized. As the press conference was over, I don't think that there was a single reporter in that room that didn't take the time to walk over to me, thank me, and shake my hand. As a rule, I had been told to be extremely cautious concerning all members of the press. But I, for one, can say that other than one person in the press, they have all shown me extreme compassion. Most of them have gotten it right and the ones with whom I have stayed in contact have continually reported the story without the spin.

People have been critical of the coverage that this issue has received in the Boston area, but without the continuing reporting and coverage that they have given this issue, there would be no public awareness. With knowledge brings power and with power comes the possibility of change. By the press covering this issue as they have, the public awareness has been heightened. Hopefully with a better educated public, there will be a change.

As the reporters gathered up their gear, we all got up and walked down the hall. I was the last one to leave and as I was walking down the hall, Bob walked over and put his arm around my shoulder. His eyes seemed moist, but he looked at me with a grin and said, "That wasn't so bad, was it?" I looked at him and said, "Piece of cake, Bob. Piece of Cake." I realize that had I actually had more time to prepare and think about talking in front of a camera, I probably wouldn't have been able to do it.

The story was out. I was to learn, rather quickly, that I had just became "public property." As I left the office and drove down Route 93 heading home at about 4:00 in the afternoon, the realization was hitting me. I called my house and let everyone know that the afternoon had not gone as planned. I wanted them to be prepared for the evening news. I tried to assure them, "Don't worry, no one watches the news anymore, especially not the early news."

Immediately after I hung up, my cell started ringing again. I didn't recognize the number so I didn't answer it, but I did immediately check my voice mail. The message was from a friend of mine Cindy, that I hadn't talked to in almost a year. She was calling me to say that she had just seen me on the 4:00 news and that she didn't know what to say except that she was very proud of me for coming forward. She said that she was there for me if I needed anything. It was a message that I would receive from hundreds of people over the months ahead, from friends and strangers, alike.

The morning after that press conference I awoke refreshed and feeling great. It took me a little while, but then I realized something. I sat down and wrote an email to Bob and Courtney which read in part:

```
Bob and Courtney,

As hard and emotional as yesterday was,
this morning when I got up, I realized that
I had slept through the night. No big deal,
right? But I have to tell you, that it was
the first time that I had been able to ac-
tually sleep though the whole night since
seeing Joe Birmingham's picture in the pa-
per that first day…
```

It was true. I'm not sure if it was because for the first time in years I was able to clear my soul or if it was simply because I was emotionally drained and exhausted. Whatever the reason was, it really didn't matter. I slept. It was May 1, 2002.

That one reporter that I mentioned, who I thought has been biased against survivors, was actually a columnist and a radio talk show host. Prior to this issue, I hadn't regularly listened to talk radio. There were one or two shows that I listened to once in a while, but nothing regularly. As far as the newspaper was concerned, I tried to read the local paper when I had the opportunity and I would pick up the Boston Globe on Sundays. So needless to say, I didn't much follow the news regularly. After the Boston Globe had the courage to break the story, I started to read the paper a bit more and follow the news much more.

One of the columnists in the local paper, who is also an editor, writes a column a few times a week. In one of his columns his advice was that the Catholic Church should give $20,000 to each of those survivors that can still work and for the ones who can't work because of the effects of their abuse, they should be able to get a job from the Church.

In yet another of his columns written prior to the first statement Ed and I released, he said, "Now all of a sudden victims are dredging up dead priests and accusing them of molesting. Of course the dead priests are not here to defend themselves." Brilliant thoughts. He also said during one of his radio talk shows that, "The first thing that the Church needs to do is stop paying these guys. These guys (the victims) need to stop thinking that they have just won the pedophile lottery." That statement was used as part of a radio commercial that ran day and night. Like my daughter learning what the press considered news, I received my first lesson in what journalistic integrity was not. The combination of the article, as well as the choice of using that line as a radio commercial, definitely got under my skin and I let him know. I wrote a letter, which I mailed to the newspaper, as well as his radio station, which read in part:,

```
Instead of using your position to cause pain to
the survivors, you could use your position to
talk about and print information about the lo-
cal rape crisis hot line or the local support
groups. Or we could use your advice. Tell you
what, why don't I give you my winning pedophile
lottery ticket? And for that matter I'm sure my
brother would give you his winning ticket, as
well. Take those tickets and give them to your
10 or 11 year old nephew. I'm sure that he
could give those winning tickets to Father
Geoghan in exchange for $20,000.00 or maybe a
job at a local rectory. But be sure and tell
him not to tell anyone about it and keep quiet
for 30 years…..
```

In the months since that first press conference, I have come to realize the power of the press and the value of keeping the issue of sexual abuse in the public eye. As I have said, without the reporters breaking and keeping this story alive, I would have remained a victim. I would never have taken those first steps of becoming a survivor. Because other men came forward, I found the strength and courage to come forward. Because of that, I started to tell my story and will continue to tell it. I tell it for my sake, for the sake of my son, for the sake of those today who can't, and for the sake of those who hopefully won't have to in the future. Maybe others who have seen and heard me have found the courage as well. In the weeks and months ahead, I would tell my story, the story which you are reading, over and over again. I have spoken to let people know that is not just a story about a stranger. It could be a story about your father, your brother, your nephew, your neighbor or your friend. If you think that you don't personally know someone that this abuse has touched, please keep reading. Should you ever see me in public, I invite you to walk over and shake my hand, because I could be *your* brother, or *your* uncle, *your* friend or *your* son.

Since that initial press conference, I have attended many more press conferences regarding Father Birmingham. I have also been asked to appear on NECN, CNN, The Today show, CBS, NBC, ABC, as well as the local cable channels. I have told my story to many, many groups of people. Groups gathered in church halls and in public halls. I have continued to tell my story in the hopes of bringing about change.

If nothing else, I can tell you this. My son will never have to write a letter to me like I had to write to my family. I will do what ever I have to do so that it will never happen. Not to my son. And I ask you don't let it happen to your son.

✼✼✼✼✼

The tennis game was over. We'd been playing for over an hour. I couldn't believe that Fr.B had actually asked me to play with him at his club. I don't know anyone else that got to play tennis with him. He'd said that I had "an athletic body, nice and tall, great for tennis." He had asked me a few times to go and my mother said that he'd asked her if it was all right. She said, "It isn't every day that a priest takes an interest in you. You should go. It'll be fun." So I said I'd go.

It was definitely cool. We went in his shiny black car. Just him and I, no one else. I'm a lucky kid. The club was nice, we even had our own tennis court. We walked into the locker room area. I knew what a locker room was because I had caddied for my dad at his golf club. There were lockers lined up, benches, and a steam room with benches.

He told me that we should strip down to our shorts. I did, no big deal. He said, "Slide over, I'll rub your shoulders and back for you. I know you've never played tennis before but we usually get a rub down afterwards." He started massaging my shoulder and back and then my lower back. After a few minutes he said, "It's time to weigh ourselves." I wasn't sure what that meant, or why, but he explained that "after a work out, you always weigh yourself before you shower off." I said okay and started to get up to go over to the scale. "Wait a minute," he said. "You have to get undressed first." I took off my gym shorts and started to go to the scale again. "Wait a minute, you have to take all your clothes off. Even your underpants. They can count for a few extra ounces." He started to undress himself.

My stomach is turning and I want to hide. He's completely undressed now and waiting for me as I take off my underpants. Something's not right, but I don't know what it is. Why do I feel so uncomfortable? Why is he watching me like this? My hands are on the bench, I get up and walk over to the scale. I feel the cold tile on my feet and the cold metal plate of the scale. There's no one else around. "Well I'm not sure what you use to weigh, but I'm sure you had a good workout out there on the tennis courts." I get off of the scale. I feel like I've been naked for hours. He hops on the scale for a minute. "Time to clean up in the shower." I'm relieved to be going anyplace that I can be alone. As we walk, I realize that they aren't individual showers. I realize that we are going to take one together. I feel sick. I want to crawl out of my skin. I want to run and hide. There is no one around. We are all alone. I have no place to hide. The water comes on. We're both standing there naked. He takes his hand and grabs the soap, Huge hands, hairy knuckles. He asks me to turn around so that he can "help wash your back for you." I turn around, he starts to wash my shoulders, then he washes my back, then his hands slide down to my bottom. As I feel those hands all over me, I close my eyes and close my mind as Fr.B begins to molest me for the first time.

*****

6.

Over the next few weeks there was continually news about Father Birmingham and his legacy of abuse. It was constantly in the news. Several times a week our local paper was running stories regarding it. It was during that time that Saint Michael's Pastor Father Capone put a notice in the Church bulletin about an open parish meeting to be held in the basement of Saint Michael's School regarding the abuse issue. He had also indicated that there would be a representative from the Archdiocese of Boston there.

I was hesitant about going at all. Partly because I had no desire to once again be in that school. I didn't feel the need to discuss this issue with a priest and I felt that if the local church realized the true issues as hand they would never have a meeting in any building related to religion. I knew that there would probably be few actual survivors there because survivors of sexual abuse, as a rule, don't read church bulletins. I only found out because my parents still attended weekly mass at Saint Michael's. It was unlikely any survivors would attend since the meeting was being held in the very school where many survivors had actually been molested.

I did decide to go and my parents decided to attend, as well. I was surprised that my father wanted to go, though. My mother was a given, but my father was another story. Like most parents, this issue has had an immense effect on them. Unlike most of the men my age who are survivors, the majority of the parents of the survivors are of a totally different generation. As a former victim and now as a survivor, the anger and rage that I felt due to my abuse was visible in my life intermittently. Most of it showed up during my younger years, in my teens and twenties. Anger and rage had been replaced by determination, fear and shame has now been matched by tenacity.

I find that switch of traits to be in most men my age who have come forward. Our parents, however, are angry. Sometimes that comes out as blind anger, and sometimes rightfully so. Our parents feel as though they let us down. I remember my dad telling me, "Of course we're bullshit. We should have known. We should have protected you." He is no different from all parents when it comes to the protection of their children. Their generation grew up with the principle that "the buck stops here." They are use to a chain of command. Their's was a generation that was taught to "pray, pay and obey." Authority had the final say and you didn't question authority. When I made the statement that I wanted Cardinal Law to heal my parents and restore their faith, I meant it. I believed it was going to be much easier to deal with men like me who were survivors, than it was going to be to deal with our parents.

That night, in the basement of the school that I had attended for eight years, there was a group of 30 or so people. There were three (as far as I know) survivors of abuse, Olan Horne, Larry Finn, and me. The rest of the hall was filled with parishioners from Saint Michael's. Fr. Capone, the pastor, was there, as well as Fr. Mario. As soon as Fr. Capone got up and started to speak, my father's eyes filled up and he got up and left the building. I waited several minutes but he didn't return. I found out later that he had walked home. I knew that he had mixed emotions about going and I gave him a lot of credit just for being there.

The emotions were running high that evening. Especially after Fr. Capone introduced a woman we assumed was a representative from the Archdiocese. The first comment she made was that she was from Catholic Charities and that "she did not represent the Archdiocese of Boston in any way." That remark definitely set the tone for the evening. There were many questions from everyone there. That evening I realized it wasn't just the survivors and their parents who were upset. There truly was a sense of rage from everyday parishioners, as well. The consensus was that the Church wasn't doing enough to address this issue. Fr. Capone had the guts to ask us exactly what it was that we wanted him to do. Olan and I had plenty of ideas.

We told Fr. Capone that we appreciated the fact that he called a meeting like this together. We went on to say that the survivors that were coming out daily, didn't have time for the Archdiocese to take their time and decide what to do. We couldn't wait for new offices to open and new phone lines to be installed. We didn't think it was right for the Cardinal to be out there soliciting funds for his annual Cardinal's Appeal when his Church was in crisis mode and he was nowhere to be found. We needed action and answers. We needed communication. We needed accessibility.

To his credit, Fr. Capone asked what we wanted him to do, we told him, and he did it. That following Sunday, in his weekly statement in the church bulletin, Fr. Capone made what some would consider bold statements. I don't consider them bold. In my mind he made the right statements. He made mention of the fact that the Archdiocese wasn't doing enough and that they seemed to be dragging their feet. He went on to say that St. Michael's would not be participating in the Cardinal's Appeal fund until they took care of their own parishioners who were affected by this scandal and in need. I gave that man a lot of credit, which is, in itself, an irony. The fact that I felt the need to credit someone for what, under ordinary circumstances, would be an ordinary act, simply saying and doing the right thing, proves what an extraordinary time the Church had put us all in.

Soon after the bulletin was put out on Sunday, the local and national press picked up his message and it was all over TV. "Local Pastor snubs his nose at Cardinal Law," was one headline." This pastor is leading a one man revolution against Cardinal Law," was another comment made by a reporter. Poor Father Capone. Here he was trying to do something, anything, and he could be made the one of the first martyrs of the year. I'm not sure what help it did, but I faxed a letter of support, both to the rectory, as well as the Chancery's office, as did others from our group. Hopefully it helped cool the heat that he must have been feeling. Father Capone is still pastor at Saint Michael's, and we still maintain an open line of communication. He is proof that there are good priests out there who truly want to do the right thing.

When we got home from the meeting that evening, I went to visit my dad to make sure that he was all right. I asked him if he was okay. I'm very fortunate that my dad and I have had a great relationship for my entire life. Most survivors I have met have had strained relationships with their fathers and other men in their life, as well. My dad has always been there for me. I'm sure that it's partly because my dad and I worked side by side, both in the office of his flooring company, as well as in the field on job sites. I started working for my dad when he opened his business in 1975 when he was 50 and I was just turning 13. We continued to work together until he stopped flooring installations just two years ago when he turned 75. Over the years we've had our arguments, but we were able to argue about the problem, usually business related, as opposed to letting it become personal. Most of my brothers worked with and for him at one point or another, as well. As close as we were, we had still never talked about this issue.

That evening when I got home, my dad was sitting in his chair. I'm sure you know what I mean by "his chair." Everyone's dad has a chair, usually an old recliner. It's that worn in chair your dad sits in when he watches baseball on TV. As he looked at me, he started to cry. My dad is a very emotional man. I have seen him get emotional many times over my life. But, I have actually only seen him openly cry twice. The first when he had to bury my Brother Rick, who was my oldest brother, and the second when he had to bury my sister Terry, who was my youngest sister.

As he sat in his chair that night, my dad, the person in my mind whose faith had never floundered, who went to church daily for 18 years while my sister fought with cancer, who I would watch say the rosary as a child, was crying. Through his tears, he said, "I just couldn't stay there in that room. As soon as Capone got up and started to speak I just had to leave." "Its okay, dad. I was surprised you went to begin with. It's okay," I said. He went on, "No, you don't understand. I might as well tell you now, even though it's too late." Dad was sobbing. I had never seen him like that. "What you and your brother are going through is all my fault. I might as well get it out. When I was an altar boy at Saint Louis , Fr.____ molested me. What you kids are going through now is punishment for my sins of silence for not saying anything."

I was absolutely stunned. My dad had just told me something that he had never ever told another person in his life. Not even my mother, his wife of 50 years. He remembered how old he was, where he was, and he remembered the priest's name. It was almost 70 years, and he remembered. What could I say? what could anyone say? I hugged him and told him that it was okay, that Eddie and I would be okay, and that we were going to get through this. I couldn't imagine guilt that my father was feeling because of this. He told me that he should have been there to protect us. Like every father of an abuse survivor that I have met, he was angry.

I could only associate my own guilt for not dealing with this issue years ago with the guilt that my dad was feeling. I had begun to wonder how my life would have differed if had I opened up that can of worms years ago. Would it have changed the divorced home that my son now has to grow up in? I wondered how different things could have been? I am not alone, this is a feeling that I have shared with many of the guys that I have grown to know. We all have that "what could have been" syndrome concerning things in our lives.

This is a not a new phenomenon that has suddenly come out. Sexual abuse of children has been around for years and years. It is not just a problem that the Catholic Church is suffering from. Sexual abuse is a problem that has touched nearly everyone's life in some way. It's just that the window that was opened within the last few years has prompted many of us to talk about it for the first time. Because of that opportunity, sexual abuse is a topic that may be finally open for discussion. My decision about publicly speaking was cemented in place that night. There would never be another child with the name of "Bergeron" that would be abused by a priest. Not ever again. I would do whatever it took to make that a reality. Not my son. Not my son's son. Never ever again.

Over the weeks that passed after that revelation, I would ask my dad whether it was okay for me to talk to others about what he has said to me that night. "What use would it do? The priest is dead." As soon as he said that, I think he realized that the priest who abused Edward and me was dead, as well. He realized that only by talking about it did we have a chance to prevent it. It was then that my father said it was okay to publicly discuss something that he had kept hidden for almost 70 years. Courage in its true form.

I would come to find out that our story, the fact that a father as well as his children were abused at the hands of a priest, was not as unique as everyone would think. As I continued to talk and tell my personal story over the next few months, I would include bits of the conversation between my father and me. Inevitably I would have a father come up to me and tell me a similar story almost every time. The guilt is real, the effects are long term, and the rippling effects of abuse are huge.

7.

Driving to the Chancery in Brighton to meet with Barbara Thorpe, I was wondering what the meeting was going to be like. Barbara seemed like a compassionate woman on the phone when I called to make the appointment, but it was hard for me to trust anyone. I was driving in my dad's car, his pride and joy. It's nothing that out of the ordinary, just a Chrysler convertible, a few years old, not nearly new, but it's his pride and joy that he washes more often than most. It was the first time that I had borrowed his car. I had never asked before and I don't remember him letting anyone else ever borrow it either.

Pulling into the Chancery grounds I could see TV camera trucks parked outside the Chancery wall. The coveted property which houses the Chancery, the Cardinal's residency as well as, St. John's Seminary covers 14 acres. There's a long circular driveway leading to the Chancery administration office which is where I was heading. As I was sitting in the waiting room, I noticed the picture of the pope on one wall and the dated waiting room furniture. It was sparsely furnished with 1970's style furniture, not a very warm waiting area. I also noticed the bullet proof glass that's separating the receptionist from the waiting room area. I thought how odd to have thick bullet proof glass in a such a place.

After a few minutes Barbara Thorpe came out and introduced herself. I followed her into her office, which was a small room with no windows, not much larger than 9 feet square. As we sat down and she began to tell me how sorry she was to see me under these conditions. She also apologized to me for the pain that I must be feeling. Barbara asked me if I was comfortable enough to tell her a bit about my personal story. For some reason, I felt perfectly comfortable with her. I started by telling her that I felt angry. Angry because of the lack of action that the Cardinal, as well as the Archdiocese was taking. As I begin to tell her a bit about my family's history and my history of abuse with the Church, I noticed her becoming emotional. At times I had to stop and relax. As much as I try to not get emotional, it just comes out. I went on to tell her that " The Cardinal doesn't need to be in Chicago at a Catholic fundraiser, he needs to be here, dealing with these issues."

I tell her that he is the person in charge of the Archdiocese and the one that can begin to heal the pain that this has caused. "It is his responsibility and he has an obligation, as well as an opportunity, to do just that." I also told her my thoughts about him staying in Boston. "The Church has no right to pack him up and ship him somewhere else and he has no right to run away from this problem that he has continued to hide from. Part of this is his mess and he needs to stay here and clean it up." I went to tell her that there needs to be complete disclosure of the files on Birmingham so that the survivors can begin to heal and go on. She asked me, "You mean you want to see the complete files on Birmingham? No matter how painful they may be?" I simply replied, "Yes." I told her that if Cardinal Law had taken responsibility from the beginning, the Church would not be in as big a mess as it was. "Barbara, I thought that in the Catholic faith, we called what I was talking about Confession. From what I was also taught at St. Michael's, if you are truly sorry, confess your sins, admit your guilt, make retribution, your sins are forgiven and healing begins. Why hasn't he done that?." Had the Cardinal done that, neither I, nor many of the other men involved in this would be involved in a law suit. The law suit started because of this wall of silence and the continued profession of innocence that the Church has put up.

I told her that the Cardinal needed to be out meeting the survivors and their families and not hiding from everyone. "He is the only one that can begin to heal the pain that my parents feel. I've become a very patient man in dealing with this issue. Barbara, my parents are in their 70's, they don't have another 40 years to heal like I do. I don't want my parents taking their guilt and anger to their grave. The Cardinal needs to realize this."

As our meeting wound down, she asked me, "Do you think that you would like a meeting with the Cardinal? Gary, when you came in here, the first thing you said to me was that you were angry, but you managed to tell me how you felt and tell me your story without directing your anger at me. I think that it's important that the Cardinal hears this and it's important that he hears it from you." I was still leery, but I said that I absolutely wanted a meeting with the Cardinal, as long as it was in a private one on one setting. She said that she would check his schedule and get back to me within a few days.

As I drove home, I felt good. Olan had told me that his religion was "optimism." If his was optimism, then mine was eternal optimism. I would be getting a call from Barbara and I would be meeting the Cardinal within a few days, I thought.

I wanted that meeting. I really wanted it. I felt that if I had the chance to see him and talk to him one on one, I might be able to get through. In the days and weeks that followed, I would tell other survivors about my meeting with Barbara and her offer to meet the Cardinal. One by one, they would tell me that I was crazy. I was told not to hold my breath and at least once I was told, "Sure, you'll get a private meeting with the Cardinal when Hell freezes over." Although Courtney and Bob thought such a meeting was a good idea, both doubted that that meeting would take place, especially considering that the Cardinal was a named defendant in a lawsuit in which I was about to become one of the plaintiffs.

Days turned into weeks and weeks turned into months. I would receive no call about my meeting. As the press coverage continued and my public speaking continued, I would talk about meeting with Barbara. I would talk about being offered a meeting with the Cardinal and not hearing from them. One of the first opportunities to speak was at Saint James parish in Salem, where Birmingham was before he was moved to Saint Michael's in Lowell. This meeting was a combined meeting of the seven parishes in Salem which was going to be an open forum to discuss the abuse scandal. Bernie McDaid had told me about it and said that it would be good if some of us were there to speak and answer questions. I told Bernie that I wasn't sure if I would be able to speak. Although I had told some of my story in the news, I had never talked to an audience of this sort before. "It's too emotional for me, Bernie. There's no way I could speak without breaking down again." I told him that I would go though and at least be there for support if he decided to speak. I also thought about what I could do that may get through to the Cardinal.

One of the many questions that I had been asked was "What can I do to help?" I really didn't have an answer. Talking with some of the other guys at our regular Tuesday meetings, I told them that we needed to do something that could involve all the parishes that Birmingham was at. There had to be a simple message that we could send the Cardinal collectively as a group, some simple message of solidarity. We went around and around for a while. I wanted something that he would read and would think about. I felt that if we had a message that everyone was comfortable sending and made it something easy and simple, that the parishioners would do it.

After talking with Olan, Bernie, and the others, I decided that I would take a step and try and come up with something simple and non threatening. Telling Bernie and the other guys that I would meet them in Salem for the meeting, I went to work over the next few days.

The evening of the meeting I met the SOJB group in the parking lot. The group now loosely consisted of about 10 of us who met at the regular Tuesday night support meetings. It is true that there is "strength in numbers," especially when you're talking about an issue as personal as this one is. The parking lot also had the usual TV and Newspaper reporters. As our group walked into the hall, the meeting had just begun. There were probably 250 parishioners in the hall, as well several priests, nuns, and laypersons. I wasn't sure how the evening was going to progress. It was an open mike platform meaning that anyone who had anything to say was invited to just walk up and talk. It would be interesting to see how other people felt about this. I had hoped that we would be able to get a random selection of opinions. At that point it was too soon for anyone to have recognized us. It wasn't announced that we would be speaking there that night so I was more interested in listening than I was interested in speaking.

One by one parishioners got up and talked about how this has affected their faith. One by one they got up and talked about feeling angry, hurt, embarrassed and distraught because of the actions that priests had taken and because of the inaction that the Church was now taking. I felt relieved, I know we all did. There are times when I've questioned whether this issue was as important to me as it was to the general public and to the everyday Catholic. To see an elderly Catholic woman get up on stage in front of a large crowd and talk about her anger and resentment because the "foundation of the Catholic Church is breaking down and the Cardinal is standing by and watching" was a pretty moving sight.

After several parishioners got up, Bernie went to the stage and spoke. Thanking everyone for their support and for coming there, Bernie went of to tell them that they had a small window of opportunity to get things done, to start change. As Bernie talked, Olan looked at me and asked if I was going to be able to speak. I said probably not. "It's too emotional here. Can't you feel it in the air?" I said. He grinned at me and slid over a napkin. "Here, it's for you. We voted you the best crier in the group," he said. His wife gave him the look of death and said, "Olan, that's awful." I smiled. Olan then got up and spoke for a few minutes, telling the people what the needs of the survivors have been, talking about the outreach that needed to be done for the survivors and their families, many of whom were finding out, like the parishioners, for the first time. After Olan spoke, he returned to the table. A parishioner got up and asked about what they could do to help. Olan looked at me and I knew it was my time. I was out of my seat and on my way to the stage.

As I got there, I took the microphone and started to talk. I'm not sure where the words came from, but they came and they flowed. With the words came the emotions, as well. I know that there was a five minute limit on anyone talking. They actually had an egg timer that would ding after five minutes. I can tell you this, I know I talked for more than five minutes, probably more like 20. I don't know what happened to the timer, I never heard it go off. I talked about my family's faith, about history of abuse at the hands of Birmingham, about my decision to go public and about my sister. I also talked about meeting with Barbara Thorpe and about her offer to met with Cardinal Law.

I told them, "It's been over two months and I'm still waiting for that call. If anyone here has access to the Chancery, please let the Cardinal know, that I'm still waiting. I will continue to wait as long as it takes. I'm not going anywhere. To that parishioner who asked a few minutes ago, "What can I do?" I would like to thank you. Not just for having the courage to come to this meeting, but to ask that question. If I can ask only one thing of everyone in this room tonight, it would be this. If you want to help me and help all the survivors, please help us in sending Cardinal Law a message, and ask him this question for me, and for all of us."

I reached in my pockets and pulled out a stack of post cards. I had shown them to some of the guys and the opinions were mixed. But I had to at least try. I pulled them out and held them in the air as I continued.

" I ask only this. That at the end of the evening you come up to me and take one of these cards. They are already stamped and addressed to the Cardinal. All you have to do is sign them and tell him what parish you are from. They ask Cardinal Law one question, which is the only question that he needs to answer in order to do the right thing."

I showed them the front of the post card, which had a stamp and an address on it, and then I flipped it over on the other side, and in large block letters the post card read…

"DEAR Cardinal Law, WHAT WOULD JESUS DO?"

"It's a simple message and it's a question that the Cardinal needs to answer to all of us. Thank you for giving me this opportunity, and thank you for your support."

I got the message out, it was simple and to the point. I felt as though I had connected on a personal level with the people there. Hopefully, I had. It was important for me to tell my personal story because I always felt that the public needed to know that we're not strangers, we're not numbers. We're human, each with a human story. As many men that have been affected by Father Joseph Birmingham, this was not a story about a priest who abused a hundred men. It was a hundred individual personal stories about the tragedy of abuse.

I walked back to my seat, after shaking the hands of parishioners who had grabbed me along the way and thanked me. Hoping that my message got across and wondering if it had, I sat down. I asked Bernie if I had done okay. "You did a great job, great idea with the post cards," he said. I looked at the tissue that Olan had given me earlier and I slid it back across the table. "Here you go, " I said. Olan, with tears in his eyes, took the tissue and said, " Fuck you, you're an asshole." I realized then, that it was actually the first time that any of the guys had heard me talk about my personal story, as well. That night would be the first night that Olan, Bernie, and myself would speak publicly at the same time. Three months before, we had been three strangers. We had become three friends. Since that night, my view has been that when Olan talks he tells them what needs to be done. When Bernie talks, he tells them how it needs to be done. And when I talk, I tell them why it needs to be done. I'm not sure if that makes sense, but that's the way it always seemed to fit together. Nothing was planned for that night and nothing is usually ever planned when we have talked since, but it just always fits that way.

As the meeting closed up, I stood in the back of the room, postcards in hand. I had printed up 300 earlier that day, although I wasn't sure how or what I was going to do with them., The evening worked all that out for me. Every one of the guys that were there as part of our group were handing them out. People were asking for the cards and they were offering money for printing, postage. Any time they offered the money, I asked them to send it instead directly to Catholic Charities which had been hit hard because of the shortage of donations. I didn't want money. What I wanted was for them to send in the post cards. I wanted this message to get across.

By the end of the end of the evening, we were out of postcards. Within the next few weeks, we would continue to speak. I would continue to ask for my meeting with the Cardinal at every opportunity and continue to hand out those post cards. Those post cards would find their way onto news broadcasts. Hopefully, they would also find their way into the hands of the Cardinal. One person doing one thing, asking another person to do one thing. Sometimes it can be that simple. Sometimes simple things can make a difference.

8.

On Tuesday, June 4, some of the files on Birmingham were finally to be released. They were reluctantly released as part of a group of files pertaining to a deposition of other Church officials, so naturally, there was a press conference regarding this. We had been asking for these files for months and even though it wasn't a complete set of files, it was some progress. Bob and Courtney called to see if I would be willing to come in, along with Olan and Bernie, to represent all the Birmingham survivors at a press conference that afternoon.

Driving into Bob's office with Olan, we talked about the direction that the press conference would take. We both felt that we only wanted to be there if it was for the good of other survivors. Neither of us wanted to start playing the "poor victim" role into which we could be cast. Talking and telling my story on a personal level was one thing, but I didn't want to be at a press conference just for the sake of having "victims" out there. The three of us had been fielding calls, which went something like, " Hi, this is so and so from group x. We would like a few victims to speak to our group. Can you get us some?." As stupid as that may sound, that's exactly the way it went.

Naturally, we all talked about it. Because our three faces were being seen more and more, we were assured that it wasn't just a case of needing a victim to face the camera. The three of us were asked for specific reasons. Our stories were connecting with people on a personal level. That being said, we were still leery of being pawns in the press game. But we all knew what was at stake. Needless to say, we went.

Even knowing what we knew from personal experiences with Birmingham, that day was eye opening. There were about 80 pages of documents relating only to Birmingham. Eighty pages of abuse allegations and admittances relating directly to him. It is one thing to know what you know from personal experience, it is totally another thing to actually see it in writing black and white. We read story after story about Birmingham's abuses, survivor after survivor, parish after parish. The names of the survivors were blacked out, but we knew who they were. In almost every story that I read, I recognized who they were talking about. I didn't need to see the names of the kids. I knew the men they had become.

In that batch of documents, I read about the meeting that Bernie's parents had with the Chancery, about meetings on behalf of other men in my group that had been abused by Birmingham which had been documented. There were documents about Birmingham's abuse relating to every single parish that he had been assigned to. Every one. There was, however, only one document that really hit me. It made me sick and flush with anger when I did the math in my head. As unbelievable as it sounds, the three of us were reading these documents and just looking at each other with astonishment. And this was only a miniscule part of the Birmingham files that we were asking for.

The press conference started. As before there were many, many cameras and reporters in that room. Bob Sherman, Courtney, as well as two other attorneys from their office were there. Unlike the last press conference that I was at, when they asked if we wanted to say anything, I said yes. Unlike the last press conference, I knew exactly what I wanted to say.

"Over two months ago, I sat in this room with all of you. That day, I talked about the abuse that my brother and I suffered at the hands of Joseph Birmingham. I told you, without proof, but having learned by meeting other survivors, that the Church moved Birmingham to parish after parish after parish. I now sit here and I have read document, after document, after document that the Church did, in fact, know all about Father Joseph Birmingham and did nothing about it. These are not documents about mere allegations, these are documents where he admitted it. Not only did they know and document it in their files, but also these files show that they knew that Father Joseph Birmingham was molesting child after child as early as 1964. The Archdiocese of Boston knew that Father Joseph Birmingham was molesting children in 1964. When I was 2 years old, and when my brother was just a year old, The Archdiocese knew that he was molesting children and did nothing but allow him to continue to molest children until I grew up. They then allowed him to continue year after year, after he had molested my brother and me. The fact is that they knew, they knew and did nothing."

That was the document that did it for me. It was unbelievable to me to think that as early as 1964, Birmingham had admitted abusing children. There were no words that could possibly begin to explain this to me. After all these weeks of meeting survivor after survivor, I was still in shock. Regardless of all of the other files that had been made public, I had never seen a more blatant disregard for the safety of children. I had never seen a more offensive show of self protection by the Archdiocese of Boston, as well. I was beginning to s realize why there had been no response from the Archdiocese about this. The plain and simple fact was that there was no defense. There was nothing that could be said, no excuse that could be given for the children's innocence that they sacrificed.

Also that one piece of paper had given, not only me, but also many other men that had come forward, vindication. It was proof. Not that any of us needed it. But I know that the families and friends of many of the men wished for it. I probably wished for it, as well. (see Birmingham Document 2.1)

There was one other piece of paper that bothered me more than most. It was a letter written by a mother in Gloucester. She had written to Cardinal Law in April of 1987. Her letter asked about rumors regarding Fr. Birmingham's transfer from her parish that had recently taken place. Parishioners were told it was for "health reasons." Subsequent to his leaving, she met a friend of hers who told her that a Fr. Joe Birmingham had been removed from Salem in the late '60s because he had molested boys in the parish. She went on to say that twice within the past six months her Fr. Birmingham had given sermons on AIDS, which she had found odd. She asked if these two Birminghams were the same man. She was more than curious, she was concerned because her son who has just turned 13, was an altar boy at St. Ann's in Gloucester where Birmingham was priest and pastor. (see Birmingham document 2.23)

The reply to her letter was written, not by Cardinal Law, but by the Secretary of Personnel Fr. John B. McCormack, who has become Bishop McCormack. The shocking reply, in short, would say that she had nothing to worry about because he had personally spoken to Father Birmingham and was assured that there was no "factual basis for her concern." This reply was written by the same John B. McCormack who graduated the seminary with Joseph Birmingham, the same Fr. John B McCormack who was also a priest at Saint James in Salem serving with Joseph Birmingham when boys were being abused.
(see Birmingham document 2.25)

The documents released gave the Archdiocese "factual basis" for concern for the safety of children regarding Birmingham as early as 1964. To me, that was pretty factual. The AIDS issue is still being investigated. Not only by survivors, but by others as well. Although Birmingham's death certificate states that he died of lung cancer, questions remain as to the validity of that finding. As of the writing of this book, the Archdiocese has refused access to the late Joe Birmingham's medical records.

On Thursday, June 13 of the following week, I was asked to appear live on the **Today Show** in New York City. I had been asked to be a part of a round table discussion regarding the abuse scandal. There were four other men who were also invited to speak, I knew none of them. As I sat in the passenger area of Logan Airport waiting to board my flight, I was thinking that three months earlier, I had told no one what had happened. And I was about to fly to New York to appear on national television to tell everyone. Three months before I was hanging sheetrock and painting woodwork. And at that moment, I was wondering if I packed everything I needed for an overnight stay in New York City. My life was suddenly not my own. At times I had the overwhelming feeling that I was thrown out into the public and my life seemed surreal. How could a guy like me from a small town like Lowell ever do right with something as important as this was? What if I totally just screwed up? What if I said the wrong thing? What if I just froze on national TV?

After checking into the hotel the show provided, I took a long walk around the city. It was lightly raining and as each person passed me, I wondered if they would be watching television the next morning. That evening I sat in the lounge and had a few glasses of wine to relax. I had been fighting a sick feeling in the pit of my stomach all day and nothing was helping. As I was sitting there, trying to just blend into the woodwork, a guy walked over to me and said, "Hey, aren't you here for the church sex thing with the Today Show?" I couldn't believe that someone actually knew me, let alone would say something like that out loud. I had just met face to face with Jamie Hogan, the first Birmingham survivor who had come forward. I didn't realize that he would be on the show with me. I wanted to crawl under the table. What could I say, but, "Yes."

The following morning, after not sleeping well, I was introduced to the other four men who would be joining me. I recognized only one, Jamie Hogan, from the night before. After a brief breakfast that nobody ate, we were all driven to the studio. I'm sure we were all equally nervous that morning but that fact didn't make me feel any better. We were shown to the green room which was where you waited until you went on the air. While we waited, we actually sat with actor Michael Gross, who played Steven Keaton, the father on the sitcom "Family Ties." Talk about surreal. For some reason out of all the people in the room that day, he looked at me and asked what I was being interviewed for. Not knowing what else to say, I told him why we were all there. I was pleasantly surprised when he walked over and offered his hand and thanked me for having the courage to be public on such a "sensitive issue." We actually had an extensive conversation about it. He was very compassionate. Moments later, it was our turn. As an assistant came in to get us and walk us to the set, I asked for the nearest men's room. Walking inside, I ended up losing the battle with nausea I had been feeling for the previous 24 hours. With minutes to go before I would appear on national television for the first time, I was sick to my stomach and I was throwing up. As I walked out of the men's room, it must have shown on my face. Someone came up and asked me if I was okay. "Of course. Let's get this done," was my reply. Thankfully before we headed to the actual set, we visited the makeup person, who coated my ghost white face with powder.

As the cameras started to roll, we were each introduced and asked a series of questions. When it was my turn for a question, I was first asked about the fact that Birmingham was buried next to my sister and brother. I didn't know that anyone had told them about that and I wasn't prepared for it. I stumbled and fought back tears, but I got through it. Someone had done their homework that day and realized that the topic of Birmingham's grave site is a very personal subject to me. They had also asked about my dad talking about his abuse. It was another very personal subject which was tough to get through. The whole segment lasted 20 minutes, which I have since come to realize is a long time on national TV. It was one of the toughest things I had ever been through. Everyone said it went well. My only thoughts were that I was glad it was over and I was glad to be going home.

Arriving home that day, I would get a phone call from Tanya, my former wife. I hadn't told her about appearing on the Today show that day. She had gotten calls from her family. Apparently she hadn't told her family anything about what was going on in my life either. They had just found out.

9.

It was shortly after the Today show interview that I got a call from the Boston Globe. Tom Farragher was doing a story on failed promises of the Church. He called wanting to know if I would be willing to talk about my meeting with Barbara Thorpe and about the empty promise of a meeting with the Cardinal.

Hoping that by doing the interview the Archdiocese might remember their offer, I agreed. Tom sat for two hours with me and my brother Ed, who had not been doing well since this story had opened up in March. Ed, who lives in South Carolina, had been staying with me for a few weeks. We talked about our family, the Church, our abuse and about the promise of a one on one meeting with Cardinal Law. Barbara had made that offer not only to myself, but also to Ed. Tom wrote a lengthy well written article. It may have worked.

Three days after the article was in the paper, I got a phone call from Barbara to see if I was still interested in meeting. I was absolutely interested. She apologized for not getting back to me sooner and admitted that it had been a mistake. Apology accepted, we moved on. She had given me a few dates to choose from, the first one wasn't good for me because my son was coming up to visit for a few weeks. We set up an appointment for July 18th. It was a couple of weeks away, which was good. It was a firm date, and the Cardinal had committed to it. Needless to say, I was a bit surprised, especially after I had openly and publicly

criticized Cardinal Law's actions of the past. I had also spoken openly about his lack of action in the present, too. After hanging up with her, I made the usual series of calls and sent one e-mail.
...

```
Courtney and Bob:

It must be freezing in Hell. My meeting
with the Cardinal is set for July 18.
```

When people heard of my meeting the first thing that happened was this surprised look on their face. As soon as the surprise factor wore off the next thing I would get from people would be advice. The first one to offer it was my father. He called me late one night and said, "Gary, it's dad. Listen I was just thinking, I don't want you to go and meet with the Cardinal by yourself. Make sure you bring someone with you. As smart as you think you may be, the Cardinal's no dummy. Don't go alone." My dad wasn't the only one I got that advice from. Everyone seemed to have an opinion. Don't go alone, bring a tape recorder, bring your attorney, bring a friend or bring anyone.

The funny thing is I remember that Bob was the only one who actually got the real reason that I wanted this meeting. Bob was the only one who advised me to go alone. He would be the one to say, "Go alone. You're having a one on one and you know what you're going for." I did know, and so did Bob.

My reason was not for a "face off with Bernie" as some called it. To me, there is a difference between publicly criticizing a person's actions and publicly criticizing a person. For several months I had been publicly criticizing the actions of Cardinal Law. I wanted to meet with him personally on a one to one basis to judge the "man" for myself. I wanted to see him eye to eye and have him answer my questions to me, directly. I'm not one to believe everything I see and read. Again, with my optimistic attitude, I believed that if I could meet with him and talk with him, one on one, talk to him about abuse on a personal level, then there may be a chance he might get it. I also felt that he was going to be around for a while.

Because I believed that for anything constructive to happen, there needed to be a dialogue. What is important to remember is that in the end, we all want to heal. I want my soul to heal, I want my family to heal, I want my Church to heal, (even though I don't go) and I want my spirituality to heal. The only way that any of that healing is going to take place is for change to take place. There are only two ways you can bring about change. By attacking, breaking down and replacing, or by changing from the inside out. I believe that there are many great things that the Catholic Church has achieved and continues to achieve. That being said, the first choice, taking the Catholic Church apart is not the option for me. That only leaves the latter, change from the inside. The only way that there can be that type of constructive change is through dialogue.

My opinion has not been the popular one, but for me, it's the right one. For change to happen there has to be dialogue and if I was going to engage in dialogue regarding an issue as important as this one , I was going to have that dialogue with the man who makes the decisions. No one else.

We were not dealing with an institution that based decisions and policies on the whim of a committee or on the popular opinion of the general population. This institution was based on the faith and belief in one man in authority. The Archdiocese of Boston was not a democracy. There was only one man that could, if he had chosen to, do the right thing at that moment in time in the greater Boston area. There was only one man who could have made institutional changes for the good of all the faithful in this area. To me, in order to deal with and get past this I would have to deal with that one man as well. Cardinal Bernard Law. Although the Cardinal was not in his position when I was abused, he was in power when others were abused. I wanted to meet with him on a very personal level. I was not sure if it was my faith of "eternal optimism" that Olan and I had talked about, or it was my belief that good, will always over come evil. In my heart, I just felt that if I had the opportunity to connect with him on this level, he would get it, realize the problem and do whatever was necessary to fix it.

This was a meeting about healing, building a dialogue and initiating a discussion for possible change. Proactive, that was my attitude. I wasn't sure if anyone in my position had given Cardinal Law that kind of opportunity before. I wanted to know the who, what, where, when, and why. I wanted to give him the opportunity to answer those questions. I wanted to hear the answers from his lips, not his attorneys, not his press people, not see them on TV or read them in the paper. I had been asking for this meeting and I wanted it. Now, given the opportunity, I would take it. I can tell you what I didn't want was to go to my grave hating a man that I had never met. There had been enough hate and destruction in my life caused by this already. The bottom line was? What was my option?

On July 18, 2002, I made that drive to the Chancery again. This time it was different, though. The apprehension that I was feeling the last time I was there meeting Barbara Thorpe was not there. My palms were not sweaty, I was comfortable. I was meeting Cardinal Law at his residency, located on the same land as the Chancery. The residency is tucked away on the right, not visible from the street. It's an old stone façade building, probably built before the turn of the century. Large and a bit foreboding. I parked in front and was a bit early, so I waited and read the paper.

As I was reading, Barbara walked up, we talked a minute or two about what was in the paper that morning, another article regarding the church scandal." She said, "We're both a bit early, but we might as well go in and get out of the heat." Off we went. While walking, Barbara asked me if I was okay. "Absolutely," was my reply. She also reminded me that along with the Cardinal and me and herself, the Cardinal's personal secretary, Fr. John, would be there. She also asked if I was still okay with that. I thought to myself, No, not really. That means it's going to be three against one That's not fair. I felt bad for their side. "Yes, that's no problem Barbara." I said.

Walking into the Cardinal's residency, I looked around and thought to myself, this looks just like I've pictured it in my mind. Large rooms, high ceilings, warm furnishings, very spacious. I was also wondering if Jesus Christ was living on earth, if this was the kind of house he would live in, probably not. I followed her into what I believed to be the dining room. Though I didn't ask, I just presumed it was a dining room. This room was probably 15 feet wide and 30 feet long. There was a long wooden table with two dozen chairs, paintings and a few pieces of sculpture scattered here and there. Nice digs, I thought.

I was shown to one end of the table, sitting in the last chair on the corner, Barbara was immediately to my left. With in a few minutes the a door to my right opened and in walked Cardinal Bernard Law with Fr. John Connelly right behind him. Maybe it's because Fr. John is such a tall and large guy, but the Cardinal looked smaller to me than the man I remembered seeing on television day after day and in the newspapers. He was wearing simple basic black clothes, the same as an ordinary priest, with a large sliver cross necklace. No taller than I, more frail that I had anticipated. This has taken its toll on everyone, I thought to myself. Walking over he extended his hand. As we shook hands he said, "Thank you for coming, Gary. I've been looking forward to meeting you." "I've been looking forward to meeting you, as well," was my reply. "I'm sorry it's taken so long for this meeting to happen," he said. "So am I," was my immediate reply.

Taking the seat immediately to my right, he sat down within an arm's length from me. Close and intimate, not a bad thing, I thought to myself. Fr. John would sit across the table on the opposite side of Barbara. So this would be it. After months of planning and asking, I was actually going to have an opportunity to ask some of the questions that had been in the back of my mind. I can remember thinking to myself, *I don't know what the big deal is here*. And I really didn't.

Everyone who knew that I had a meeting with the Cardinal was almost in awe of it. To everyone else it was as if I was meeting God himself. "You're going to actually meet the Cardinal?" They would ask me in disbelief. What was the big deal with all this? To me, this was what he was supposed to be doing.

In my on mind, I compared this reaction to the same reaction I get when people find out that I travel to Virginia every other weekend to see my son. It's as if I was doing something extraordinary. I don't see it that way at all. Regardless of how it may seem to others, the fact that I'm on a plane every other weekend only means that I have a few more frequent flyer miles than most. My flying to see him is the least I can do and I wish that I could do more. To me, it's a shame that because of things that have happened which have nothing to do with my son Evan, he only gets to see me every other weekend. It's a shame that in today's society, suddenly you're branded an "exceptional father" just because you're doing the right thing. And it's not the right thing. The right thing would be for my son to be raised in a normal family household, the right thing is not for me to be a weekend father. A long time ago before my daughter was born, someone said to me, "Always remember, kids don't ask to be born." He was right, that was something that I have never forgotten. For my sake, and my son's sake, me going to see him, regardless if he lived in the next town, or 20 states away, is the right thing to do.

The fact that the Cardinal had agreed to meet with me and the reaction that I had received from people who found out about it was strange. This was an ordinary event, but it again proved what an extraordinary situation the Archdioceses had put us all in when the fact that the Cardinal is meeting with someone had been raised to such an event level. Simply put, he should be meeting with me, it was the right thing to do.

We talked over the next two hours. This wasn't a prepared meeting for me, anyway. Though I had waited 30 years for it, I didn't prepare anything. "Talk from the heart," as Bob Sherman had once advised me. That's exactly what I did. I told the Cardinal parts of my story, the abuse and the effects it had had on my family. I told him about Birmingham being buried near Terry and I told him about my father's pain. I held nothing back. I also talked about the effects that it had on my own life. In doing so I had admitted to myself. for the first time, that there had been effects. Up until this point I had refused to give Father Birmingham credit for almost anything that affected my life. Through therapy, I was starting to learn that nothing could have been further from the truth.

When I looked at my family as a whole and then looked at the aspects of each life individually, I couldn't help but wonder what would have been different if my past had not been touched by an evil predatory priest named Joseph Birmingham. What would it have been like if my life had instead been touched by a priest whose concern was spiritual nurturing, not sexual gratification? The effects of sexual abuse are wide and varying. The sexual abuse of a child, at such an age, by a a priest, someone who is often considered "Godlike," is devastating. In the past few months, I had to take a hard look at my life, although I was extremely reluctant to do so. I had never been the type of person who wanted to point blame at someone for things that I had done. Now, sitting in front of Cardinal Law, after refusing to even address or discuss the "men we could have been" with my brother Edward until several months before, I was about to break through that wall.

In some aspects of my life, I am truly (as people of faith would say) blessed. I am healthy. I have an exceptional family, two incredible kids, a roof over my head, food on my table and I am alive. I realize that there are many in this world that don't even have the basics. At times in the past I have felt guilty even thinking about "what could have been" and "about the men we all could have been." Now that I had taken a long hard look at my life through the help of a therapist and with the help of other men within our support group, things could have and should have, been different. For the first time in my life, after taking an honest look in the mirror, I realized that for many years I had just been going through the motions. I had always felt that I was really "one of the lucky ones." I never believed that there was anything wrong in my life. Many times people have come up to me and say that "you seem to be doing okay, you really have it together." That may be the appearance, but it's not the truth. Not by a long shot. When I finally did do that "look in the mirror," no one was more shocked than I. After almost 30 years, I was finally ready to sit down and connect the dots. What I found was definitely not what I wanted to see.

I told Cardinal Law that after growing up in a family whose parents have been married 50 years, I had two failed marriages. My relationships with both women and men have been anything but successful. My family life was very grounded, yet since moving out of my parent's house at age 18, I had moved 22 times in 21 years. Yes, I have had 22 different addresses, 22 different phone numbers, and 22 different sets of neighbors. Was I running away from something? Or was I running, looking for something? I have lived in three different states, sometimes moving several times in a single year. I had never realized any of that until I was asked to put all my addresses on paper by Bob and Courtney that day in March. Then it hit me, something wasn't right.

I talked about the fact that I was the first person in my family who didn't attend a Catholic high school. I refused to go. I went to a vocational school, and although my older brothers and sisters attended private parochial schools, I refused. I also had no intentions of going to college, which was odd considering I had been an A-B student for most of my eight years at Saint Michael's. Oddly, I almost flunked out of high school. I have older brothers that have graduated college and are newspaper publishers and chief engineers. My younger brother Steven graduated Harvard, yet Edward and I barely made it out of high school.

Unlike the circle of friends who surround my parents or my other friends, I have always been a loner. In high school, I never played any team sports, nor joined any group. I never participated in sports or gym because I didn't want to have to hit the locker room and I absolutely refused to have to take a shower in one of those open shower rooms. If anyone thinks that sexual abuse is forgotten in the minds of those abused, think again. The first shower incident that I had with Birmingham remains as clear in my mind today, 30 years later, as it did that day. I can still remember the feeling of the cold tile under my feet, the musky smell of the locker room, and the clanging of the metal scale that he made me stand on, naked, to get weighed. I remember everything. To this very day, if I go to the gym, I'll take a shower after, at home.

The effects that he had on relationships I had in my life are even more apparent. Some men who have had this kind of abuse have had problems regarding their sexual identity. For me, part of the result of that sexual abuse was a disassociation of sex and love. Sex was the mechanical act. Love was something "out there" that should have had a connection, but didn't. Where some men would wonder whether or not they were gay because if because of what they went through and what they did with Birmingham, there was no doubt in my mind that I was not. I spent the next few years of my life proving it. Sex was mechanical, and women, for the most part, were a means to an end. From one, to the next, there was no stopping me. If she walked and she talked, then I was interested in sleeping with her. To me, there was definitely a disconnect between love and sex. I loved rarely and sexed frequently. Sex became almost an obsession, one after another, after another. Many survivors of sexual abuse suffer from sexual addictions as well as alcohol and drug addiction.

It comes in all forms, destructive sexual behavior, excessive masturbation and dangerous sexual behavior, just to name a few.

Some I have personally dealt with. Addictions, in general, whether to drugs, alcohol or sex, are very common among abuse survivors. Every single abuse survivor whom I have met has had an addiction problem, of some sort. Every single one. Some have been able to work through them and would be considered "in recovery," but the majority of them, like me, have just begun to realize that their lives have been anything but normal.

Whenever I was involved in any kind of long term relationship, as soon as the relationship turned serious and there was a possibility that the term "love" was creeping in, a wall automatically went up. And any interest in sex was lost. No matter what my partner did, nothing would be able to break through that wall of protection that had formed around me. Not even while being married. These are issues that I continue to work through to this very day. And I am not alone.

As I continued to talk with Cardinal Law, the conversation turned to my sister Terry and my emotions took over. The fact that while my parents were caring for my sister, Birmingham was taking the opportunity to abuse her brothers is one thing. The fact that he is buried near her is another. I had a hard time admitting that after helping her, as did all my family, through her 18 year battle with cancer, flying back from Florida to be with her in the last month of her life, and standing next to her when she passed away in our family home, I had not visited her grave for almost 10 years. I wanted him to know that. To put it simply, it just isn't right. That is hallowed ground and Birmingham had no right to be there. I had learned that I was not alone in that arena, either. I discovered that there were other survivors of Birmingham who would come to the horrible realization that their family members were buried in the same cemetery. I was not alone.

Other effects, such as anger and rage, had become commonplace in my life. I remembered being 13 and having an argument with my mother. At one point, I became so angry that I literally picked up the vacuum cleaner and threw it at her. Thank God it missed her, but it did go through the wall. After that, I sat on the front steps outside, crying. I didn't know why I was so angry. When my father and older brother got home, I was still sitting on the steps crying and when they asked me what was wrong, I couldn't answer them. I was just full of rage. In my teen years my temper would get out of control many times. Edward and I would be at each other's throat. One time, after a fistfight in the driveway which my father broke up, I walked down the driveway and with my fist, punched out all the windows in the van. I then turned around and walked to the hospital, numb. I would hear similar stories of excessive anger and rage from other men. No, I was definitely not alone.

The last part of my personal story that I told Cardinal Law was something so personal, that I had never told anyone. And although I had never mentioned it, I had thought about it often. I would think about it every other weekend when I was getting on a plane to see my son. It is definitely one of those "what if" things that I wondered about. What if this abuse had never happened?

After my wife and I had separated, she informed me that if and when our divorce was final, she intended on moving back to Virginia, which is where she grew up and which is where her family was. "No way," was my reply. There was no way that that was going to happen. Evan was not going to grow up without his father nearby. It wasn't even a possibility. I was going to do anything possible to prevent her from leaving with our son. Or so I thought.

When the divorce papers were delivered to me, not only was she requesting that she be allowed to move out of state, she was also seeking full legal custody of my son and supervised visitation, which meant that I was not to be left alone with him. She was asking that I be forced into court ordered psychotherapy. I was completely shocked. I had no idea why. I had never ever done anything that would make her ask for these things. I was devastated, I was angry, I was sick. When I asked her about it, she simply said that I had "issues" I needed to deal with regarding what I had told her about the sexual abuse. I couldn't believe that she had even remembered it. We had talked about it years before that and it wasn't even a 10 second conversation.

When the court date approached, she let me know that if I didn't try and prevent her from moving, she would drop everything else. I hated to admit it then and I hate to admit it now, but I was so fearful of that fact becoming public, I was so afraid of my family finding out that dirty little secret, I was so mortified about it, that I said okay. The fact that my fear and shame about the abuse came before any other consideration is something that is with me always. In hindsight, I realized that, like all mothers, she was in what I call protection mode. In her mind, she was doing what was right for the sake of her and Evan. I wished I could have lived a marriage without the baggage of sexual abuse that I brought with me. And I wondered what if. These were just some of the personal stories of my life and the effects that sexual abuse had on my life that I wanted Cardinal Law to know. Not through depositions, not through attorneys, but through me, personally.

As we went on I also asked him questions like, "What can you say to me when I read a letter that was sent by a woman concerned because Father Birmingham had left her parish because of reported medical reasons, after giving two sermons on AIDS? In her letter she asked if she had to be concerned for her son because her son had served as an altar boy under Birmingham in Gloucester. After she had written you, she got a letter back from McCormack who is now a Bishop, but was then your personal director. That letter said that she had nothing to worry about because he had personally talked to Birmingham and Birmingham said there was no truth to it." I also gave him a copy of both the mother's letter, as well as McCormack's reply letter.

He looked at me and said, "There is nothing I can say about that. There is no excuse for it." There were many things we talked about during that two hours. As we talked, I noticed the aged look about him. I could tell that this crisis was draining him. The man that I had seen in public before was not the same man that was sitting in front of me now. Gone was most of the pompous demeanor, gone was the "holier than thou" attitude that I had seen many times on the television. It may have been due to the opening remarks I had made when I asked him "What should I call you? I'm not comfortable with calling you Your Eminence." Or it may just have been that he was ready to relate on a deeper, personal level. For whatever the reason, I noticed a humility that he did not reflect when he was addressing a group in public.

During those two hours we maintained direct eye contact. There was a time or two when I could tell that he was uncomfortable, and rightfully so. This was not an afternoon tea chat. He should have been uncomfortable. He had made some horrible and inexcusable mistakes that had resulted in the pain and suffering of me and my family, and hundreds, if not thousands, of others. I told him exactly that.

When I told him that he needed to apologize to every person that this had effected, he started to say that he began doing that in a public sermon in January. But before he finished, I told him, "You need to realize that the people that you need to start apologizing to don't go to mass and don't hear you. You need to start doing it the same way that you're doing it here, one on one, regardless of how many times you have to and regardless of how long it takes." I told him that he needed to cut the red tape regarding access to therapy for the survivors and their families. I related a story about a survivor that had gone through hell just to get into therapy, which was not acceptable to me.

I also offered what I had hoped he would take as a "ray of hope." I told him "I realize now the effects that this has had on my life and the life of my family. I'm not asking you to change the past for me. I know that you can't do that. There is nothing that you can do which will erase the horrendous abuse, not only by Birmingham, but also by the Archdiocese of Boston's lack of response for over 30 years. I am asking you to change the future. I am willing to do whatever I can to make sure that this never happens again, you have the opportunity to do that, as well. Don't let this history of abuse be your legacy in life." I urged him to start meeting with survivors and to start going to every parish and meet the people that this had affected. By that, I mean not only the survivors, survivors and their families, but the parishioners, as well. I had heard them talk and I had felt the breakdown in their faith. He needed to, as well. "The Catholic religion is based on one thing, faith. If you want anyone to have faith in your willingness to make it right, you have to have faith in them, as well. Tell them the truth, they can handle it."

There were many topics which we covered. There were topics that I had agreed would be kept private. Do I think that what was said that day changed anything? It won't ever change the past, but I hoped it could begin to change the future. One thing that it did change, I released the hate and anger in my heart that I had carried for a long time. But he was not off the hook that easy. I let him know that I was going to continue to "hold your feet to the fire," regarding promises that he had made to me. I would continue to publicly speak concerning all the issues as long as it took for change to happen. I did tell him that there were two separate issues at hand. One was the legal issues related to the lawsuit and responsibility of the Archdiocese regarding the abuse. The other was the moral and spiritual responsibility facing him. I would continue to let the attorneys handle the legal issues. I would continue to hold him responsible for the rest.

I was finished. As we got up to shake hands, he asked if he could say a prayer and a blessing for me, I said, "Yes, but don't say it for me. Say it for my family and my children." A short blessing, a prayer, and the meeting was over. As he shook my hand, I offered one thing. "My cell phone is always on, If you have any questions about anything that you're doing regarding the survivors, please call me. I don't make that offer lightly, I mean it." His reply was, "Thank you, I have a feeling that I will be seeing you again."

"You can count on it," I said. As I got up to leave, he asked if I would accept something from him. I said I would and he then pulled out a Bible, a book entitled "Catechism of the Catholic Church," and several sets of rosary beads for my family. I thought that they were an odd set of parting gifts to be giving out, but I accepted them.

As I walked away I was struck by the gentle nature of Fr. John Connelly. Fr. John, a giant of a man, had often been seen with the Cardinal. Some have thought that he was his bodyguard, he was definitely big enough to be. He was actually his personal secretary. Though I had seen Fr. John many times at the side of the Cardinal, it was the first time I had met him. I was impressed at his frank willingness to express his opinion. Regardless of who was talking at the time, if he felt you were correct, he would agree. There were several times in that meeting where I would make a point and Fr. John would speak up and agree as in, "Gary, we've been trying to explain the same thing to the Cardinal."
I was impressed with that.

After that meeting, some people doubted that Fr. John was even a priest, and that if he was a priest, they believed he was just one of the Cardinals "yes men.". Two things I can tell you about Fr. John. Yes, he is a priest, and no, he's definitely not a yes man. Before I left I gave Fr. John my number, as well. In the months that followed that meeting, I would have more conversations with Fr. John. Some over the phone and some in person over dinner. I would find the answers to my questions about him becoming a priest and answers to my questions about what he thought had happened over the last 30 years. I have not been impressed with many men of the cloth, Fr. John definitely left an impression. I respect his frank and honest answers and his willingness to listen and offer help. The open line of communication that developed that day was a valuable one.

As I walked away from that meeting, my only other thought was, "Did he get it? Did Cardinal really get any of it?" I wondered.

*****

It's Thursday, Sister Noberta tells the class that because tomorrows a Holy Day of Obligation, one of the priests will be here to hear everyone's confession. It's going to be an open confession, that's where the priests will just sit in one of the closed class rooms and one by one you can just go in and tell your confession. A few hours later, the classroom door opens, we all stand up and say "Good morning Father Birmingham." He tells us what room he going to be in to hear our confessions. One by one, off we go. As one child returns, another gets up and goes.

It's my turn. I walk out the classroom, close the door and go across the hall. Father B is sitting in a chair. He has on the purple sash over his shoulders, under that he has on a vestment robe. It's the same one that I help him put on, and take off when I help him serve mass. I sit down, now facing him. Our knees are almost touching. He has his head bowed, and his forehead is resting in his hand, his elbow is resting on his knee. "Bless me father for I have sinned, it has been 2 months since my last confession, these are my sins" I begin. I don't know what to tell him, I make things up, just like I usually do.

Sometimes at recess we would talk about what we made up to tell the priests at confession, sometimes we wouldn't. I made it up. Father B reaches down and pulls my chair closer to me. Our knees are touching, and he has one hand on one of my knees. I can't see his other hand. "Tell me about masturbation" he says. I don't know what he means. "You must masturbate, everyone does." I don't know that that word is.
"When you masturbate, do you play with yourself in your bedroom, or in the shower." I tell him yes, even though I don't know what it is. He must know what everyone else does, he hears their confessions too. "Do you think of other boys when you masturbate?" "It's ok if you do." Father B starts rubbing my knee and unzipping my pants. I notice that his other hand is under his vestments. .... Today I learned what masturbating is.

*****

10.

"I used to see the world in black and white with shades of gray, now I'm seeing the world as it really is, in color." That statement was said a long time ago from a recovering drug addict when she was asked how she felt now that she was in recovery. Until lately, I had never given that much thought. Recently though, it has been floating in my mind constantly.

Put yourself in the mind of a child. You're 10 years old. Think of someone that age that you know. Your son, your grand son, your nephew, your godson, your brother, or your friend's son. As a 10 year old, up until now, you've been living the life of a normal, happy child. School work, Little League, music lessons, running around with neighborhood friends, getting into the typical things that all 10 year olds do. You go to school, go to church, ride your bike. Your Friday nights are spent in front of the TV and Saturday mornings, you're watching cartoons.

One day you're serving mass as an altar boy with a priest that you know from school, a priest that your family knows and trusts, a priest that's been around the school and is trusted by you. After mass, you're in the sacristy changing out of your altar boy uniform and helping the priest change out of his vestments. He asks you if you want to wrestle. "Sure," you say, it's cool. Here's a priest that's revered by everyone else and that is looked up to by you. You're thinking that I'm so lucky, I can't believe that he wants to wrestle with me, wait till the guys hear this. You begin to wrestle with him, and it's fun. He's like a big brother, he's like your father. Everyone likes him, everyone trusts him. You do, your parents do, and everyone else does. You're grabbing each other, pushing back and forth, he's throwing you around and you're giving it back to him, as well. He's grabbing at your clothes, and you're grabbing back because it's okay for him, and he said it's okay for you too.

Suddenly you find yourself on your hands and knees. He's behind you with his arm around your waist and an arm around your neck and shoulders. You feel his arms wrapped around you, his hands are starting to slide slowly down your chest, over your belly, under your pants. You don't know what's going on now. Something's not right. You feel sick, you're sweating, and your stomach is in knots. "I don't like this" you tell yourself over and over and over again. All you can feel is something hard pushing against you and you're frightened. You're scared and you don't know what to do. You're trying to get away but you can't. Your first instincts are to fight harder to get away, but the harder you fight, the harder he presses against you. You want to fight harder, but can't move. You want to run, but you can't get away. You want to scream, "Get off me, get away from me." But you don't, you don't because you're afraid. You want to kick and scream and punch. You're only 10 years old.

Maybe you do tell your friends a little, but maybe you don't tell anyone. Not a soul, not your parents, your teachers, not anyone because you're afraid of what they may think, you're afraid they won't believe you. It's his word against yours.

Think about that for a minute, now think about this, as awful and as repulsive as that may seem, not only is that not the worst of it, but it happens more than several times at more than several locations and with different degrees of severity. Over and over again it happens. Your 10 or 11 when it starts, you're 13 or 14 when it ends. You graduate from grammar school, or you move away, or maybe he leaves the parish. For whatever reason, he's gone and you move on with your life. In your mind, it's finally over. Or you try and forget about it, as if it never happened to you. But it did happen. Your first sexual experience was at the abusive hands of someone that you looked up to and trusted. And you were at such a young and impressionable age. The pattern has been set, the mold has been made.

Soon after that, there's a change. You're no longer interested in lots of things. Your parents may have noticed a slight change, but "it's normal, he's growing up," they say to themselves. You're no longer interested in music, or Cub Scouts, or Little League. No big deal. "Every kid loses interest in things at that age," your parents tell themselves.

While in high school, trouble begins to start. You're fighting with your parents, you're skipping school, you go from class clown to class troublemaker. You're not interested in music anymore, you're not interested in sports, and you're not into anything that's group related or team oriented. You know that you're not like the other kids because you just don't feel like you fit in. You're not interested in anything that has to deal with structure or authority. As a matter of fact, no one is ever going to tell you what to do again. You do find yourself interested in girls, though. They're not challenging, they like you because you stand out. You stand out because you don't fit the mold, maybe you're the rebel that bucks authority. Maybe they like you because you smoke pot or drink. It doesn't matter why, it only matters that they like you. You like them because you realize that girls = sex, and sex means love. You want love, you want to feel that closeness and you don't feel that closeness at home anymore. Your parents tell you that you have to learn to control your temper, but it's not you, it's everyone else. They need to stop bugging you. They tell you that you'd better straighten out in school because if you don't clean up your act you'll end up with nothing.

The pattern continues. Somehow you make it through high school, maybe. You're still drinking, women are coming and going and it's great. You're the guy that other guys think is lucky.

You're cool, drugs, women, booze, you have it all and its easy for you. You're liked, and you fit in. When people disagree with you, it's settled in a fight, or you just move along and forget them. If you fight with your girlfriend, and you do fight, who cares? They're all the same anyway. You think that no matter what you do, it's never enough for them. You know that eventually the right girl will come along, the one that will accept you for who you are and what you are, without trying to change you. Year after year you cruise through life this way.

In your 20s, you're working. College wasn't an option for you. There was no need for it. You had a chance, some of the colleges may have been interested in you. You showed "promise." They may even have offered you a partial scholarship, but it wasn't for you. You've had enough with the rules and the teachers. You're working now, you're independent. You left your family, moved out after the last time you heard the "this is my house and as long as you live under it you'll live by my rules" speech. Screw it. My life, my rules, and my apartment.

You are working a few jobs here and there. Why does there always have to be that kind of boss everywhere you go? The one who is always on your back, always on your case about stupid stuff. You leave your last job for the last time, saying, "No one's ever going to tell me what to do again. I'm not going to ever punch a time clock again. Screw it. I'll work for myself from now on." In between high school and now, you managed to meet a girl and she got pregnant, but things didn't work out. You tell yourself that "she was the screw up," At least you have a child that loves you now. It's no big deal that you're living in one bedroom apartments. Your kid doesn't mind it, either. You've moved a few times by you're in your mid 20s. It's no big thing, you just have itchy feet. Weeknights are spent having a few beers, maybe doing a few lines of cocaine to keep you up. It's all under control, though. You're your own boss. You set the rules, nobody tells you what to do. Sure there have been a few fights, a few arrests, but its normal, everyone goes through it.

The pattern continues. You're in your early 30s now. Your parents still worry about you. They wonder if you'll ever settle down. They wonder if you have cleaned up your act. You realized you had to after you lost a few friends to car accidents and drug overdoses. You're seeing a woman, it's been a few years that you've been together. Sure you fight, but everyone does. She doesn't understand you. She wonders why you're distant a lot of the time. She wonders why there are always money problems, wonders why you won't just settle down. Wonders why you wont just get a real job and start growing up. You decide to try it. Maybe you should get married, maybe not, but you settle down. In your mind, you do. You're in a committed relationship. You have a few kids, try to put the booze and drugs in check, try and build a life. You move along in your 30's, knowing that the big 40 is coming soon. You have a few marital "indiscretions," but it's no big deal, everyone does, right? Whenever you feel the walls closing in, you have to do something. You move, change job paths, find a new female friend and go out on a weekend of binge drinking, whatever it takes to feel good. It's normal, Your life is normal because you're getting your life together.

But it doesn't work out. You and your partner split up. She's tired of the loss of intimacy. She figured eventually you would come around but she's tired of you being unsettled. She's tired of the half truths you give her when she asks you a question. All it is is that she doesn't understand you. She wants more.

You don't understand it. You're working, you've cleaned up your act, and life is normal. She wants perfection out of everyone and everything. Everyone fights, what's the big deal if she doesn't feel close to you? It's her problem, she needs to deal with it. She's talked about counseling but you don't need it. You don't have a problem. Sure, you've had some ups and downs, but everyone does. Why can't you just find someone that wants and loves you for who you are? Why can't people just leave you alone and let you live your life? There is nothing wrong with you, you don't need to see a shrink, for Christ's sake. Sure, maybe you told her jokingly that a priest had "tried to grab you." It was a long time ago, though, and it had no effect. You were one of the lucky ones that got away. She doesn't really love you. They're all the same anyway.

Suddenly it happens. You wake up, you're tired. You don't know why, maybe its because you're turning 40, maybe its because something else happened in your life. Whatever the reason is, you know that something's not right and you start to ask questions. Maybe you meet other people that you used to know. You see them in their lives. They seem happy, they have stable marriages, they have great kids. They're working and they're happy. They've been in stable relationships for a while. You wonder, what's the deal here?

What you just read is a sad account of 30 years of a life. Parts of it reflect my life, but it's a composite of what many survivors of clergy sexual abuse have lived. For many of us, for the first time in almost 30 years, we have decided to take that "hard look in the mirror." For many of us, it's the first time that we have realized just how we have lived our lives It seemed normal, but in reality, it wasn't at all normal. We spent 30 years simply going through the motions. We now realize that our life was only normal in our minds. No one else knew what was going on, no one else knew what was wrong with us because we didn't think anything was. This was "normal." Our views of trust, love, sex, relationships, authority and even right and wrong were twisted 30 years ago. The amount of effect that any type, let alone this type of sexual abuse has on a child at that age, can never be underestimated. There are literally thousands of what we call the "walking wounded" that have been just going through the motions.

There is nothing that has been more painful than looking into the mirror, realizing and facing the fact that this has been your life. In essence you have lived a lie for 30 years. It is not normal for someone to live this way.

Seeing it laid before you is one thing, seeing it explained is another thing, realizing it by connecting the dots in your life is yet another thing, but admitting it to yourself, that's the painful part. It's also the point when you begin to mourn and wonder about the life you may have had. It's when you start to ask yourself, what if? It's also a point when you start to realize all the damage that this has been caused including the damage you have caused to others who have come and gone in your

"I use to see the world in black and white with shades of gray, now I'm seeing the world as it really is, in color." Now, when that sentence plays out in my head, I know what it means. The men who have made the journey of discovery to look into that mirror have taken that exceptionally painful honest step of discovering that they are not the same men they were before.

11.

On July 20, the Friday following my meeting with Cardinal Law, I was invited to speak at a three day convention in Boston which was put together by a group known as Voice of the Faithful. This group was formed in the early part of the year by Catholic parishioners from the town of Newton. What had started as a small group of concerned people had now grown chapters all over the state and all over the country. As many as 5,000 people from all over the country were expected to come to this event.

I had talked at some of the private VOTF gatherings held at some the parishes in the area, but this was going to be different. I, as well as other Birmingham survivors, did have concerns and reservations about this group. We wondered what they actually represented, as well as what their agenda was. We agreed that their heart was in the right place and that was a great place to start. Whatever we could do to keep the pressure on and keep the public awareness up on this issue, we were willing to do.

What an awe inspiring event those three days turned out to be. I was struck that so many people from so many places around the world had come together for a common good. Regardless of what their total actual agenda was, this was a good thing. When I had talked to the smaller groups in parish halls before, my advice to them was to stay focused, and stay on track. I told them not to get bogged down with commissions and panels, not to let egos get in the way of the good that they were trying to accomplish. "Don't become so organized that you become a hierarchy. Doing so would mean becoming the same thing that you are criticizing. Keep focused and keep it simple." Some people listened, some did not. Part of the problem that many groups "trying to do the right thing" have is that they become so large, everything gets tied up in meetings and discussions and platforms and agendas.

During those three days, I watched egos jockeying for position on the stage, but I also watched and listened to many people who only wanted to help. We had the opportunity to address several of the smaller groups in separate areas during that three day convention. Originally, we had been asked to address the entire crowd, but as the week before the convention progressed, we could see things changing. SOJB had gone from a 20 minute time slot of addressing the entire group, to a 15 minute time slot, then to a 10 minute time slot, and finally, to not getting the opportunity of addressing the group at all. We were concerned greatly about this. If this was a convention put together in order to address the "needs of the survivors", then we wondered why they were not letting the survivors of the Boston area address the group.

We went back and forth on this issue. In the end, we realized that we had to continue with our efforts, regardless of their agenda. We had to pursue and push our own agenda. Never again, that was our agenda. We would get our message through, somehow.

That Friday, the first day of the conference, we were able to do just that at what was supposed to be a general "meet and greet" in one of the smaller conference rooms. In one of those rooms we met with the leaders of VOTF and the leaders of other smaller groups as well. There were representatives there from all over the US.

What was supposed to be an hour long informal introduction meeting turned into a three hour intense emotional session on the real reason why we were all there. Straightforward questions from all parties involved were asked and were answered. As a survivor support group, we asked them what their intentions were. As a group of survivors, we trusted no one. One of the biggest issues on our minds was the fact that we wanted to be there to make sure that the real message got out, not be a part of a procession of victims, to be on stage and presented as such. Early on in the planning of this event, one of the things that VOTF wanted to do was to present us with a ribbon/award to be worn for the entire convention. I couldn't imagine such a thing. In their minds, they were paying us homage and giving us the credit for coming forward.

In my mind, this wasn't a badge of honor. All I could picture was walking around with this ribbon around my neck and people looking and pointing, "Look, there's one. Let's talk to him." The thought of that made me nauseous. Tom Blanchette put it best when I met him for the first time. "This is not something I'm proud of, but it is something that I'm no longer ashamed of." They just didn't see it that way. I know that their intentions were good, but I continued to wonder, did they get it?

Another one of their well intentioned ideas was to give an honorarium for any survivor who spoke. This honorarium would be in the form of money. I know that they felt that this would be a good thing to do, that giving a small cash honorarium might cover the expenses that we had incurred, i.e. cell phones, gas. It was a nice gesture on their part and well intentioned but to me and many other survivors out there, accepting money to tell our personal stories wasn't even a conceivable option. When it had been offered to anyone that I know of, we had suggested that they donate the money to a charity. I'm not faulting anyone else from accepting money, but for me, this was the first time that I had had the opportunity to do something for the greater good of society. I couldn't accept money for speaking of my pain and my family's pain.

There were many important basic issues that we discussed that day. Most importantly, we questioned what the direction and intention of this group was. If it truly was the intention to put survivors first, then we told them that they had to ask us what our needs were, and not assume. As the meeting was coming to an end, a representative of SNAP (Survivors Network of those Abused by Priests) was looking in my direction. I had not met him before, but he was pointing at me and giving me a signal. I thought that he was signaling me that he wanted to talk to me after the meeting broke up. I was wrong. As I was nodding yes with my head to him, he got up and said, "Gary Bergeron had an opportunity to meet with Cardinal Law privately for two and a half hours yesterday. I've asked him to say a few words." The room suddenly went silent. I guess I had read his signals wrong. I'm sure I turned pale at that point, this was not something that I was prepared to do. It had only been a day, and I hadn't talked to anyone about it yet. I thought for a minute, then took Bobs advice, and just talked from the heart. "No matter what happens, if you talk from your heart, you'll never say the wrong thing."

There was a woman present filming that meeting for a documentary concerning the abuse scandal. I asked her to turn off the camera and I started to talk. I had been getting a lot of heat from some people who had questioned my reasoning for seeking a meeting with Cardinal Law. I guess that this was my chance to explain. Most of the people in that room were there in opposition of the Cardinal. I was about to discuss, what in many of their minds was "meeting the enemy." I did the best I could though.

In what was an extremely emotional 30 minutes, I told them all about my wish to confront the man closest to the man who had molested my brother and me. I tried to explain that it was just something that I had to do. I shared some of the questions that were asked and some of the answers that were given. I told him of the advice that I had given the Cardinal regarding the access of survivors to counseling. More importantly, I tried to explain that I needed that meeting to try and understand what had happened over the last 30 years, and why this awful cycle of abuse had been perpetuated for over 30 years. Most importantly, I told them that I needed to meet with this man, face to face, to tell him how this affected my life, as well as the lives of my family. I also told them that I needed this meeting to make an attempt to begin to heal my life, my mind, and my soul. As I said these words, my eyes filled with tears, but I managed to continue. "I needed this meeting because there has been so much damage in my life, I couldn't carry the hate in my heart for the rest of my life. I won't carry it. I'm not going to go to my grave with the regret that I've lived with."

It was painful to say, but it had to be said. My goal throughout this painful journey has been simple and perhaps selfish. Some people have said it's too simple. I will do whatever I have to do to prevent this from happening again and to make sure that my children never have to go through this again. And I will do whatever I have to do to heal. The healing has to start somewhere.

When I was through, the room was pretty silent for a few minutes. In that silence, a man approached the group. He was the father of a survivor from New Jersey that had traveled to be there. I admired the work that he and his wife and their son had accomplished. They had been very active for more than 10 years in this cause.

As he walked over, he started to speak. His voice was loud, almost screaming, and was directed at me. **"Cardinal Law could stand on a stack of bibles a mile high, from the highest mountain and could say, 'I'm sorry,' and I wouldn't believe him. He's nothing but a liar and if you believe anything he says, you're nothing but a fool. He's just trying to con you again, like he did before."**

I let him speak and said nothing. There were many people who came up to me after that and apologized for his actions, but they didn't have to. That man had nothing to be ashamed of. He and I did end up speaking privately later on in the day. He felt bad and apologized, but I told him that he didn't need to. He made me realize two important things that afternoon. I know what it feels like to be a survivor, but I don't know what it feels like to be the father of one. I pray that I never will, which is why I'll continue on. The other important thing I realized is that I don't want to be that angry man. I need to heal and I need my parents to heal. That man's message to me was that there had to be healing. Somehow, when the day is over, to get through this, we all had to heal. His message would stay with me and his message that day would have a direct effect on things that played out in the future.

Over the next two days no matter where we went or who we were with, someone would come up to us and tell us how thankful they were that they had been in that room. People that weren't in that first meeting would come up to us and tell us that they had heard about us speaking and wanted to know if we would speak to their groups as well. We seemed to be making progress in getting our message out. As simple as our message was, it was powerful enough for others to want to hear it. Maybe it was because we weren't as polished as some of the speakers and they could relate to us easier. Maybe it was the fact that all of us talked from the heart. For whatever the reason, they started listening.

At one point we had the planners of the event come up to us and apologize. "We realized that before we planned this, we should have actually been talking to more survivors. We got your message loud and clear. Next time it will be different." Finally even they were getting it. Maybe, just maybe, we were getting something done there.

We continued to tell them, that their intentions were noble, but they needed to keep it simple, keep their eye on the goal at hand and not get bogged down by committees or hierarchies. I would say those exact words every time I would address a group from VOTF. I would tell them that one on one, as well. Somehow I had to get it through that the emotions of this issue had to be engaged in a one on one level, person to person, not through the chain of command, not through endless letters. This was a human issue, these were human feelings, and it had to be dealt with on that level. It seemed so simple to me, why complicate it?

As the convention wound down, I had yet to make it to the main auditorium. While they were in there listening to speakers, Bernie and I would be working the halls. We would meet people from all over the world that day. At one point we decided to go into the large hall. As we walked in and looked around, I couldn't believe that all these people were there because of this issue. They weren't all survivors, it was actually just the opposite. These were ordinary church going people who just wanted to do help. They were angry at finding out that the same priest that had been telling them that if they ate meat on Friday, they would go to hell had actually been making the lives of hundreds of children a living hell. They wanted change, they wanted to help, they wanted to do something. They just didn't know what to do. The convention was a start. Standing there with Bernie, I looked at him, turned around and quickly left.

As he saw me bolting to the door, he asked me later why I had left. I just couldn't do it, standing there and realizing that these good people were there in part because of me, in part because of us. It was too overwhelming for me. It was Sunday afternoon. We went there with a goal in mind. I think we accomplished it. We got them to realize that we were not just numbers, we were people, and before you assume the needs of someone, take the time to ask.

12.

There was another thing that happened following that convention. Up until that point, neither Bernie nor Olan had any interest in sitting with Cardinal Law. Neither of them saw the benefit in it. I had still been publicly stating that I wanted Cardinal Law in Boston to deal with this and they had both been leaning towards his resignation. And although they supported me 100% for wanting to meet with him, it didn't make sense to them. That was changing, though. The first time they had heard me talk about it was that Friday. At our next regular Tuesday meeting, we talked again about it. They had both grown to see the value in it I was glad. I felt that if they gave up a chance to, at the very least, confront him, they may regret it later.

Over the coming weeks, I would answer questions from a lot of people regarding my decision to meet with Cardinal Law. Not everyone agreed with my decision, but not everyone is me. At times I would have to answer questions like, "How come you were the one chosen to see him, why didn't I get called?" Over and over I would have to tell them, "I didn't get called in. Nobody opened the door for me and said come on in. I've been knocking at that door for months. I've been asking for months. If you want a meeting, then call and ask for one."

In time, others would decide that they wanted to meet with him, as well. Things were finally happening. Would these one on one meetings change the past? Definitely not, but they could help change the future. I still felt that if Cardinal Law, a person known as a civil rights advocate in his early career, had taken the time to really meet with survivor after survivor and hear story after story, maybe, just maybe, he would get it. Needless to say, after my visit with the Cardinal, there was a flurry of press interest. I was asked all kinds of questions. They wanted to know everything. There were things that I shared with the interviewers and things that I did not. There are things that remain between him and me. Because of this meeting and the press interest, I was able to further awareness of Birmingham and his legacy. Keeping the public interest was important. The most difficult question I was asked in those interviews came from Victoria Block. She's comfortable to talk to and her integrity is intact   not always an easy thing to maintain in the news business. At the end of her interview, she asked me if I trusted the Cardinal and I couldn't answer it because I didn't have an answer. Then she asked me if I thought that the Cardinal was "doing his penance in meeting with survivors." Probably, I answered. Finally she asked me if I was ready to "give the Cardinal absolution." No, not yet was my answer. Penance and absolution, two words from my Catholic past taught to me, in part, by a priest that sexually abused me. I hadn't heard them in years and now they were asked of me regarding a Cardinal that I was suing by a female reporter who happened to be Jewish. Irony?

I wasn't sure if he was getting it, but someone in the Chancery was. The week following my meeting with the Cardinal, I got a call from Barbara Thorpe. She called to let me know that a problem a survivor was having getting into therapy was all taken care of. That same day, she called again, this time to let me know that Cardinal Law had called from his car and that he was heading to Canada for the papal visit going on that week.

He was calling so that she could set up appointments for Olan and Bernie that I had asked her about. I thanked her, but I also used the opportunity to ask about the Cardinal coming to Lowell. In my meeting with him, one of the things that I had asked about was getting him to Lowell and to all the parishes that Birmingham had effected. I wanted him to meet with groups of survivors and their families. I knew that I was reaching for the stars, but if you don't ask, you don't get. I asked. Barbara said that she would work on it, but that it would take time. After 30 years of waiting, time I had. Patience is one virtue that I learned. I had no choice.

These two calls were different than the ones in the past. First of all, I hadn't called her for anything. She was calling me. That may not seem like anything, but it was a major step. After weeks and months of having the Archdiocese dodging my calls, they were calling me. There was also a different tone in the conversations. I'm not sure what it was, but something was changing. No matter how slight the apparent change was, it was a step in the right direction and I was going to take advantage of it in every way possible. They had made the offer of telling me to call them should I, or any other survivor, not be happy with any statements that were coming from their direction. In the next several weeks and months, I, and others, did just that. Step by step, one at a time, we were pushing forward and making headway. I realized that nothing would happen overnight, but I realized that it was progress and not perfection. Any dialogue taking place to further help the needs of the survivors and their families was a good thing. In the weeks that followed, there were lots of conversations between SOJB, Barbara's office and me. Olan and Bernie would get their private meetings with the Cardinal and others would, as well. Olan, as only Olan could, went in with a list of questions to ask. He asked nearly everyone involved in the crisis to come up with one question that they would like him to ask of the Cardinal. He wrote them down and went in there with a written list. The first question he asked the Cardinal was, "Can you tell me what your PIN number is for your bank account?" I thought that was the funniest question I could imagine. The odd thing was that the Cardinal didn't even know what a PIN number was. I know his questions just got harder and even more direct from there, though. When Bernie went in for his meeting, he brought his mother in and she brought in a loaf of Irish soda bread. One of Bernie hopes was that his mother, a staunch Catholic, would get some type of healing.

We all had different ideas and reasons for going. We would learn later, and only after all of us talked about it together, that as different as our approaches were, we all relayed similar messages to the Cardinal. He needed to be visible if he truly intended on seeing this through. He needed to visit every parish where the abuse took place. He also needed to own up to his mistakes and apologize to the survivors and their families, as well. We all also told him that we had to heal and that we were going to continue to pursue healing and change, as well as the legal avenue. We were going to pursue each avenue with equal interest and we were all going to hold him accountable for his actions of the past, as well as the promises he made to all of us for the future. We had no choice, we had to.

Because of those series of meetings, the Archdioceses began to address our request to have the Cardinal visit the parishes in a series of group meetings with survivors and their families. There were many issues on the table, but the Cardinal agreed, in theory, to have the initial meeting in Lowell. As the days progressed, we all realized that we were actually about to finally see some progress. It did take us several weeks to address certain issues regarding the press, locations, as well as security which in this situation was a real issue for all of us.

In addition to the planning of this first of its kind meeting, there was talk about depositions. As a plaintiff in a lawsuit, it was my right to witness the numerous depositions that were about to take place. From day one, when I was told that I could do this, I asked to be on the "A" list. I knew that there would probably be lots of people who may have wanted to as well, so I put my name in immediately. I had many reasons for wanting to do this. One was that I wanted these men, the men who had made those horrendous decisions that effected so many lives, to realize that this was not about numbers, it was about lives. When they were asked repeatedly about decisions they had made which ultimately affected me years ago, I wanted them to see my face and to know my name. I wasn't a plaintiff, I was a person. I knew that they hadn't thought of that years before, but it was time to realize that now.

One of the other reasons for wanting to be there was to let the Cardinal, the attorneys and the Archdiocese know, that even though I truly meant what I said when I told them that I planned on getting through this, there were separate issues at hand. There were the moral and healing issues, but there were also the legal and responsibility issues for me.

There were other depositions before ours that had taken place and there were other lawsuits that had been settled. One of the differences in my mind was that we, as a group, had decided that we needed to address all issues, not just the legal ones, and not just the spiritual healing. Collectively we all agreed to that point. There were many groups that were speaking out regarding either one issue of the other, but we seemed to be the group interested in addressing both issues. When word hit the street that we had actually been able to schedule the first public meeting at which the Cardinal would be addressing a group of us, some others were rattled by this. There was criticism both public and private. Eventually, as we became successful, criticisms became tremors and the tremors turned to an earthquake in the form of hate mail. I was personally condemned as a traitor, someone that was caving to the will of the Cardinal and the Archdioceses. Nobody knew that in our own group we had had discussions regarding this same subject. Some of us wanted the press to cover the meetings, some of us didn't. We had open and frank discussions about the format, the location, who would handle which details, who would be invited, who wouldn't be invited. There were many deep and heated discussions regarding all of those issues. Olan, Bernie and I would disagree loudly with each other several times while planning that meeting to the point that others would be uncomfortable at some of the Tuesday night meetings. None of us took it personally, though. In the end, we didn't agree on all issues, but we trusted the judgment of each other and we made it happen. The criticisms of some of those groups continued, but we kept our eye on the ball and kept pushing for our goal. Those criticisms increased at 11:00 on one Sunday morning.

The Friday before the Cardinal's first public meeting with a group of survivors and their families, we got a conference call from Barbara Thorpe and Fr. John. There was a scheduling problem. The Cardinal had been requested by a family in Rome to attend the expected funeral mass of a family friend. We all realized that things may come up like this, we were disappointed, but we also understood. We all agreed to reschedule the meeting for another day, but the day hadn't been agreed upon. They would get back to us with his schedule. Not trusting anyone, we naturally checked out his story and learned that there was a bishop in Rome who was in fact in the hospital and did die within the following few days. It's awful to have to feel as though you have to check on something as private as that, but we did it.

Days went by and another meeting date was not set. Days turned into weeks and still no date. One Tuesday I called up Olan, and said, "Olan, it's me. I know this sounds crazy, but I'm thinking of going to see the Cardinal say mass on Sunday." There was dead silence. "I don't know why I have this feeling, but I want to go and I'm going to." After a moment, he said, "Good for you." Not a bad good for you, a good good for you. When he realized that I was talking about going to his public mass that he says at the Holy Cross Cathedral, he was a bit cautious. He reminded me of all the protesting that had been taking place there, week after week, month after month. I hadn't given it much thought and it really didn't matter to me. I had the urge to go and I was going. I hadn't felt that kind of feeling, a sense of wanting, for a long time. The only problem was that we were still in the middle of trying to commit the Cardinal to come to Lowell, and those protestors were part of the groups that we were feeling the heat from. My response? "That's their problem, not mine. I'm not going there to make a political statement, I'm going because I want to go to mass. I can't believe that I have to think about all these things just because for the first time in 30 years, I have the urge to go. And besides, we haven't heard from them about a firm date yet. It may be good for the Cardinal to see me, as well. Maybe he'll realize that I'm really not going to go away until this mess is cleaned up." Olan's only suggestion was that I call Bob Sherman's office and let him know of my intentions. I wasn't sure if Olan had thought that Bob would try and talk me out of it or what. I did call Bob and he seemed surprised, Not so much surprised that I was going, but surprised that I had called. "Good for you," was his only reply. Again, not the bad good for you, but the good one.

So, on the following Sunday at 11:00, I drove to The Cathedral of the Holy Cross, but I didn't go alone. A few days before, Olan had called me and told me that Dave Lyko told him that when he heard I was going, he wanted to go, as well. So heading into Boston that day, was Dave, myself, and Olan, the professed agnostic of the group, as well. I had called Bernie and invited him, but he just couldn't do it, even with the three of us there. I understood and respected why he didn't go. He understood and respected why I did go. I think we were all a bit on the nervous side. It was probably the first time in many years for all of us to go to mass on our own, no funeral, no wedding, just mass. Driving by the cathedral, we all watched as the protestors with their signs and bullhorns as they walked the picket line just as they had done every Sunday for the previous 10 or 11 months.

I had called Barbara Thorpe and let her know that we were going. The only reason I called her was to give her the courtesy of knowing we were going for personal reasons, not to protest or make statements. We didn't want anything special that day. We just wanted to go to mass. She seemed truly touched by this. She offered the use of the side door of the church in order to bypass the protestors. Even she knew the fine line we were all walking and the risk to our cause we may have been taking.

We didn't use the side door. That Sunday, through picket lines and bullhorns, through protestors' screams of "hypocrite" and "the Cardinal's a pimp," we walked to the front door. The Cathedral of the Holy Cross is an exceptionally beautiful church. The sight of the marble columns, the smell of the candles and the sound of the organ music would be extremely moving for anyone, let alone someone who hadn't been to church for years because of what we had been through. We walked down close to the front. After noticing the beauty, I first noticed the fact that the church was almost empty. In a church that size there were, at most, 100 parishioners in it. What a sad state for the church to be in, I thought. Even the normal everyday parishioners, they weren't even going to mass either. How long was it going to be before the Cardinal realized that everyone felt this wound?

The mass was beautiful. The choir music, the candles, the incense, my senses were flooded. It was interesting to see the Cardinal in what I considered to be his "natural habitat." He seemed quite different from the man I had met with just a few months before. Father John was there on the altar as well. As we had hoped, there was nothing special said regarding our presence there. At the end of the mass, Barbara, who had been sitting next to us, leaned over and said that the Cardinal wanted to know if it was okay if he spoke to us for a few minutes after mass. We waited until he returned from meeting the parishioners at the rear of the church and he walked to the front to meet with us. This was a different man. No longer in his normal black garb he was wearing when we all met with him one on one. Now he was in full regalia. As he walked in our direction I noticed all the vestments, his pointed hat, and his long foreboding staff. I was waiting for him to, at least, remove the hat, or maybe his hand off the staff, but it didn't happen. This was his realm, there was no question about it. It was odd to me that he could seem so different. Either I didn't get him or he didn't get me. I didn't understand why there had to be such a different attitude and posture. What struck me that day was that here was a man, who may have been a good man at one time, but nonetheless a man very involved in the trappings of the position.

When he got to the place where we were all standing, he shook hands with all of us. Aside from the Cardinal, there was Fr. John, and several other altar servers and deacons, as well as two men I assumed to be plainclothes police officers. As soon as he shook hands, he said excuse me and proceeded to speak to a man that was probably 35 feet from us. "Did you get all the microphones and the tape?" he shouted. I knew that Catholic television was there taping and I knew that they had microphones that they passed around so his question, though asked at an odd time, wasn't inappropriate. "Yes I did," the man answered. A second time the Cardinal asked, "You got all the mikes and the tapes?." Again the man answered, "Yes." Odd, I thought. Then the third time came around and the Cardinal asked again, "Are you sure that you got everything, ALL the mikes and tapes?" and the man answered, "Yes I got them all." After the man answered for the third time, the Cardinal looked at no one in particular but my eyes met his and he said, "Excuse me, but I have a habit of asking questions in triplicate to make sure it gets done. I'm particular about those kinds of details." I'm not sure if there was any expression on my face or not, but in my mind I was thinking, son of a bitch.

We then had general chitchat regarding nothing in particular. He thanked us for coming and we talked briefly about his coming to Lowell. There was light chatter regarding a few aspects of the mass itself, but nothing too heavy was discussed. After 20 minutes we all shook hands again. The Cardinal invited us to exit with him via the side entrance of the church, but we opted to go out as we came in through the main doors. Much to our surprise, when we got there, fully prepared to again meet our share of protestors, we found that everyone had left and gone to the side entrance. They had realized months ago that the Cardinal exits from that door and to get their point across they would meet him there after mass.

As we walked to the car, I looked at Olan and asked him if he had

just got what happened in there. With out even giving him time to answer I said,
" Olan, son of a bitch. I can't believe that just happened. When I met with him privately, part of his defense was that he was not that detailed, that he relied heavily on the trust he put in others and in their ability. In other words, he delegated and gave me the impression that he wasn't very detail oriented. Let me ask you, did that seem like a detail oriented man in there? He said he asked that guy about the mike and the tape three times out of habit. I don't know why, but man that hit me like a lead pipe."

Olan's just looked at me and didn't say a word. He simply stared.

I had really wanted to give him the benefit of the doubt, especially before I had the opportunity of reading the depositions. Something just didn't sit right about that statement he made. Something didn't sit right, at all.

The following Monday I called Bob and Courtney's office just to make sure that I was still on the A list for depositions. When they asked me how Sunday went, I said it went well and nothing more. I did have a renewed desire to sit in those depositions, though. I had to listen to those questions and hear the answers for myself. Within another month or so, I would have my initial opportunity to do just that.

13.

My "normal" life continued through those weeks and months. For almost 30 years I had packed the thoughts of abuse away. They were in the back of my mind. I had put them on a shelf and had avoided opening that box at all costs. Suddenly for the past eight months, the thoughts of it consumed me. I knew what had happened. Now I had the need to know why. Why me? I had spent my entire life up until that point convincing myself that Birmingham did not affect me and that the abuse had no impact on my life. Over the previous few months I had realized just how devastating the effects had been. And I wanted to to fix it. Besides therapy, I started to read. I read books on sexual abuse, I read books on addictions and I also read books on religion. What I didn't read were books on the effects of sexual abuse of men by priests. I didn't read them because there were none. I searched but found that there had never been any studies on this topic. I was still going to therapy, still peeling open that onion. Some appointments went better than others. After 30 years it was tough to open up, but little by little it was happening. Hopefully, little by little, change for the better was happening, as well. Meeting every Tuesday night at our support meetings was definitely helping. What a strange band of brothers we were becoming. We had gone from a group of guys that in the beginning couldn't agree on what kind of pizza we wanted to a group of guys that were on the phone daily with each other. Whether it was calling each other to find out about a survivor's therapy, calling about the details of the Cardinal's upcoming visit, or just calling each other to see how things were, we were always on the phone.

For some of us, our home life was getting better, for others, as they peeled back the onion of life, it was painful and things weren't improving at all. Everyone heals at different speeds. We all definitely learned that. What worked for one, may not work for another, but at least we all had each other to bounce ideas off of and to vent to.

The Cardinal's visit was fast approaching. The new date had been set for October 29. The meeting itself was going to be held at the parish hall of a church in Dracut. The plan was simple. Get the Cardinal in a room with a dozen or so survivors. Let him feel and hear their pain that this has caused. Maybe he would finally understand. In actuality it was a little more complicated than that. We had to issue a press release in order to keep the press away. That meant we had to write it and release it. It sounds easy but it wasn't. We also had to worry about keeping order and flow in the meeting itself. This was our one chance and it was an important one. We didn't want it to be three hours of screaming with nothing getting resolved. My personal goal for the evening was to be able to get my father in a room with this man and to get both my parents to let their guilt out and start the healing process for them, as well. Although it was my personal goal, it was also available to lots of other parents and family members, too. The image of that survivor's father screaming at me at the VOTF conference several months before was not forgotten. I had told my parents that Ed and I were going to get through this, we were survivors, and we were going to make it. Things were going to get straightened out and we would go forward. There was no other option for me. For me and for many survivors, it was important for our parents to heal and for us to know that they were going to be all right as well. This night was more about them than it was actually about us. It was important for the Cardinal to know the extent of the damage. Not just for the survivors, but for their mothers, fathers, sisters, brothers, children and ordinary parishioners, too.

We proceeded with planning our meeting. It was a pretty basic format. I would open the meeting by making introductions and giving a small speech that would hopefully set the tone for the evening. Bernie would be the moderator. Cardinal Law would have 15 to 20 minutes for an opening remark and then the rest of the night would be an open question and answer session. Olan would give the closing remarks and the Cardinal would do a meet and greet afterwards to anyone that wanted to. We had several prepared questions in case the crowd got quiet, but we ended up not needing them. The only change that was made from our original plan was that after I did the intro talk, Paul Chimitaro, whom we called the baby of the group, would stand up and ask for a moment of silence for the survivors we all knew who couldn't make the journey and took their own life. When he was done, he handed the mike to the Cardinal. It was only fitting that he asked for that moment of silence, it was his suggestion.

On the Monday before and the Tuesday of the meeting, the phones were ringing off the hook. Our press release was sent out on the Friday beforehand. The weekend was quiet and we figured that apparently the press wasn't concerned about the meeting, especially with the election ahead. Monday and Tuesday we found out differently. In the press release we informed them that there would be no press allowed in the meeting. As a matter of fact, we held the meeting at an undisclosed location. We had planned on having press availability afterwards at another location. My cell phone started ringing on Monday morning and didn't stop ringing until Tuesday night. I must have fielded 50 or 60 phone calls. It was still news. Almost 11 months after the first story broke in the news, they were still interested. Good for us, good for the cause, good for a chance of change.

Tuesday night, standing outside the basement of St. Francis Church in Dracut, Massachusetts, I was having my before the meeting cigarette. People were arriving and there seemed like there was going to be a good crowd. We expected around 100 people to show up. Out of that, there were only 15 or so survivors. The rest were mothers and fathers and family members. As I was finishing up my smoke, the black sedan pulled up. The air was frigid, but as Cardinal Law and Fr. John got out of the car and approached, I waited. We all shook hands, I thanked them both for being there, and they thanked me for inviting them. With that, we headed in to what would be the first and only public meeting ever between Cardinal Law and a group of survivors and their family members. For many of them, it was the Cardinal's first acknowledgement of their existence, let alone their pain.

After we walked in, the Cardinal spent a few minutes shaking hands. I found Olan and Bernie and we all made sure that everything was set. I walked over to my parents, they were there along with my sister Cathy, my brother Tom, and my daughter Katie. My mother said to me, "I can't believe it, he walked in with you and acted just like one of us." It was something only my mother could say. I bent down and said, "Mom, he is just one of us. That's the problem. He's forgotten it too, but he's about to find that out." Find it out he did. It started from the very moment the meeting began. I opened up the meeting by introducing everyone. I also explained my personal reason for wanting this kind of meeting to take place. I told everyone the story of the man who had screamed at me during the Voice of the Faithful gathering in Boston. That man was still so angry that almost two decades after finding out about his son's abuse, he was screaming at me because I had met with Cardinal law for the first time. I looked at Cardinal Law and then the crowd of people and said, "I wanted this meeting for a very personal and selfish reason. When I see that man in my mind and I remember that anger, I see my father. I don't want my father, or any parent to have to live with what that man has been living with. Everyone here has an opportunity to get some of this off their chest. It's going to be painful and it's going to be emotional. If you need to scream, or if you have to cry, do it here. You don't have to feel this pain alone. You're all among friends tonight."

I then Introduced Bernie who went over the basic ground rules. Paul came up and asked for a moment of silence, just as we had talked about, then at the suggestion of another survivor, Paul make a statement saying that if anyone wanted to stand up and represent a relative who had actually committed suicide, please do so. Six people stood up. When it was over, a woman stood up and asked if those people would stand back up, she then said *"CARDINAL, YOU DID'NT EVEN LOOK UP AND ACKNOWLEDGE THOSE PEOPLE. YOU HAD YOUR HEAD DOWN. I WANT YOU TO LOOK UP AND LOOK THEM ALL IN THE EYE."*

There were many, many questions that were answered that night. They ranged from questions about his zero tolerance policy, questions about the future reporting policy, questions about who knew what and questions about his effectiveness. There were also more than several suggestions about how he could be more effective in helping. There were survivors, parents, as well as priests, who made suggestions. There were heated exchanges and demands for his resignation, but there were also deeply moving moments of intense emotion. One parent got up and read a poem that his son had written. I had listened to it months before, but that night it took on new meaning and it was as if I had never heard it before. There was a sister of a survivor who had committed suicide years before who spoke of the tragic effects that Birmingham had had on her brother, and on four other siblings, as well. There was a mother who pleaded with the Cardinal to publicly speak and apologize and to admit his faults and to ask for forgiveness. There were many moments where there was not a dry eye, including my own. There was tremendous pain in that room, but there was also a desire to heal and move forward. In order to get forgiveness, you must admit your mistakes and ask for forgiveness. This time it wasn't a parishioner telling his confession to a priest, it was a Cardinal, hopefully, learning what he had forgotten years before. I try to give credit where credit is due and he deserved credit for being there. I know it wasn't easy, but it wasn't easy for anyone else to be there either and it hadn't been easy for many of us for over 30 years.

The last suggestion to the Cardinal was a request for him to make a public plea that if any priest knew of any details relating to the sexual abuse of a child, past or present, to come forward. In the end, the Cardinal thanked everyone for their suggestions and said that he would try and do what he could do to honor their requests.

Almost three hours after we began, Olan got up and made his closing remarks. In a style that only Olan could pull off, his last remark was a suggestion that the Cardinal sell the Chancery to help offset the costs of the Archdiocese. No fear. Those are the words that I would proudly use to describe my friend Olan. No fear. With that, and the agreement that other meetings would take place, the meeting was over. There was a lot of pain expressed that evening, there were a lot of tears shed, as well, but I felt that there was also some healing that took place. Many parents were there, including my own.

Leaving the meeting and heading to the press availability, I wasn't sure who would be there. We were almost a half hour behind schedule and they had a deadline to meet. Arriving a little before 10:00 p.m., there was still plenty of press waiting. I was very proud of the guys in the press that night. This group of Birmingham guys that, a year earlier, hadn't been able to talk about their pasts, now were pouring their hearts out about it. They were healing, as well. My comments to the press were pretty simple that night. "Tonight wasn't about blame. We know where the blame lies in this. Tonight was about assessing the damage that it has caused. This is only the first step back in a journey that took us a long time to get here." There were many questions asked and many answers given that night. Driving home, for the first time in a long time, I had a sense of accomplishment. I was proud of what we had accomplished, but I also knew that we had miles to go. I sill wondered if Cardinal Law had gotten it. The impact of what we achieved that night did not surface until the weekend. That following weekend, I started to get my answer.

It was Sunday morning, I had left for a few days between the

Wednesday following the meeting and the following Saturday. I was tired, but got up early. I was also restless. I went up to see my mother and decided to turn on the TV. The Cardinal's mass on Sunday is televised live and I wanted to take a look just to see if he would say anything. There was a ton of press over the previous week about his meeting with us and I just had the thought that he may say something. As the mass opened up, after the opening prayer, he said that he would like to address the assembly for a moment. I called Bernie and had him turn on the TV. I called Olan, as well, and he already had it on.

The Cardinal started to speak. I immediately felt and noticed a difference. He wasn't the pontificating man, the pompous man, he wasn't Cardinal Law, Archbishop of Boston. The man who walked down from the altar, walked away from the podium, this man was, as we called him, Bernie. There was a different tone in his voice. There was a different air about him. I could tell it in his appearance and in his voice. On that day, Sunday November 3, 2002 on television, for the first time we heard the words and sensed the remorse that we had longed for and sought for many years. With tears in his eyes, and at times with his voice trembling, he spoke:

Earlier this week, I was privileged and blessed to meet with a truly inspiring group of people who had been sexually abused as children by a priest. They had invited me to join them and their family members and friends who gathered with them as they continued their own efforts to deal with the devastating effects of the abuse they endured. That meeting, although difficult and painful at times, was truly an occasion of grace for me and, I hope and pray, for all of those with whom I gathered. It was suggested during our time together that it would be good for me to address, more publicly and frequently, a number of issues that came up in the course of our time together. After all, there are many other people who have been abused by other priests. I told them that I would be willing to do just that. What follows now is a sincere attempt to honor the spirit of our meeting. I am indeed indebted to all of those who contributed so much by their presence, words and actions earlier this week.

It almost seems like an eternity away, yet it was in January of this year that the crisis of sexual abuse of children by clergy began to dominate our consciousness. Ten months later, I stand before you with a far deeper awareness of this terrible evil than I had at that time. No one who has not experienced sexual abuse as a child can fully comprehend the devastating effects of this horrible sin. Nor is it possible for someone else to comprehend the degree of pain, of confusion, of self-doubt, and of anger that a mother or father feels with the knowledge that her child, that his child, has been sexually abused by a priest. Who can know the burden of a wife or husband of someone who was abused as a child?

I do not pretend to fully comprehend the devastating consequences of the sexual abuse of children. Over these past ten months, however, I have been focused in a singular way on this evil and on what it has done to the lives of so many. As I have listened personally to the stories of men and women who have endured such abuse, I have learned that some of these consequences include lifelong struggles with alcohol and drug abuse, depression, difficulty in maintaining relationships and, sadly, even suicide. It is impossible to think of an act of sexual abuse of a child in isolation. There is inevitably a ripple effect from this evil act that spreads out and touches the lives of all of us. Clearly, these evil acts have touched our life together as an Archdiocese. Our relationships have been damaged. Trust has been broken.

When I was a young man different priests profoundly influenced me. They represented all that was good to me. During my high school years, Father Mark Knoll, a Redemptorist priest, was a great mentor. During my college years, Bishop Lawrence J. Riley and Father Joseph Collins made a lasting impact on my life. Like countless others, I placed great trust in them.

One of the insidious consequences of the sexual abuse of a child by a priest is the rupturing of that sacred trust. For some victim-survivors, not only is it difficult to trust priests again, but also the Church herself is mistrusted. Many victim-survivors and their family members find it impossible to continue to live out their lives as Catholics, or even to enter a Catholic Church building.

Once again I want to acknowledge publicly my responsibility for decisions, which I now see, were clearly wrong. While I would hope that it would be understood that I never intended to place a priest in a position where I felt he would be a risk to children, the fact of the matter remains that I did assign priests who had committed sexual abuse. Our policy does not allow this now, and I am convinced that this is the only correct policy. Yet in the past, however well intentioned, I made assignments which I now recognize were wrong. With all my heart I apologize for this, once again.

An apology in and of itself is not sufficient. I hope that the efforts that have already been made and which are in process in this Archdiocese to insure the protection of children as we move forward will serve as a motive to accept my apology.
Today, however, I would also ask forgiveness. I address myself to all the faithful. Particularly I ask forgiveness of those who have been abused, and of their parents and other family members. I acknowledge my own responsibility for decisions that led to intense suffering. While that suffering was never intended, it could have been avoided had I acted differently. I see this now with clarity that has been heightened through the experience of these past ten months.

I ask forgiveness in my name and in the name of those who served before me. We turn first to God for the forgiveness we need. We must, however, also beg forgiveness of one another. The dynamics of the evil of sexual abuse of children are very complex, and can often generate deep shame within those who have been abused. There are times, strangely enough, when those who have been abused wonder whether they themselves were to blame, and there are times when their parents are plagued with self doubt about the manner in which they exercised their own parental responsibilities. I would want to say a word to such survivors and to such parents. Realize that the sexual abuse of a child by an adult is an act of exploitation. When the abuser is a priest, it is a profound violation of a sacred trust. In order to experience healing from the pain and all the sad consequences of such abuse, it is necessary to recognize that the blame lies with the perpetrator.

For us as a community of faith, forgiveness is always seen in the context of the forgiving, reconciling love of God made manifest by the cross of Christ. Christ draws us to Himself and draws us closer to one another. For whatever wrong we have done we turn to God for forgiveness, even as we extend forgiveness to one another. The forgiving love of God gives me the courage to beg forgiveness of those who have suffered because of what I did. As I beg your forgiveness, I pledge my unyielding efforts to insure that this will never happen again.
Finally, once again I urge all those who live with the awful secret of sexual abuse by clergy or by anyone else to come forward so that you may begin to experience healing. The resources of the Archdiocese through the Office of Healing and Assistance Ministry are available to you. I am happy to see that Mrs. Barbara Thorp, Director of that office, is present. Obviously, anyone with knowledge about past abuse should make this information available to appropriate public authorities. No one is helped by keeping such things secret. The secret of sexual abuse needs to be brought out of the darkness and into the healing light of Jesus Christ.

I could not believe what was happening. I just could not imagine that this had just actually happened. The Cardinal had just actually done something that we had asked him to do. He actually had addressed every single aspect of the meeting that we had attended and he did it from the heart. I wasn't sure from the beginning if he completely got it, but I was completely sure that he was beginning to get it. There were times as he spoke that he broke down, I broke down at those times, as well. For the first time I felt as though he had pain and remorse in his heart. For the first time I felt that he actually believed in what he was saying. For the first time I felt that there may be hope.

My phone was ringing as well again, It was Olan. "Can you believe what just happened?" It was Bernie. "Oh, my God. I can't believe what just happened." It was many people that attended the meeting Tuesday night. it was also all the major news agencies calling. They had seen it too and wanted interviews and responses from us. They couldn't believe it either. For the first time, I heard from reporters who didn't know what to say. We were getting somewhere, we were moving the ball forward. We were achieving change. It didn't matter if it happened one step at a time, it happened, and that's all that mattered. I had said from day one, that if we could just get the Cardinal to feel the pain that he would begin to do what was needed. Well, after months of working to do just that, we were finally beginning to see a glimmer of light at the end of the tunnel. We weren't there yet. No, not by a long shot. But we were definitely making progress and with me, it's progress, not perfection.

We were all ready for a rest that day. I was exhausted and only wanted to kick back. It was the first Sunday in a while that I had no plans, but plans changed. When I made that decision to do "something," that something involved making a commitment and that commitment meant keeping my promise about change. I knew that without public awareness there would never a chance for change. Public awareness meant dealing with the press, even on Sundays.

I showered, changed, and headed out the door. I picked up Olan and Dave and made plans for Bernie to meet with us. We had several interviews to do that day. It was important for us to get our point of view across. One thing we learned was that when a reporter wanted a question answered, many times it didn't matter who answered it. Thus, if they wanted to know what someone thought of the Cardinal's statement, it didn't matter if they got that answer from us. If not us, then they would get it from someone else and they would probably get it from someone that hadn't attended the meeting or who didn't see the entire statement he had made. Many times over the previous months, survivors would be infuriated because there were people being interviewed talking about an issue that directly affected survivors and survivors. The only problem was that the person being interviewed wasn't a survivor or a survivor, but they thought they were doing us a favor by giving their opinion of what we needed. Wrong answer. Dealing with the press has definitely been an education. The only problem was that it was a hands on kind of job that you learned as you worked.

And then there's the story of the water buffalo and the scorpion. Bob Sherman told this story to me in the spring when he was giving me advice regarding the press. It was a story that had been repeated by him to me as well as others on more than one occasion.

There was a water buffalo sitting on one side of as stream. He noticed a scorpion on his back. The scorpion said to him, "Listen, I can't swim. Will you take me across the stream?" The water buffalo replied, "Hey, but you're a scorpion. You could sting me." To that the scorpion replied, "Listen, if you take me across the water, I promise that I won't sting you." The water buffalo thought for a minute, told the scorpion to hop on, and then started across the stream. Suddenly in the middle of the stream, he felt a sting on his back. He looked around at the scorpion and said, "What are you doing? You said you wouldn't sting me, now we're both going to drown. What did you do that for?" The scorpion immediately replied, "Well what did you expect? I'm a scorpion, that's what I do."

That story came to mind on more than one occasion when I felt the sting of my remarks being taken out of context. It also immediately came to mind, with Bob's reminding, after our meeting with the Cardinal that Tuesday night. Prior to our meeting with the Cardinal, we had issued a press statement requesting the privacy of meeting be kept. This was a real concern of all of us. There were men and families that were planning on being there that had not talked about their abuse in public. We wanted to assure them that their identity would be kept in private. We went to what we thought were extremes so as not to allow anyone to know where the meeting was taking place until a day or two before the meeting. That is one of the reasons why we offered press availability at another public location afterwards.

We thought we had that under control. There was one reporter who found out where the meeting was being held. She was from the Boston Globe and had showed up at the meeting that night. The reporter had done a remarkable job in reporting on this issue for the previous 11 months. Olan cut her off before she got in. What we learned later was that she was only the bait and we definitely bit. While Olan was walking her out the door, another junior reporter snuck in among the survivors and their families and sat with them. Nobody knew she was there. It wasn't until the next day that they published their article that we found out. Why it especially irritating to me is that only a few days before, I had had an extended conversation with Walter Robinson, editor for the Globe, justifying the reasons why we were even having a meeting to begin with. There had been questions, criticisms and rumors circulating for a few days before regarding our "true intentions" about meeting with the Cardinal. Instead of avoiding the issue, I personally called Walter and had, what I thought, was a frank and open discussion about it.

I was shocked to find out later that the reporter did what she did with the complete authorization and approval of the Globe. Walter himself told me that it went up the "entire chain of authority of the Globe." I called him several days later regarding it. I was upset and he knew it. His response was that we should have opened the meeting and asked if any reporters were present. In other words, it was our fault. He went on to say that the reporter didn't quote anyone that didn't agree to it afterwards. My reply was that she quoted the exact words that the Cardinal had said throughout the entire article, and I know that he didn't give permission for any of it. We had planned this meeting for months. It was our integrity that was on the line. I had made promises to other survivors and to representatives from the Chancery, as well, regarding keeping the privacy and anonymity of everyone in that room. I also forwarded him several emails that I had received, which were actually abusive hate emails criticizing us for "asking a Globe reporter to attend and not informing anyone in the room of it." His tone changed a bit when I explained that because of his article several survivors who had planned on attending the next meeting had since changed their minds. He asked me what he could do. I asked him to publish a letter to the editor. He asked me to fax it to him and he would personally walk it up to the office. While he was on the phone I faxed this letter over to him:

```
The Boston Globe
To the Editor,

I would like to thank the Boston Globe for its
in depth reporting on the abuse scandal, which
has affected so many lives. Without this kind
of reporting, the public awareness, as well as
the apparent newfound willingness of the Arch-
diocese of Boston to deal with this, would not
be possible.

It is unfortunate that after months of profes-
sional journalism on this crisis, the Globe
would put its own interest before the requested
privacy of the survivors. What had taken us
months to build, mainly a dialogue to establish
the beginning of healing for survivors and
their families, could have been severely dam-
aged in a minute's time because the Globe
choose to disregard our request, the survivors'
requests, for privacy. "A Globe reporter was
present," does not do justice to the truth.
Your reporter wasn't invited and should not
```

```
have mixed in among the survivors and their
families. The healing and yet painful journey
that was braved by survivor and family members
that night was one that we have walked down
step by step, mile after mile, for decades. It
is unfortunate that your reporter was just
there for a ride.

What is equally unfortunate is that when the
integrity and trust in one reporter is broken,
the integrity and trust in all reporters is
questioned.

Sincerely:
Gary M. Bergeron
```

He left to get the letter off the fax machine. When he got back on the line, he read it and said again to me, " Gary I have it and I've read it, I'm going to personally walk this up to the office and get it done." I thanked him and hung up.

An edited version of the letter was published a week later. My education in the art of dealing with the press continued. I felt the sting of the scorpion and I would remember it.

Keeping that story in mind, Olan, Dave and myself drove on to what would be our first interview that day in a series of interviews regarding our response to the Cardinal statement made an hour or so before. My cell phone started to ring again. Thinking that it was another reporter, I grabbed it to answer it. This time it wasn't a reporter. It was Fr. John, the Cardinal's secretary. He asked me if I had time to talk to the Cardinal. The look on my face must have said it all because suddenly the car went quiet. Neither Olan nor Dave said a word.

"Good morning, Gary. I was wondering if you had the chance to hear me this morning at mass?" he asked. "Yes, I did. I actually watched you this morning with my mother. I know that what you did this morning was not an easy thing to do, but it was the right thing. I would like to thank you for my parents as well as my brother and I. I know it was painful, but it's been painful for all of us," I replied. The Cardinal went on, "Gary, I want to thank you for all your effort that you've been putting forth over the last few months. As you have said, this is a journey, it's been a journey for you and a learning journey for me, as well. This is just a small step, I plan on doing a lot more with you and your group in the future. A lot more. I hope that you'll continue to give me the chance to make things right. This was just one step, we have a lot more planned for the future." I thought for a split second and said, "I hope that there are many more occasions like the one we had last week. We do have a long way to go, but your comments this morning touched on a lot of requests that were made of you last week and it did not go unnoticed. I've had several calls this morning from survivors and their family members. Thank you." "Gary, thank you for taking my call this morning. I look forward to talking with you again and getting this done. Have a good afternoon."

I hung up, and sat in silence for a minute. Olan and Dave were silent, as well. It wasn't the fact that I was talking to the Cardinal that hit me. To me, that was no big deal. What hit me was a combination of things, the therapy that we were able to get for survivors over the last few months, the meeting that we were able to hold the previous week, the Cardinal's apology that we had just listened to that morning and the fact that six or seven months ago, the Archdiocese was dodging phone calls like a group of school children playing dodge ball. We would call over and over again, getting only a promise of a return call that, for the most part, never came. Here we were driving in the car six months later and the Cardinal was calling me on my cell phone.

We had come a long, long way from the basement of a club where we all began meeting for the first time the previous spring. I had come a long way, as well. I had seen subtle changes in my attitude, just as I had begun to see subtle changes in the attitude of the Archdiocese. Mine came out of necessity of healing. I didn't care what the reason was for their changes. The only thing that mattered was that it seemed like they were coming. I had a glimmer of hope. The only problem was that we couldn't let it slip backwards. We had to continue to keep the pressure on. I may forget things, on occasion, or put them on the shelf for years, but the one thing I won't forget was the promise I made when I first decided to come forward. Not ever again, not to my children, not to anyone's children. I would do whatever it took to make sure of that.

So off we drove. A little bit higher than were a few days ago, but with the sting of the scorpion still burning. My general thought throughout all the interviews that day was, cautious optimism. I was thankful for the initiative that he had taken that morning, but I was also left with a deep desire for more. I wanted this man, who had in his early career been known as an advocate for civil rights in the '60s, to finish up his career as an advocate for children. I challenged him to do it. I wanted more healing for more survivors. I wanted his apparent compassion to extend to every official and clergyman who represented him. And I meant everyone, including his staff and his attorneys. Within a week, I would have the opportunity to see if my comment was getting heard.

14.

The week following the Cardinal meeting was filled with phone calls and questions. They came from every direction and from everyone. I knew that what had happened was an important step for all of us. I didn't realize the extent of the interest that continued to be there regarding it. The story of our meeting and the apology was carried everywhere, and I mean everywhere. I was questioned about it by the press from California to Australia.

The funny thing was that even with everything that was going on, others saw it much larger than I did. While I would sit there and listen to what a tremendous thing it was, my life still went on. I was still dealing with the everyday issues that the effects of the abuse had on me. Others were doing the same thing. We all still had demons that we were fighting. I was still making my bi-weekly trips to visit my son, and I was still doing my weekly visits to my therapist's. This wasn't over for me. This wasn't over for the other survivors, as well. I learned that people heal at their own pace. One day we would hear about what a tremendous job we were doing, the next day we would get criticized for it. Everyone had their own opinion on what needed to be done. It was hard to ignore the emails and phone calls, but we all agreed to continue to keep our eye on the ball and keep pushing the ball down the field. Several people accused me of being soft on the Cardinal. I tried not to engage any of them, I would try to let my actions speak for themselves. It wasn't always easy.

On Thursday of that week, I got a call from Courtney. They were deposing Bishop Banks in the morning and they were going to be introducing Birmingham documents. She wanted to know if I wanted to be there. "Absolutely," was my only reply.

Bishop Banks was the Vicar For Administration for the Archdiocese of Boston for over two decades. He was, in other words, the person who handled personnel. Any "problem priests" were under his control and he was one of the key persons who had been reassigning known pedophile priests under the administration of several of the Cardinals. He was part of the group in the era that included Bishop McCormack and Bishop Jennings.

I had never met this man before, but I had read enough of the subpoenaed documents to know that he was personally responsible for horrendous decisions that were made on his say. The last 10 days may have seemed like a "feel good" week for many people, including myself. Friday, it was going to be back to business. If anyone doubted that I meant what I said about dealing with both issues, the goal of healing and the legal consequences of it, they were sadly mistaken. I would be there, Bernie would be there, and Paul would be there, as well. I had been waiting months to sit across from the players in what they decided would be the game of life for many survivors. I had started that journey months ago at the Cardinal's residency when I met with him face to face. I could continue it the following day, sitting across from Bishop Banks.

Sitting in the offices of Greenberg Traurig that morning, Thursday, November 7, I was sipping coffee. Courtney came out and by the look on her face, I knew something was wrong. She told us that the attorneys were not agreeing to let us in. I was pissed, to say the least. I thought everything had been agreed to the previous day. She went on to say that that day they decided we were only to be allowed to be in the room after they were finished deposing him in the Shanley matter and when they could go into the Birmingham matter. The problem was that they didn't plan on completely finishing up the Shanley matter that day, so they couldn't go into the Birmingham documents. I was even more pissed. Here we all were. We had taken the day off from work and headed into town when the attorneys for the Archdiocese could have voiced that concern the day before.

The next person who came in was Eric MacLeish. Eric was the lead attorney in the Fr. Shanley lawsuit. He had a long history of representing clergy abuse survivors that went back over 10 years. He litigated the Fr. Porter case early in the 1990s. I was equally impressed with the way he handled himself and his representation. He was the one that was going to be asking the questions in the deposition today.

If I thought I was pissed, Eric was fuming. He couldn't believe that this was going on after everything that had happened the previous week. Neither could I. Apparently neither the Archdiocese nor their attorneys got it when I said that I wanted "to see the compassion that the Cardinal was showing to extend to everyone that represented him." I couldn't believe that after that week, the attorneys would want to piss us off even more. Apparently they still didn't get the fact that we were there for the long haul. We were going to see this through and get it done, whatever it took. We were going to be in that room.

"Do you want me to call someone, or would that be out of place?" I asked him. He told me he didn't care who I called, but that I had the right to be there and if I could call anyone, "do it," he said. I'm not sure if he actually thought I was going to, but I did. I found an office and called Barbara Thorpe's office. I was going to actually call the Cardinal's residency, but I wanted to start with Barbara. I knew that she would do what she could. If she couldn't get anywhere, my next call would have been there. I explained the situation to her. It was important for us to be there. In my mind it only added credibility to all parties involved. Aside from our personal right to be there, we owed it to represent all survivors by being their representative. And it only added credibility for our continued public dialogue with the Cardinal. Barbara, the ever patient person, thanked me for calling her first and agreed with me. She said she would look into it and get back to me. Ten minutes later she was on the phone and said that she had made a call. I won't share the details of that call, but a few minutes later Eric came in and after a conversation with the attorneys for the Archdiocese said that we were "pretty much all set." Two minutes later, the deposition began with us present.

For nearly four hours I watched a man that represented the faithful of the Church for many years, answer questions. For four hours I also felt the hope that I had felt in the week before slip backwards. "I can't recall ", I heard the Bishop use those words almost 100 times in four hours. I understand that the memory of people may lapse over the years but there was no way to believe the extent of this memory loss. We were reviewing document after document, after document, hour after hour, after hour. These were documents that he, himself, had written and signed. These were documents, not only having to do with Fr. Joe Birmingham, but documents relating to priest, after priest, after priest. How any human beings could have sat there, after reviewing his own hand writing for hours on end, and show absolutely no emotion, is beyond me. There were documents in which Joe Birmingham admitted to Bishop Banks on more than one occasion that he had molested boys. There were documents that showed that Banks has stated that there were no apparent problems with Birmingham and that he should be made pastor. These documents were in his own handwriting. Incredible as it seems, it didn't end with Birmingham. There was a another priest who had not only abused boys, but had been arrested on two separate occasions. One occasion was in the bathroom stall of a department store where he was arrested after "doing an immoral action with another man." As incredible as this seems, he was returned to the priesthood. A few years later he was arrested again. This time at a public park after sexually confronting a police officer in a sting operation in an area known for male sexual activity. These were only two of the many, many priests we found were documented that afternoon.

In one document there were notes written concerning 12 boys who had come forward on one singular priest from one parish. When questioned about this document which was again in Bank's own handwriting he stated that he did nothing because there was not enough credible evidence. This was after all the boys were interviewed and after he wrote down specific details of each of the boy's instances of abuse. It got to the point where he would be writing about a priest and addressing him on a first name basis. and He would link that priest by describing a survivor of abuse as "one kid was only touched under his pants, another kid …." They weren't survivors to him. They weren't children to him. They weren't even people. They were a problem that needed to be dealt with, as quickly as possible.

Document after document, priest after priest. I had been involved in this kind of detail for months and had reviewed many documents. I had never imagined that there were that many instances with that many priests and this was only the beginning. There were over a dozen depositions with other Bishops and Cardinals regarding many other priests. It was unimaginable to me. After over three hours of this we broke for lunch. During lunch, Eric said that he had just about finished the Birmingham part of the questioning, but that if we had any questions we would like asked, to let him know. When the deposition resumed, there were only two questions left to ask. They were my two questions. Regardless of everything that I had heard asked that morning and everything that I had seen that morning, I had only two questions. They were questions of faith and redemption, at least to me. They were also questions of hope.

Question : Bishop Banks, as you sit here today, after seeing all the documents before you, given what you know now, do you think that in the past, you have made any errors in judgment concerning the safety of children?

Answer : No.

Question : Bishop Banks, As you sit here today, if you had the information and knowledge during those past years that you have now, would you have made different decisions regarding these priests?

Answer : No.

For me, everything that I had heard this morning was summed up in those two questions and in those two answers. He had no issues with what he had done. No remorse, no guilt. The only feeling which that man showed that day was arrogance. There was no way he was going to admit that he had done anything wrong, ever. Regardless of the fact that it was clearly shown to him that priests he had assigned and reassigned had, not only been arrested, but had repeatedly molested child after child, at parish after parish. He didn't get it because he didn't care. He didn't care before, and he didn't care then. Leaving that afternoon, my head was spinning. I couldn't believe what I had heard and seen. If this was the type of man that represented the Church, then the Church was in deep trouble. Deeper than even I could have imagined. If the public saw what I had seen and read that day, the churches would be empty, and if the Church was represented by that views and beliefs of Bishop Banks, then they deserved to not only be empty, but perhaps they should be taken apart brick by brick, and rebuilt.

A few days before I had been thinking how far we had come. By the end of that afternoon my only thought was how far we had to go. The previous week began with optimism, it ended in reality. God, did we have far to go.

15.

By the middle of November there was a firestorm of events that started unfolding. I knew that there were ongoing negotiations regarding a settlement between the attorneys. I also knew that the heat was being turned up, as well. The battle in the courts regarding the release of 11,000 pages of documents was coming to an end. It seemed as though it was going to be resolved in our favor. Months before, a petition had been filed in court requesting the release of all documents relating to sexual abuse involving priests in the Archdiocese. This motion had been filed on behalf of the survivors of Rev. Paul Shanley, who was currently in jail awaiting trial. Shanley had been extradited from California to face charges in Massachusetts. Judge Sweeney had granted the request, but there had been an ongoing battle for months. It finally seemed to be ending and the Archdiocese had been ordered to release all of these documents.

The court of public opinion would soon find itself buried in documents that continued to reveal the extent of the problems within the Archdiocese of Boston, and throughout the Catholic Church, as well. I could sense the tension that had been building up in the press, as well as the new "victory at any cost" mentality that was developing among the attorneys for the Archdiocese. Unfortunately, at times. it seemed as though it could develop with our attorneys, as well. This was extremely unsettling for me.

Fighting the good fight, for me, did not mean victory at any cost. There was no doubt that when this was over, it would end with a new sense of responsibility and public awareness, however, I was finding myself asking, at what cost? Would the additional price include "life lost due to friendly fire?"

The week before Thanksgiving, I was talking to Olan about this. We both agreed that at that point, more than ever, we needed to keep the dialogue open. That Tuesday, we met with Barbara Thorpe at her new office. The creation of the Office of Healing and Ministry was one of the positive steps that had been taken in this whole mess. In the beginning, survivors would go to the chancery to talk with counselors regarding their abuse and to arrange for therapy. Thankfully, someone had listened to us when we explained how difficult it would be for survivors to be going to this kind of setting. For some survivors, the simple sight of a church would bring about anxiety, let alone an actual visit to the seminary grounds. The Archdiocese then opened up this office in a separate location. What did strike me as odd though, was the fact that in order to get in, you had to press a buzzer and next to the buzzer was a video camera taking your picture. What a weird way of welcoming people I thought.

During the two hours we were there, we asked for another meeting with the Cardinal. For me, it was about letting him know that in the weeks ahead, if these documents were going to be released, it meant the pain of the survivors, as well as ordinary parishioners, was going to be at an all time high. At that point, more than ever, if he intended on staying the course and seeing this through, he needed to be out there in front of it. There was no question, in my mind, that as long as he held that office, he had to do something. I knew that the effects of the release of these documents would be devastating, for him, the survivors, their families and the three million Catholics of the Archdiocese, as well.

Olan's point was that we were reaching a point where a line had to be drawn in the sand. Christmas was coming, and neither of us wanted to go into a new year without a definitive direction regarding this whole situation. I couldn't have agreed with him more. We both tried to stress to Barbara that this meeting had to happen sooner, rather than later. I also told Barbara about my thought of the "victory at any cost" mentality that I saw developing. To me, this mindset was beginning to take on a life of it's own, and I sensed danger in that. If this was turning into a battle of egos between all the attorneys involved, we were all in trouble. Barbara, compassionate as always, assured us that she got the message and that she would relay it to the Cardinal. Hopefully, she said, that she would get us an appointment before Thanksgiving. She realized and agreed with us that the documents that were coming out would have the most negative effects possible in escalating an already volatile situation. She was also concerned that for many of the survivors of the older cases already settled, this would trigger revisiting their trauma. She told us that she had been fielding calls from them and that some of them were concerned that their names would be made public. Many of them had been un-identified or "John Doe's" and wanted to remain that way. We all agreed about the importance of the truth coming out. The problem was whether or not the Church was ready and able to handle the truth. Based on the actions or actually lack of actions taken to this point, none of us thought they were.

Thanksgiving came and went. We received no call. The weekend following Thanksgiving, I awoke on Sunday morning at 3:00 am. I don't know why, but I couldn't sleep. I had a nagging thought in my head. I don't know where it was coming from, but it was persistent and wouldn't go away. I tried to go back to sleep, but the message continued. This is stupid, I thought, but I couldn't ignore it. The message was, go to the 11 o'clock mass. At times like this, I felt foolish. I wasn't one to believe in prophetic messages, but I had always felt that, like Bernie had been saying all along, "There is a higher power in this and there is a hand guiding us." I knew that someone was telling me that it was time for the Cardinal to see my face again. I tossed and turned, trying to go back to sleep. Finally at 6:00 a.m., I got up, made coffee, and sent Olan an email.

```
Olan,
I got a message at 3:00 am from God last night.
He said to "Go to the 11 o'clock mass today."
Gary
```

I sent it, and thought to my self, when he gets up and reads this, he's going to think that I'm crazy. I laughed to myself, but then something very weird happened. I had no sooner sent it, than my phone rang. He didn't say hello, he just started in with, "I can't fucking believe that you just sent that to me. I've been up all morning. I was waiting until 8:00 to call you because I didn't think you were up yet. Gary, this is too weird. I was going to call you and tell you the same thing. Have you read the papers yet?" Read the papers? I said no, it was too early. "You have to read the Globe online. I was thinking the same thing this morning, but I thought I was crazy, then I read the Globe," he said.

I checked the Globe online. The headline was "Catholic Church weighing the factors of Bankruptcy." It was too strange and too weird for me, but I knew where I would be going today, and I knew Olan would be going with me. I was pissed, we both were. The article said that an unnamed source at the chancery stated that the bankruptcy subject was being discussed. Unnamed source. That was part of the problem. Bankruptcy was a non issue as far as I was concerned. It was a tactic that was being use to put fear in the survivors and turn the public's attention away from the imminent release of the documents. On the Friday after Thanksgiving, the Church and their attorneys, in their infinite wisdom, had filed an emergency motion at 5:00 p.m. to stop the release of the documents. It was a last ditch effort which was poorly planned and received. They knew that it was no use, but tried the tactic anyway. Realizing that it wouldn't work, they were now using the bankruptcy plan.

The Boston Herald had done a detailed story listing excess properties that the Archdiocese owned. The total assessed value was $1.3 billion. To think that for the first time in the two thousand year history of the Catholic Church, an entity which has valued its privacy and gone to every length to protect its inner works from view, would have to open its books to the public, was difficult to imagine. Furthermore to think the Church was sitting on that kind of money while people are walking around in Massachusetts hungry and homeless, was both shocking and sickening to me. Yes, I was definitely going to see the Cardinal that day. I thought of calling Bernie, but decided against it. He had been in Florida with his family for the past week, and was catching up at home. I wasn't sure what his reaction would be to my late night "message from God," and thought I would just call him later and fill him in.

Olan called Barbara Thorpe. He thought that we should let her know we were coming. I agreed. I called and spoke to Barbara, as well. There was an edge in her voice. I knew it was because of the documents that were going to be released soon. She asked me candidly if we had any say in the release of the documents. We talked a bit further. This was an interesting turn in the conversation. To me, the fact that she was asking meant she realized the significance of what their release would mean. The fact that she phrased the question the way she did seemed like someone was reaching out. I wasn't sure if she was reaching out on her own, or reaching out for someone else, but I took it at face value. I told her that we all had a say in the release. We were always willing to do whatever was in the best interest of everyone affected by these documents. I went on to ask her if she had anything in mind. She wasn't sure, but she just wanted to know what I thought could be done. I told her that time was continuing to run out, and that if she had something in mind, there was no time like the present to talk about it. She ended the conversation with, "It's definitely a good thing for you guys to be at mass today. The Cardinal needs to see you. I see that more clearly now today than ever."

It was incredibly cold that Sunday morning. Not the normal winter day. That day it was bitterly cold. As Olan and I drove, we talked about the possibilities regarding the documents that were coming out. I told him about my conversation with Barbara and we both thought that there may have been a hidden message in that conversation. Only time would tell. Time, and the Cardinal.

The protestors were out in front again, in full force with signs and bullhorns. This time, just like last time, we took our share of jeers shouted in our direction. This time, just like last time, we didn't avoid them. We walked past them saying hello to some and dismissing the anger of others. There were camera crews there from all the local and major networks. Apparently they had all read the Globe, as well. We took the same seats as last time, second to front row. That day was different though, I was not there under the same pretext as last time. Unlike last time I was definitely there to deliver a message. Olan knew it and I think Barbara knew it, as well. The Cardinal walked down the center aisle at the beginning of the mass as normal but when he got to our pew, he glanced over, nodded his head and winked. This guy winked at us. I looked at Olan, as if to say, "this guy thinks we're here to sing today, he has no idea." Olan had the exact same expression on his face. The Cardinal apparently knew we were going to be there, but I doubted he knew why. I started to think that this was going to be a waste of time. That simple gesture, to me, meant that my conversation with Barbara was just that, a conversation. There was no hidden message, the message was plain and simple, please come and do whatever you guys can do to get through to him. Not only was there no hidden message, now it seemed like she was almost begging us to try and do something. I asked her if the Cardinal knew the reason why we were there. Barbara assured us that he would meet with us after mass, so we waited.

As mass progressed, we noticed camera crews setting up to the front left of the altar. We didn't know why, though. It was extremely unsettling watching communion being given out and cameras being set up at the same time. Call it Catholic guilt, or call it decency. The fact was that, to many people, the inside of a church was no place for a TV crews. I'm probably one of them.

The mass ended, and, as it did, Donna Morrissey, the spokesperson for the Cardinal walked in. We realized that she was going to have a press conference. Olan and I were both puzzled, I was actually shocked. This was neither the time, nor the place, for it.

The Cardinal came over to greet us. Shaking both our hands, we asked if he had the time to speak with us. Nodding, he said, "Absolutely. Why don't you meet me in the side of the chapel?" We waited for a few minutes and then followed him. We walked around the camera crews and the press conference that was in full force by then, following Barbara to the side chapel. As we walked in, I knew that we were going to get absolutely nowhere. Here, in the side room, the Cardinal was being undressed of his regalia by several nuns, along with several other priests. This was no place for the kind of discussion we needed to have. Definitely not in front of all of these people. I knew it, and Olan knew it, but we tried anyway.

Once he got undressed, he sat down on a bench. Immediately Olan sat on one side of him and I sat down on the other. At least we had him between us, and, for a few minutes, he had to listen to us. We started to tell him that it was important for us to meet together and talk. He agreed, but said that he didn't have time that day. Not a problem. We said that sooner was better than later and he said that he had gotten that message the previous week. Olan looked at him and said, "I thinks it's vitally important for us to get together this week. I think we're a good barometer out there and the tension is getting extreme." The Cardinal actually looked at both of us, patted each of us on the knee, and said, "No, I don't think you're a good barometer, but I do think you're both good guys." I could feel my blood pressure rising, and I could see Olan's rising as well. "When is a good time this week?" I asked. The Cardinal said that we would have to check with Fr. John. "He has my schedule." Looking at Fr. John, Olan said, "You're a big guy, but I'll take one side of you, and Gary will take the other side of you and find that schedule." He laughed and said that he didn't have it on him, but that he would get back to us. He gave me a look, a look that said, "Don't worry, it'll happen." We were just about finished, I knew that we had at least let them know we were still not giving up on this. Walking away I said to Olan, "We definitely met with Cardinal Law today," He replied, "Yes, we definitely didn't see Bernie today. He was pure Cardinal. Did you see the way he patted us on the knee?" I laughed and said, "Hey, at least we'll be seeing him this week. I'm pretty sure of it. He knows that it's time."

We walked out of the sacristy. It had been a long time since I had ever been in one, let alone been in the sacristy of the Cathedral. So many of the survivors of Birmingham had been molested right there in a sacristy just like this one next to the altar, I couldn't help but think of it. Had it been too long? Definitely not. Not long enough? I wasn't sure. But there was definitely a tightening in my stomach as I was leaving. It was that weird feeling that you got when you realized that something had happened, but you realized it after the fact. It didn't last long, but it had lasted long enough that I had noticed it. I hoped that what I was feeling inside wasn't visible outside. We managed to get past the camera crews and press conference without much notice. There were a few eyes raised as some of them noticed where we were and who we were with. We had been interviewed, at some time or another, by all of them. Not that day though. We continued to walk past them and get outside. It was still frigidly cold, but I welcomed the fresh air.

We got back to Lowell around 3:00 p.m. that day. There were a few calls from the press to both of us. They wanted a survivor's opinion of the bankruptcy issue. As always, I tried to play it right down the middle. The quote for the day, which was repeated whenever we were asked, was, "This is nothing but a thinly veiled threat used to change the public's interest away from the release of the documents and towards the issue of bankruptcy. The fact that it did not come directly from the Cardinal, but was rather leaked from the Chancery, does nothing but take away whatever credibility is left." That Sunday ended later than either of us had planned and it didn't go as well as either of us had hoped. It was the beginning of a long week and it was only Sunday. I had no idea what was in store for any of us in the few short weeks ahead. No idea at all. I would start to find out the next day, and it was only going to get more intense.

Monday I got a call from Eric Macleish's office. He wanted to make sure that I, along with Bernie and Olan, was going to be at the office that evening. Eric was going to be doing a preview of the documents that were to be released in the press. He wanted us to know everything that was going to be happening regarding the documents and he wanted us there in person. It seemed odd that it wasn't Bob Sherman who called. I said I would be there and then made the usual round of calls to Bernie, Olan and Paul, who all agreed to go. I called Bob's office later in the day and asked if we needed to be there. Bob wasn't in, but Courtney said that if we were invited, then we should go. There was a strange tone in her voice, as well. My interest was piqued. She didn't reveal anything else, but something weird was going on. The four of us arrived, one at a time, that night. As I walked into the lobby, I noticed lots of familiar faces in the crowd. The leaders of many of the local advocacy groups were milling around in the lobby on the first floor by the security desk. What a coincidence I naively thought. I said hello to those whom I knew, and was introduced to those I didn't. Some were friendly faces, some not so friendly.

One International Place, which is the address as well as the name of the building, had a grand marble lobby. The lobby included dozens of shops, restaurants, a flower shop, copy shop and a few newsstands. Those shops surround a huge 3 story waterfall. It was definitely a grand lobby, to say the least. There were many other firms in the building, which encompassed two separate towers. Maybe they were there seeing someone else, there were many other tenants in the building.

Ever since the tragedy of 911, the security of the building was high. I checked into the security desk, got out my license and received my visitor's pass and took the elevator to the third floor. As I got off the elevator, I noticed some of those same familiar faces that were downstairs. As I walked around the offices, I spotted Olan, Bernie and Paul. I looked at them and gave them a "what the fuck is going on?" look. I couldn't believe that all these advocacy group representatives were there. They all gave me the "I have no fucking idea either" look. We all milled around for a while. I was looking for Bob or Courtney or someone who would tell me what the hell was going on. I started to realize what was happening. Eric had invited all these groups to attend this meeting. They, along with actual survivors, had been invited to the preview. The only clients, though, that the firm represented were Olan, Bernie, Paul, Paula and Rodney Ford and myself. As these documents were actually being produced officially in the Ford case, I knew why they were there. As for the other advocacy groups, I had no idea why they were all there. It was a strange sight to look around the room and realize that the advocates outnumbered the survivors almost 4 to 1. Strange setting, I thought.

As always, I didn't have an issue with any of the other advocacy groups. As always, they had issues with me. I thought that it was strange that they would have been invited, not only because of the flack we had taken from them, but also because no one had told us that they would be here. I always considered the office our territory. It may seem strange, but it was a safe haven for us. I had spent a lot of time there over the previous nine months and it almost seemed like home to me. I was annoyed that we were not notified they were going to be there. Given the fact that I had personally received hate mail from some of the very same people now sitting in the same room as me, yes, I was definitely a bit annoyed. I was also annoyed because the office knew about the criticism some of these people had been sending our way and that they had been invited, regardless. I looked around for friendly faces from the office. There was no Bob, although I found Courtney and I sat next to her.

As the evening progressed, I realized why there was no Bob. This was definitely an "Eric Macleish production." Eric's presentation in the press had been a turning point months before. There was still talk regarding his PowerPoint presentation which had taken place regarding the documents about Rev. Paul Shanley. Some thought it was overkill, others thought it was masterfully done. I thought it definitely triggered a change in the public's perception of what these file encompassed and what a rampant problem the sexual abuse scandal was. I did wonder, though, if it was all still necessary at that point. As the evening progressed, we went over several files. We would see document after document, file after file, and priest after priest. It was horrendous, it was painful and it was incredible. Time after time, there would be transfer after transfer of one abuser after another. There were literally dozens upon dozens of priest that had been abusing hundreds of children over decades of time. I understood why Barbara was concerned. Now I was concerned, even more. The public reaction to this was going to be outrage, and it should be. I would find out that cardinal after cardinal and bishop after bishop fully knew what was going on and did nothing. Not once that evening, in the literally thousands of documents, did I ever see an instance of someone doing anything to put a stop to it. Not once that evening did I see anything to indicate that they had ever taken the child into consideration. It was truly sickening to me. As deeply as I was involved in this, I still couldn't believe that there was more. I would find out as I personally took the time to go through these documents on my own, that there was much, much more. What would the public think? What would the everyday Catholic think? There was no way possible that the Church could ever have considered what the release of these documents was going to mean to the 60 year old Catholic. The one who goes to Church every Sunday. The one who continues to place money in the basket, money they thought was going to help feed the poor. What the public would learn is that that the Church had done everything but the right thing.

These documents were more damaging than even I could have

considered and we were only looking at the tip of the iceberg that night. The evening went on. A few hours into it, we all took a break. I looked at the guys and said I was going out to have a cigarette. As I got up, I noticed one of the advocates getting up to have one, as well. Olan grabbed me and said, "Do you know who that is?" Yes, I knew exactly who it was. It was the guy with the bullhorn that had been sending the emails busting my hump for months. "Yes, I know. I'm actually going to try and talk to him when I grab a smoke outside," was my reply. Olan just looked at me and said, "Be careful." "No problem," I said. He asked if I wanted him to go with me. "No thanks, Olan." I thought that since we were both there, it was an opportunity to say hello and maybe clear the air. It was an opportunity, just maybe, for him to realize that we were on the same side. I was wrong.

I took the elevator downstairs and walked outside. As I lit up, a few of the others joined me, as well. They all knew the dynamics of what had been going on between me and this guy and I told them all that I actually wanted to talk with him and maybe put an end to the bullshit that was going on. As he walked out, one of the others who was with me yelled for him to join us. He glanced at me and said, "No thanks. The air is better over here." So much for my attempt at diplomacy. I guess he wasn't ready yet. I finished my cigarette and went upstairs.

The meeting went on for another two hours. As it wound down, comments began flying around the room. Everything from, "I told you all that these guys were doing nothing but pimping children," to "I want everyone here to be at the cathedral this Sunday to join me in protesting Bernie Law the Pimp." These comments were coming from the same advocates who had been sending these messages for months. It started to get out of hand for a while. It almost got to the point where one group would make one suggestion, and another would try to "one up" the other with a suggestion even more outlandish. All the while, I was looking at our guys with the same "what the fuck is going on" look. I was waiting for someone from the firm to say something, but no one did.

No one, that is, until Courtney.

One person said, "This is why I expect everyone in this room to continue to be more vocal at the cathedral every Sunday, and I mean everyone in this room." This was yet another comment from an advocate who was neither part of our lawsuit, nor even a survivor. I found it funny that some advocates on this issue feel it necessary to tell the survivors what they should and shouldn't be doing. I knew that the last statement was directed to us, the Birmingham guys, but I let it slide. It wasn't important. But it was to Courtney. Courtney started to make a point. "I think it's important for everyone in this room to respect each others feelings regarding the decisions they make as individuals regarding protesting. We do have a wide group of survivors that we represent here and some of them don't want to protest. They have that right. We all need to respect each other's decisions here." Courtney didn't even finish her sentence. This guy, the same guy who was outside, the one that had been criticizing us for months, the same guy that wasn't even represented by our firm, and yes, there as a guest, started yelling and pointing fingers.

"I know where this is coming from. It's you guys (as he pointed a finger directly in my face). This is bullshit! If you think that I'm going to stand here and take this from you, you're fucking crazy! If you think that I'm going to start listening to lawyers tell me what I'm going to do, forget it. It ain't never gonna happen. This is coming from you guys, this is bullshit."

He went on for a few minutes. He continued to stand there, with his finger inches from my face, ranting and raving about me and about us. As he went on, I remained seated. I didn't need any help in restraining my emotions, even though the minute he stood up. Olan put his hand on my arm, as if to say, "Don't get up Gary." And I didn't get up. I just sat there patiently and said, over and over again, to him, "You're out of line here. You're a guest here and you owe this woman an apology." He continued to rant and rave and I just repeated the same thing to him over and over. I think that's why he kept going. Now looking back, it was kind of funny. Back then, It wasn't, but as they say, he was a small fish in a big pond and I had much bigger fish to fry. I really wasn't pissed at him. I was extremely pissed at the firm for even inviting this guy. There was no way I should have to deal with that kind of mentality in this kind of office. As everyone got up to leave, almost everyone in that room apologized, on his behalf, to me. Everyone that was but him, not that I actually expected it from him. It was another example of people allowing something to go on and not having the balls to stand up and say, right then and there, "This is wrong." Here I was, sitting with a group of advocates, with all their names and titles, telling me, after the fact, that he was out of line. No one would get up and stop him when it happened, yet, there we all were, sitting in a room criticizing the Church for doing the very same thing. For not standing up and saying, "This is wrong and it shouldn't be." It was one of the reasons why I hadn't aligned myself with any of those groups. To this day, I have no idea what the deal was with this guy. But to this day, I don't lose sleep over it, either. He's continued to email me with his criticisms, which range from, "You're nothing but a patsy for the Church," to one of my personal favorites, "The first thing I'd advise you to do is stop wearing that turtleneck sweater." Hey, what can I say? I loved that turtleneck.

I didn't engage him that night, though. I waited until everyone left and I engaged Eric about it, instead. The following day I also told Bob about it. I let them both know that this was wrong. Plain and simple. The fact that we were set up that evening was incredible to me. The fact that no one stood up when this guy was ranting and raving and screaming at Courtney was wrong. The fact that they were even invited was wrong. These people had no right to be there. That night was as classic an example of a "dog and pony show" as I had ever seen. It was the type of event that was done by other people, for other reasons. It was not the type of event that any of the SOJB group was interested in. It was actually the reason why we had gone with the Greenberg and Traurig firm. Something called professionalism. One thing was for sure, last night was about anything but professionalism. I hated to be thinking about issues of integrity at this stage, but I definitely was. I was livid and Bob knew it. Not only did I never want this to happen again, I said that if it did, I was walking. And I wouldn't be alone. I wasn't the only one pissed off. Olan, Bernie and Paul couldn't believe the way the night went. They were all as mad as hell. My God, if our own lawyers wouldn't stand up for us in their own offices, we started to question how else they might fail us. None of us wanted to have to make that choice whether or not to stay. Not then or ever. I would find out that day that everyone in the office did not agree upon the events of the night before, which is why Bob and several other attorneys weren't present. This didn't help. This didn't help at all. I felt as if we had been hung out to dry and it infuriated me. This was not about doing anything that came to mind that might work. This was about doing the right thing. This was not about the publicity of a dog and pony show, this was about my integrity and the integrity of every survivor that I unknowingly represented. Over and over again I would hear myself telling them, "When the Archdiocese or their attorneys can start questioning my integrity, I can no longer question theirs." I didn't work for the law firm. I hired them to work for me. Maybe it was time for that reminder. Maybe it wasn't, but they got it anyway. It seemed like instead of Bob's "Scorpion and the Water Buffalo story," it was time for Gary's "the tail don't wag the dog" story.

Tuesday morning I headed back into Boston. It seemed like it was becoming my second home. I had called Bob early in the morning to let him know that I was heading in. Walking into his office, he had an idea of my reason for being there, but I had to clear the air anyway. For the next few hours I blasted away and for the next few hours Bob listened. Bob also apologized, said they had made a mistake, and let me know it wouldn't happen again. I had meant what I had said and I felt he had meant what he had said. I trusted him and he needed to know that trust didn't come easy for me. Within several weeks that trust would be tested again.

[Notes of Monsignor Finnegan] **GT REDACTION** 4 Nov 64

Fr. Birmingham was present at the Chancery Office to be confronted by the two boys and their fathers who had accused him of improper conduct. Fr. Hurley, the pastor, had come to Chancery a few days before to bring this matter to official attention and Msgr. Sexton interviewed Fr. Birmingham to acquaint him with their complaint. Fr. B. denied them and today's meeting was arranged.

Present were Msgr. Sexton, Msgr. Finnegan, Fr. Hurley, Fr. Birmingham, Mr. ▮▮▮▮▮, Mr. ▮▮▮▮▮.

Mr. ▮▮▮ related how his son ▮▮▮ told that Fr. B. "put his hands inside his pants and touched his private parts." It had also happened "last year" in the sacristy and in the kitchen. ▮▮▮ had erection and "Fr. B. asked if it felt good." One occasion Fr. B. asked if he was ticklish - but the janitor walked in and no touches took place at that time.

Mr. ▮▮▮ - told similar story regarding his son, ▮▮▮. The incidents happened on two occasions. Most recently, about a month ago, when altar boys' meetings had started. ▮▮▮ went to his mother and told the story. She told Mr. ▮▮▮ and it was brought to pastor's attention.

Fr. Birmingham at first claimed these accounts "were not true." He claimed the circumstances were different. These two boys had been concerned with mutual sex play - but Msgr. Sexton and Mr. ▮▮▮ spoke up to restrict Fr. B. to the alleged incidents themselves. Fr. B. then said that, with ▮▮▮ - "it was a spontaneous gesture of grabbing him around the waist." Did not touch his p/parts. [The boy answered, in reply to question by Msgr. Sexton, "Fr. B.'s hands _were_ inside my pants, inside my underwear]. Fr. B. then was questioned regarding the incident with ▮▮▮ and he "did not remember", "honest to God".

It was then brought out that these incidents could have involved other boys with Fr. B. A Sgt. ▮▮▮ of ▮▮▮ police had stated it could have happened to his boy. These two boys and an ▮▮▮ said "this had happened to all the boys." The ▮▮▮ boy had said that Fr. B. had once tickled him Fr. Hurley pointed out that another boy had denied it.

The Sgt's boy had told his father "it _did_ happen and it _did_ occur twice" - "Fr. B. put his hands inside my pants and touched my pr/parts."

Msgr. Sexton asked for and received Fr. B.'s apology for the "impropriety".

Further talk with the boys' fathers and Fr. H. indicated that this knowledge is widespread. Boys have talked of it. Parents (of at least 5) are aware of it. Boys won't go to altar boy meetings, CCD, etc. Mr. ▮▮▮ "not a real practicing Catholic, wife very upset, etc. etc." Msgr. Sexton told Fr. H. to speak with Mrs. ▮▮▮.

Msgr. Sexton assured the fathers that Fr. B. would be transferred immediately. Fr. B. asked if he could stay until Feb. so it would appear to be a routine transfer, and he had many projects, etc. etc.

Msgr. Sexton pointed out that this was impossible and that Fr. B. was to make immediate appointment with Cath. psychiatrist to get to the root of this problem and seek help from his Spiritual Director. He was given the name and phone no. of Dr. Quinn (?) and told to make the appointment right away. His transfer would be in the mail within a day or so - and he would be placed on sick leave, in all likelihood - and the people were to be told that he had been "working too hard" and "needed a rest." Every effort would be made to send Fr. H. a replacement, but "we're short of men at this time of year," Msgr. Sexton pointed out, and, possibly, be might not get help until Ordination in Feb.

But, in any event, Fr. B. is to be transferred.

TJF

BIRMINGHAM 2.1

Birmingham Document dating to 1964

ARCHDIOCESE OF BOSTON
RECEIVED
APR 8 1987
OFFICE OF
MINISTERIAL PERSONNEL

GT REDACTION

Mass
4 April 87

Bernard Cardinal Law
Archbishop of Boston
Chancery of the Archdiocese
Boston, Mass.

NOT ACKNOWLEDGED
AT RESIDENCE

Your Emminence:

I am a member of St Ann's Parish, Pleasant St, Gloucester, Mass.

About a month ago, our pastor, Rev Joseph Birmingham resigned for "reasons of health."

Subsequently, the Pilot mentioned that Rev Birmingham had submitted his resignation from the priesthood — which you accepted.

A colleage of mine, in passing, mentioned a Fr Joe Birmingham who was taken out of St James' Parish in Salem during the late 1960's to early 1970's.

This man said that Re Birmingham had been removed because he had molested boys in the parish. As a matter of fact, this man's brother was one of the boys who were molested.

I now request that you inform me if this is the same Rev Joe Birmingham. My friend described him to a tee.

I have a son who is on altar

BIRMINGHAM 2.22

Parent writing to Cardinal Law about concerns regarding a Father Birmingham
who has been giving sermons on AIDS
First Page Received April 8th. of 1987

boy in the church and have a rightful
concern about him if this is, in fact, the
same person.

Twice within 6 months our Rev.
Joe Birmingham gave sermons on AIDS, which
I found rather odd.

If it is the same person, how
do I bring up the subject of molestation
with my son who just turned 13
years old?

Please respond to me as I have a
real, and rightful, concern about this
whole matter. I am concerned about
the (AIDS) situation; and about a priest
possibly molesting my son.

Thank you for a prompt reply;

GT REDACTION

BIRMINGHAM 2.23

Parent continues to write asking if this is the
Same Father Birmingham that served in her parish.

THE INSTITUTE OF LIVING

William L. Webb, Jr., M.D.
President and
Psychiatrist-in-Chief

March 25, 1987

Reverend John B. McCormick
2121 Commonwealth Avenue
Brighton, MA 02135

Re: Reverend Joseph E. Birmingham
Birth Date: 04/30/34

Dear Father McCormick:

Pursuant to our meeting to discuss Father Birmingham, this letter will summarize his treatment and progress at the Institute of Living.

Father Birmingham has been extremely cooperative with all facets of his treatment. Although it is undoubtedly a difficult and traumatic time for him, he has been open in therapy and a solid therapeutic alliance has been established. This has allowed us to focus on the necessary issues. As a result, Father Birmingham has made significant progress. In addition to individual psychotherapy three times a week, he has attended a general psychotherapy group three times a week. He meets once a week with the clergy group and once a week in a group focusing on increasing patients' self-awareness. He also participates two times a week in a group that focuses specifically on sexual concerns. Father Birmingham has interacted well with staff and other patients. It is sometimes difficult for patients to relinquish control of their activities, and they sometimes see it as having no control over their lives. However, Father Birmingham adapted well to having to ask me for "permission" for various activities.

In addition to being cooperative, Father Birmingham is highly motivated. He is not only motivated for treatment here, but is also motivated to put together a discharge plan that maximizes the likelihood of his having the support and guidance necessary to consolidate the gains he has made at the Institute of Living. When this discharge plan is in place, it will of course include outpatient treatment.

BIRMINGHAM 2.20

Report on Father Birmingham from the Institute of Living, sent to Father McCormack Dated March 25th, 1987.

Annunciation Rectory
Danvers, Massachusetts

REGISTERED MAIL - SPECIAL DELIVERY

PERSONAL

17 January 1970

Archdiocesan Personnel Office
Chancery Building
2121 Commonwealth Avenue
Brighton, Mass, 02135
   Attn: Rev. John J.

Dear Father:

    I write you concerning a Brother Priest, about whom I had phoned you for advise on two occasions (around last Thanksgiving and again, on last Tuesday morning). You recall that our telephone conversations did not identify the Priest.

    The problem presented was one of a "rumor of possible homosexuality" - and the rumor concerns Father Joseph E. Birmingham (class of 1960), presently stationed at St. James' Parish in Salem. The reason why I bring this name to your attention now will become apparent as I spell out my knowledge of the case, and the action I have taken regarding it.

    The rumor first came to my attention around Thanksgiving time by way of a St. James' parishioner. This man indicated that the rumor was knowledgeable among the youngsters (boys and girls) at St. James' School, and among some of the parents. He also indicated that the problem surfaced about two years ago - but subsided shortly thereafter.

    Having heard this, I phoned you to find out if Personnel Office had any definite mode of action in such cases. We deliberately refrained from identification of priest involved. Following our conversation, I visited Father Birmingham in his Rectory, indicated the existence of this rumor, and pointed out the following: He would either have to trace the rumor out and put an end to it - or, in the event that the rumor had any foundation in fact, he should consult with a psychiatrist. I offered my own service in making contact with a psychiatrist for him, should he feel that this would make things easier for him. As I expected, he denied any foundation in fact, and assured me that he would study the matter thoroughly.

    Last Monday night (12 January), Sister Superior of St. James' School phoned me. She had been visited by my informant's wife and one/or several other wives. (It was from the informant's wife that she learned that the subject was discussed with me some 5 or 6 weeks previously). Sister was deeply troubled, felt that she had an obligation to act, and didn't quite know where to turn. I scheduled a meeting at her convent on Tuesday morning, and discussed the matter with her and another Sister for about an hour and a half. Her "research" seems to point out that the rumor is founded on facts - and that these facts have occurred

BIRMINGHAM 2.5

Letter From a fellow priest concerning Father Birmingham Dated January 17, 1970

Annunciation Rectory
Danvers, Massachusetts

page 2

even since I spoke to Father Birmingham at Thanksgiving time - indeed, as recent as within the past two weeks. I suggested that, on behalf of the Sister, and in view of the fact that I had been earlier approached on the subject, I would discuss the matter with the Pastor of St. James' Parish.

It was at this time that I made my second phone call to you, and pointed out my intended visit to the Pastor. Again, no names were mentioned. In our conversation it came out that, since you are presently working on a list of proposed transfers to become effective within the next few weeks, it would be also possible to transfer the priest in question - as a normal routine matter - if his name were presented to you. I felt that such a presentation should come from the Pastor, rather than from me.

My visit to the Pastor took place Tuesday afternoon. I told him what I have just spelled out above. The Pastor indicated that he would send a letter immediately to the Personnel Office, requesting a transfer of Father Birmingham - feeling that, as I do, Father's effectiveness in the Parish would decline in proportion as the rumor may spread. All the more reason for a transfer if the rumor proved true in fact.

And so, the matter stands. No doubt the Pastor's letter has already reached your Office. For this reason, I mention the name of the subject-priest - so that you can identify my phone calls with the Pastor's letter. It will also give you an up-to-date survey of what I have tried to do in this case. I feel that I am not betraying Father Birmingham since I had confronted him first with the situation - and now that several weeks have passed, the situation does not appear controlled.

Inasmuch as the Sisters, and the parents mentioned abov, look upon the situation as one of extreme urgency, I feel that there was no other alternative but to visit the Pastor, and to follow up that visit with this letter to you. The possibility of re-visiting Father Birmingham is impossible at present - nor could I schedule another meeting with him within the next week and a half.

Trusting that the above will be of help to you in helping Father Birmingham, I am

Respectfully
Rev. Patrick J. Kelly

Copy to:
Reverend Pastor, St. James' Church, Salem.

P.S. For your information, Father Matthias, OFM, of the Formation Center in Andover is also acquainted with the situation and has discussed the subject with me.

BIRMINGHAM 2.6

Letter From a fellow priest concerning Father Birmingham
Dated January 17, 1970

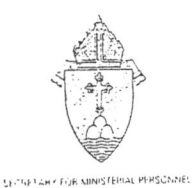

ARCHDIOCESE OF BOSTON
2121 COMMONWEALTH AVENUE
BRIGHTON, MASSACHUSETTS 02135
(617) 254-0100

SECRETARY FOR MINISTERIAL PERSONNEL

GT REDACTION

April 14, 1987

██████████ Massachusetts

Dear ██████████

His Eminence, Cardinal Law, received your letter and asked me to look into the matter for him.

I contacted Father Birmingham and asked him specifically about the matter you expressed in your letter. He assured me there is absolutely no factual basis to your concern regarding your son and him. From my knowledge of Father Birmingham and my relationship with him, I feel he would tell me the truth and I believe he is speaking the truth in this matter.

From my perspective, therefore, I see no need of your raising this question with your son. But if you feel drawn to do so, for whatever reason, I suggest that you contact Mrs. Mary Byrne at North Shore Catholic Charities in Peabody (532-3600). She is the Director of Professional Services and is experienced in these matters.

I hope that you find this helpful and that it allays any concerns you may have.

Sincerely yours in Christ,

Reverend John B. McCormack
Secretary for Ministerial Personnel

JMc:mo'1

BIRMINGHAM 2.25

Father John McCormack's Reply
Even though he had received reports on Father Birmingham less than 30 days prior.

Hand written notes from Father Birminghams file.

Additional hand written notes.

Archdiocese of Boston
Assistant to the Secretary for Ministerial Personnel

PERSONAL AND CONFIDENTIAL

MEMORANDUM

TO: File
FROM: Rev. Brian M. Flatley
DATE: March 2, 1995
RE: Father Joseph Birmingham

███████████ from the Spiritual Development Office came to see me at Chancery about Father Birmingham. The notices "Do you remember Father Birmingham" have been appearing in the Brighton newspaper, and she is concerned. Her sons were extremely close to Father Birmingham, even going to Europe with him.

███████ had concerns back then. Something didn't seem right. He undermined parental authority. She even called Lowell to see if there was anything she should be concerned about, but got rave reviews.

She said that this has been the main topic of conversation at their home these past few days, and among their children's peers. I shared with her that there are some areas of concern about Father Birmingham, and that we know that these ads are connected with Father Porter's victims, but that is all we know. She does not think that anything happened to her sons, but she would like to know if we learn that there is going to be a public issue. I told her that I would not be surprised. They certainly are digging, but we don't know what they are going to do.

BIRMINGHAM 2.86

Interoffice memos, quoting
"They certainly are digging, but we don't know what they are going to do."

182 *Don't Call Me A Victim*

Archdiocese of Boston
Secretary for Ministerial Personnel

MEMORANDUM

TO: File

FROM: Father McCormack

DATE: December 20, 1994

RE: Rev. Joseph Birmingham

GT REDACTION

In mid-December, Mr. ▇▇▇, telephone number ▇▇▇, telephoned me. He had been in to see Sr. Rita McCarthy, CSJ, a month or two previous.

▇▇▇ wanted to know what dates Father Birmingham was at St. James in Salem and where he could get a copy of the death certificate.

After doing some research, I informed him that Father Birmingham was at St. James in Salem from November 1964 until February 1970. I also informed him that he could get the death certificate at the Department of Vital Records and Statistics, 150 Tremont Street, Boston, Massachusetts, 02108.

JBM:ah

BIRMINGHAM 2.78

Memos detailing questions on the cause of death.

```
Alert Memo:

     An old case is surfacing again regarding Father Birmingham which dates
back to 1968-72 at St. James in Salem. The case first came to our attention
October 13, 1992.  Sister Grace Kenney called the Chancery and spoke with
Sister Catherine regarding a call she had from a "Globe" reporter. The
report is attached.

     Sister recalls that possibly 8 altar boys were involved.  She recently
received a call from one of the parents from St. James.  Her son
                              At that time he spoke with
         ?? who revealed that he is gay and that he, too, was molested
by Father Birmingham.  He mentioned other men who make the same claim;
namely,
              It seems that they have all been communicating regarding this
problem.  Sister Grace thought we should know. Only three people are alive
who know about this: Father John Jennings, Dr. Arthur Cavanaugh of Salem, and
Sister Grace.  Sister can be reached at St. Mary's Beverly.  Her telephone
numbers are:
     School:   508-927-3259
     Home:     508-927-4649
              508-927-4819
```

BIRMINGHAM 2.82

Interoffice "Alert Memo" stating that,
"There are only 3 people alive that know about this"

184 *Don't Call Me A Victim*

Left to right, Olan Horne, Bernie McDaid, Gary Bergeron
At a press conference the day the Birmingham Documents were released.
Photo by George Martell
Courtesy of The Boston Herald

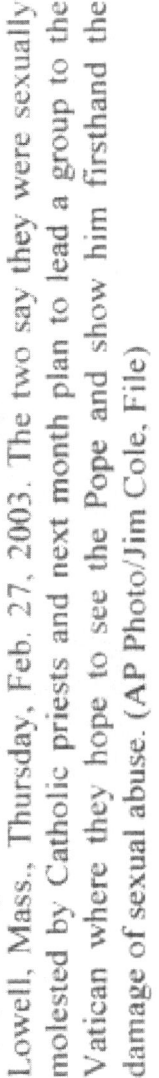

Joseph Bergeron, 77, left, and his son Gary are seen at their home in Lowell, Mass., Thursday, Feb. 27, 2003. The two say they were sexually molested by Catholic priests and next month plan to lead a group to the Vatican where they hope to see the Pope and show him firsthand the damage of sexual abuse. (AP Photo/Jim Cole, File)

Photo by AP photographer Jim Cole
Photo and caption courtesy of the Associated Press
Article by Associated Press writer Jason Hirsch

Bernie and Gary, heading from the first floor to the second floor inside the Vatican. You can see Gary, holding the "Vatican Letter" in his hands.

Don't Call Me A Victim 187

From left to right, Gary Bergeron, Olan Horne
Front page Boston Herald / Photo by Nancy Lane
Courtesy of The Boston Herald

188 *Don't Call Me A Victim*

Photo by Dominic Chavez Courtesy of the Boston Globe

Don't Call Me A Victim   189

*****

I'm in the 7th. grade. Sitting in class I feel myself getting sick. I have a headache and my stomach feels queasy. I ask if I can go to the nurse's station. She says yes. Down the corridor I walk. I go to the nurse's station and they send me to the principal's office. Sister Rose Francis decides that I should go home and calls my mother. I'm sitting on a chair now because there's no place to lie down. Fr. B walks in and asks what's wrong with me. Sister tells him that I'm sick and that she called my mother but that my mother wasn't home. He offers to bring me to the rectory so that I can lie down. Sister thanks him and he holds my hand and walks with me, out the school doors, across the street and over to the rectory. We go inside and he brings me to the cellar door and tells me that because I'm sick, he'll let me go down to the drop-in center.

Wow, the drop in center, only teenagers get to go there. He opens the cellar door and we walk down the stairs. He brings me over to the couch. It's a black vinyl couch, wooden arms, and buttons on the back and seat. There is a red plaid shawl that he bunches up like a pillow and puts it at one end. He tells me to lie down. " It's ok, go ahead, lay down and rest." I'm lying down, he sits down next to me. He's asking me to "show me where it hurts." I tell him that my head hurts and that my stomach feels sick. He said that he wants to help me and he starts rubbing my belly with his hand. He pulls up my shirt and rubs my stomach. He starts to undo my belt and I look up at him surprised. " Oh, don't worry, it's ok. I'll loosen it up a little and it will make you feel better. It's probably too tight anyway."

He undoes my belt, as he slides his hands under my underpants, Fr. B begins to molest me again. I close my eyes and in my mind, I'm somewhere else.

*****

16.

Wednesday morning started as usual. Well, it was actually the new usual. Normally, I would have gotten up, grabbed the morning coffee, hit the shower and gone to work. That was the old usual, the usual I hadn't actually seen in almost a year. This year was nothing like last year. Last year I was focusing on turning 40 and buying my Harley. I had talked about buying the Harley for a few years. I had bought, fixed up, and sold a few houses in the previous few years and had put enough money aside for the bike. I only had one piece of property left. A four family house that was in constant need of work and I loved doing it. There was always something about taking a rundown piece of property, or an old piece of furniture and making it new again. Over the past summer, though, I had sold the four family. I had actually sold the Harley, as well. It had been my pride and joy. There was nothing like taking off for the afternoon, putting in a tape, and cruising for hours on the back roads of New Hampshire. I loved it. But by that point in time, I could only love the thought of it. By the tail end of the summer, I had decided to sell it. I knew that dealing with the Church was taking up more and more time and giving me less and less time to work and to enjoy the bike. The bike was gone and the money I received from it was paying my bills. I was working less and less for myself and yet, I was working harder than ever it seemed.

So this Wednesday was actually not like any Wednesdays of last year. This Wednesday was not going to be like any of the rest of this year either. I hadn't slept well the previous night and I knew why. My sessions at therapy were getting more and more intense. In my mind I had clearer memories of what had happened to me when I was with Joe Birmingham. In therapy as the weeks went by, my memory had been jolted back more than several times. Some faded memories were clearer and clearer and my therapist had been challenging me to face them. I didn't want to. I didn't see the necessity of it, but she did. I awoke that morning from a dream. more like a nightmare, actually. It jarred me out of my sleep, I realized that there was much more that I would have to face regarding my abuse. I didn't like the thought of it.

That Wednesday morning started with the usual round of incoming phone calls. The topic was the documents. They were officially being released that day and all hell was about to break loose. We were all asked to be at the office for a larger than normal press conference. With the memory of Monday night still clear in our minds, none of us had the desire to be there. Bob said that some of us should be there as "the voice of reason," as he called it. Olan decided not to go, as did Paul. Bernie and I headed in.

Arriving at the office that day I found all the usual media there. By now most knew me by sight, if not by name. Aside from the media, there were representatives from most of the advocacy groups there, as well. Just about everyone, except my screaming friend from Monday evening, was there. Soon, one by one, the files of each of the priests that had been received were brought out. That day only 15 or so were going to be released to the public. The 15 that were released, however, were more than enough to give the public a taste of what was in the rest of them. The damage about to be caused would be devastating and there would be no turning back. There was room in front of the cameras for everyone that day but some of us decided against it. It seemed like overkill. Bernie was asked to sit down in front of the press to comment as the documents were being reviewed. He sat down, then a few minutes later, got up. "This is bullshit," he said, and I agreed. He ended up leaving within minutes. I stayed off camera and made no comments. Nor did Bob, Jeff, or Courtney. I ended up leaving without saying a word. I had had enough. I left. Looking back now, I would call that week the beginning of the end," for Cardinal Law. No one could begin to imagine how those files would maintain the public's interest in something that had begun almost a year before, yet it would. Even I couldn't imagine the changes that would be coming. I had taken the time to sift through 40 or 50 of the files that had been received and I was astonished, but I would find myself surprised, more and more often, as the days turned into weeks, and the weeks turned into months. That week and those files would begin to change the history of the Catholic Church. From that point after, there would be the Catholic Church of my parents, before the scandal broke, and there would be the Catholic Church, as I knew it.

After that press conference, the flurry of media interest continued to increase. Pressure would continue to increase on Cardinal Law and on all of his subordinates and former subordinates, as well. Men like Bishop John McCormack, then Bishop of Manchester New Hampshire, Bishop Banks of Minnesota, Bishop Daly of New York, and many others. The abuse was so widespread, no wonder Will Rogers, the lead attorney for the Archdiocese had tried so vigorously to prevent these files from being released. Not only were priests, bishops and cardinals implicated, Wilson Rogers Jr., himself, had known for years what was going on. These files would ultimately implicate the Vatican, as well.

Days after the files became public and published, the call came from the Chancery. Cardinal Law wanted to meet. Fr. John Connolly had called and asked us to come in the following Wednesday, December 4. Olan and I would be going in. We were asked specifically to be there. We had also gotten calls from Barbara Thorpe asking us to do whatever we could to get through. "You guys are the only ones that have been able to make any progress. Every time you meet with him something positive comes of it. You have to do whatever you can." I remember her almost pleading on the phone the Tuesday before.

Olan, Bernie and I had been meeting and talking on the phone constantly. None of us knew what more we could do, but we all knew we had to continue to try and do something. This was becoming an all out war, at times, and the casualties on both sides were continuing to add up. Tensions were getting higher for everyone. Our lawyers and the Archdiocese lawyers weren't even on speaking terms. Survivors had stopped going to therapy, and every survivor that called me seemed to be in crisis, including my own brother Ed. Honestly, I didn't know what I was going to do that day, but I were going to do whatever I could to get through. Both Barbara and Fr. John made one thing clear that week, every time we had met with the Cardinal and advised him to do something proactive, we warned him that if he didn't, the results would be horrendous. Every time, we were right. We had warned him for weeks that if something positive didn't come directly from him, that the release of these files and documents would have horrific consequences. We had been telling him for weeks that there had to be a clear indication that the Archdiocese was more interested in mediation than litigation. That sign wouldn't come. Sometimes I hate being right, sometimes I don't.

I picked up Olan early that Wednesday morning. We grabbed coffee and wanted time to talk about what the plan would be. Not that we had ever had a plan. We both knew that this was becoming a "do or die" situation. We knew it and most everyone else knew it, too, except Cardinal Law. We both felt, that it was up to us to change his mind. This was going to be one of the most important meetings we had had. Neither of us knew why, yet we both just had that feeling. Bob had called and asked us what our plans were. Plans? Our plan was simple. Make him realize that he had to do something dramatic. He had to make a huge statement, symbolic or otherwise. It was that simple to us, at least. The walls of the Archdiocese seemed to be falling around them and they were more worried about saving the artwork than saving lives. Bob had given us a few suggestions about what might work. They were, however, suggestions relating to litigation only. Olan and I were thinking more of the bigger picture. Litigation was important but the bigger picture included not only the litigation, but also the healing yearned for by so many people.

Driving in, I told Olan that I was going to try a different tactic that day and asked him to just "go with it." He gave me that "are you out of your mind look?" but I asked him to trust me. That had been a running joke between him and me. Trust is one issue that every single survivor of abuse has. Survivor/survivors often say, "We trust no one." Every once in a while when he and I didn't totally agree, and yet had used every possible excuse to win the other one over, we would revert to "Trust me." I had this interesting thought early that particular morning and I was going to pull out all the stops that day. Olan, though, not knowing what I had in mind, agreed to go with it. We tossed around ideas back and forth on the way there. We discussed bold things like Olan's continued suggestion to sell the chancery grounds to simply asking the Cardinal to sit in on a face to face mediation meeting. Both of these suggestions hung in limbo although we both agreed that this was going to be a "balls to the wall" kind of meeting. We either had to get through, or, well, we had to get through.

This was going to be the day. Olan, Bernie and myself had talked over the last few weeks about drawing a line in the sand. There was a breakpoint coming. We were all tired. It had been a long year for us. We had all gone from a life of anonymity to a life of phone calls, press interviews, diplomacy and advocacy, not to mention the part time social workers we felt obliged to become. Olan had talked about Christmas time which was fast approaching as that defining juncture. This was a time for family and friends, not lawyers and litigation. We had all expected that, by that time, the Archdiocese would be engaging in what was morally correct however, as each day passed there was less and less attention on what was morally correct, and more and more to legally protect. We had a challenge in front of us again today, and we both knew it.

We arrived at the Cardinal's residence at half past noon. We were welcomed into the foyer. After all these months, now they just buzzed us in, since everyone knew us. We were escorted into the dining room, which is where every one of our meetings had been. I remained standing, but Olan sat down. Barbara was there and a few minutes later, in came Fr. John and Cardinal Law. He was dressed in simple black garments that day and seemed to have aged years, although it was only weeks when we last had seen him. We all exchanged the customary handshakes and the Cardinal asked us all to sit. "Bernie, I have a favor to ask," I began to say. "Before we sit down and chat, is it possible for us to all walk to your private chapel and say a prayer today? I think we need all the help we can get on this one." Olan looked at me like I had three heads and the Cardinal looked shocked, as well. I said, "I haven't asked my agnostic friend (Olan's self proclaimed religion) about this, but I'm sure he'd join us."

The Cardinal said that he would be happy to. Olan got up and said, " Bernie, know you know that I am an agnostic, but, in the spirit of the coming Christmas, and, because my friend Gary has asked for us all to join him, I, the agnostic, will be happy to share in the spirit of joining you all in prayer." With that we all followed the Cardinal into his personal chapel. The Cardinal, placing a hand on my shoulder, said that he was happy to lead us in a prayer, but I looked at him, eye to eye and said, "No, Cardinal. Today I would like to lead you in prayer."

We all walked into the tiny chapel at the end of the hall, knelt down and Cardinal Law began to pray. I had planned a simple prayer like " God give us all the strength to do what needs to be done today", but Cardinal Law had his own idea. Before I could begin, he began reading scripture and went on to reciting several prayers of his own. After 15 minutes of his speaking, I thought we were just about through, when he asked us to pick up a songbook, and asked us to join him in singing. With that, he began singing Christmas carols. Yes, Christmas carols. I looked over at Olan and he was staring wide eyed at me. My God, the walls around him are falling and here he is singing Christmas carols. Those 20 minutes were either a testament to his faith, or a testament to his break with reality. .

We returned to the dining room. "How are you doing?" I asked him. He slumped down in the chair, in exaggeration, and said, "Awful," but he meant it. "Good, that means your human. If you had said that you were doing great, I'd be more worried than I am now." Every one grinned for a few minutes. It was the last bit of light heartedness that would happen in that meeting. What happened over the next 90 minutes was the most direct and frank conversation Olan and I had ever had with Cardinal Law. From simple statements like "Bernie, it's time," to both of us telling him about drawing a line in the sand. "Bernie, we've been criticized for being too lenient with you over the last months. Now you know that's not the case, but once we both draw that line in the sand, we won't cross over it, and trust me, you don't want us to be on the opposite side of the table on this. We're not into the good cop, bad cop routine, but God help you once that line is crossed. Once we become the bad cops, we're really bad," Olan said.

We were hitting him from every angle we could. The air was getting heavier and heavier. "Time for talk has run out, Bernie. You HAVE to do something bold, even if it's symbolic," I said. Olan talked about the pain that the documents would continue to have on everyone. Each set of priest's documents that were coming out were worse and worse. I talked about my family, which is always my soft spot. I told him that my first grandchild was due in February and that my daughter and I were in a disagreement regarding her baptism. "I do not want my grandchild baptized in a Church that hasn't recognized its mistakes. By your lack of action you're preventing healing from happening." We went round and round that day. As the meeting progressed, the eye contact was as intense as the conversation. There were times he would agree with us, and times he wouldn't. At times he seemed intently listening and other times his mind seemed to wander. I almost got the feeling that he was making decisions in his head as we were speaking that day. Almost 2 hours had gone by, and we had taken that conversation as far as we could. We wound down and our last comments to him with Olan saying " You need to make a statement. Sell this house, you don't need it, and its ugly anyway, it's too big for you," followed by me saying " Cardinal (and I hadn't called him Cardinal all day) you need to do something bold, time has run out."

His final comment that day to us was, "Thank you guys for coming in. You both gave me a lot to think about today and I'll think about everything you've said. Thank you." With that, he asked if he could give us a blessing. Olan declined, I accepted, and we were done. The Cardinal and Fr. John left. Barbara, Olan and myself talked for another 30 minutes. We weren't sure if we had gotten through. Barbara assured us that no one, but us, could have said what was said in that room and if anyone could have gotten though to him, it was us. We would find out less than two weeks later we were the last two public people who met and talked with the Cardinal that day, Wednesday December 4. Maybe we had made a difference.

The days that followed were a blur of press interviews regarding additional documents that were being released that corroborated everything from priests who had abused children to priests that had fathered children. The more information that came out, the more damaging it was. A huge protest was being planned for Sunday at the Cathedral of the Holy Cross. I had seen a flurry of emails regarding it. I had my fill that week and was looking forward to flying to D.C. to visit Evan that weekend. A few days with my son always refreshes me. There's nothing like the innocence of a child to bring the world into perspective. Flying into BWI airport Friday night, I was looking forward to a quiet weekend.

Chuck-E Cheese, the pool at the hotel, a movie, anything would be fun. My weekends with Evan were becoming as much a getaway for me as a visit with my son. My life was becoming more and more complicated by the hour, it seemed. I had just lost a labor contract that I had had for more than seven years. My brothers and I were raised in the flooring business. Most of them had gone on to college and other businesses, but I had still maintained several contacts and contracts. The main one was a contract to do the flooring repairs for a chain of supermarkets that had 37 stores across Massachusetts and New Hampshire. As an independent contractor, my schedule was flexible and the pay was more than good, averaging $ 65,000.00 a year, which wasn't bad for a flexible work schedule. But it was over. During the previous few weeks the job orders had been getting less and less. I wasn't sure what was going on and my contact didn't know either. One thing was sure though, working in supermarkets and being in the press as much as I had been in recent months didn't make some of the store managers happy. Several people working in the company told me that there were those in management who weren't not happy with the public role I had taken. This was not news to me, but I hadn't thought it was enough of a problem for my contract not to be renewed. I'm not even positive that was the reason, I never got a direct answer. In the end, I wasn't even told that the contract wasn't going to be renewed. The work orders just stopped coming.

I wasn't overly worried about money. I had sold a piece of property that I had owned in the early fall, as well as my prized motorcycle. I had also saved up a little. I felt conflicted about being able to find work to replace the lost contract. At times I felt like I was on call for the cause and almost guilty if I wasn't there when I was needed. I would find work again. In the meantime, I would live "close to the fist," as my father use to say. My only concern was that I had enough money to cover supporting my son and the traveling expenses that tended to add up when I visited him every other weekend. Things would work out, that's what I told myself. That was my mantra.

Flying into BWI that Friday night, I slept. It was only an hour long flight, but I was beat. I grabbed a rental car, turned my phone back on and it started ringing. Press calls. The Fr. Foley file had been released and everyone wanted my reaction to it. Fr. Foley was the priest that had fathered three children with a woman who had mysteriously died while in his presence. The file showed the woman had become unconscious while he was there with her and that he had "gotten dressed and left the home, and then called 911." The children of this woman, who died that day of a drug overdose, did not know that Foley was their father. The ironic twist in this story was that several months before, there was a 7 parish meeting held at Saint James Hall in Salem, where Bernie McDaid was abused by Fr.Birmingham. That evening, before I introduced the "What Would Jesus Do?" postcards, a priest had gotten up and said a few opening statements, thanking us for coming to speak. He talked about how unfortunate the turn of events were for the Catholic Church and said a few prayers. We all realized that this was the same Fr. Foley. It was unbelievable that this man was still a practicing priest. He had fathered three children, admittedly, and was still in ministry. Those poor three children. On the way from the airport I was asked to do an interview at an affiliate CBS television station in Washington. I called Bob and told him what was going on. He said that it was up to me, I know I could have just said no, but Bob's voice kept ringing in my head, "You have become the public voice on this issue, people will be looking for your comment." My personal opinion was that without the pressure of the press, we wouldn't have gotten this far, so, naturally, I agreed.

The next day was a relaxing day with Evan, at least, until early afternoon. My cell started ringing again. Rumors were starting that the Cardinal was heading to Rome. Speculation was that he was going there to get permission to file bankruptcy. That was only speculation. I knew different. I had already gotten a call from one of my Chancery sources telling me that Cardinal Law had left and was flying to Rome via Dulles in DC. We had talked about the possibility of me meeting him at Dulles, but I had decided against it. I did whatever I could on Wednesday. I learned in that call that the Cardinal wouldn't be saying mass on Sunday, that he was going to Rome and that it was all over. I was told that Cardinal Law had made his decision to resign Wednesday evening. It was over. "Do something bold," I had encouraged him that Wednesday. I guess he listened to us that day.

That evening I got a call from Barbara, as well. She wanted to tell me before I read it in the papers that the Cardinal wouldn't be saying mass and that he may be on his way to Rome. I didn't tell her that I already knew what was going on. I could feel the pain in her voice, but I also knew that this decision was definitely best for all. Flying home that Sunday evening I remember thinking to myself, "Christ, are you in deep on this one." Olan and I had talked and, for the first time, most of the conversation was filled with silence. Neither of us could believe the sequence of events, which were not only surrounding us, but involving us, as well. I was holding something that every reporter would give their soul for, an inside scoop about Law's resignation. Every day that week I would get a round of phone calls about my opinion. When asked directly, I gave direct answers, but no one asked me the right question. The question I was asked, repeatedly, was, "Will the Vatican give Cardinal Law permission this week to file bankruptcy?" My answer was always emphatically, "No."

I knew why he was there, but I wasn't sure of the time line. I didn't know when the official resignation was going to be made public. If I was to have guessed I would have said Tuesday, and I would have been wrong. Usually the Vatican releases important information on Tuesdays. It's one way that they can control the rumor mills. Releasing information on Tuesdays only means that you can usually figure that any press released on the other days is mere speculation. Not that week though. Every television station that had a camera was in Rome that week. There were Cardinal sightings, Cardinal experts, Cardinals walking, and Cardinals running away from the cameras. Each day went by, and each day I waited to hear. I told only those I trusted what I had learned, and I trusted almost no one. With the Cardinal on his way out, I was looking forward to laying low over the upcoming holidays. Bernie could handle the press, and handle them well. He was just getting back from Florida and was well rested. Olan had said that he was swearing off the press for a while. He and I both decided that we would take a few weeks to kick back, recoup and regroup. Sometimes I'm right, sometimes I'm wrong, but I was wrong on this one, and I didn't even know it.

On Friday, December 13, at 6:00 a.m., the phone rang. It was my mother. "The Cardinal resigned. Have you heard? Do you want to come upstairs for a minute?" I told her that I hadn't heard anything yet and that I would be up in a minute. Before I had time to throw water on my face, my phone was ringing again. Every local station was calling for my response. Some calls I took, others I didn't. There were plenty of people that day with plenty of opinions about his resignation, they could surely do without mine. I was actually numb that morning and it would have been hard for me to put that feeling into words. I went upstairs and walked in to see my father in sitting on his infamous chair. The television station was broadcasting the news. *"The highest ranking Roman Catholic official in the United States, Archbishop Cardinal Bernard Law, resigned Today...."* My father was in tears as he watched. I remember thinking that as the reporters continued to cover the news, at times, they ignored the real story. The actual story was that crisis continued to touch the hearts and souls of millions of people. It continued to touch their faith, as well. The news of the Cardinal resigning was not celebrated in my home, nor was it celebrated in my father's home.

"All I can say is that they had better not make this man the scapegoat for this. There are too many others that are to blame as well," my father said. He could barely get it out. I remember thinking that it reminded me of watching him in tears the night that Richard Nixon resigned amid the Watergate scandal. I knew why he was crying. I also knew that there was nothing I could say to console him. He was letting some of it out and I knew that. I sat with my parents for half an hour. After he composed himself a bit, he said, "Well, you're going to be busy today. You'd better get ready for it." He was right, I didn't know what the day would bring. As I sat and watched the TV with them, it started to sink in. I had known for over a week what would be coming, but in the end, it had surprised me, as well. I knew that Cardinal Law had finally done the right thing. He had been stuck in fear and the Archdiocese was stuck in shame. If he couldn't do something to remove the fear and shame, then he had to move aside and allow someone else make the right decisions, those that would heal the pain that he, himself, had caused. I knew it, I had known it for months, but it was still a shock to my system. I can't say that I had grown fond of this man, but under different circumstances I very well could have. I had seen this man transform over the previous six months. Gone was the arrogant approach he had taken when I had first met him. At times I would see humility, and I would also see pain in his eyes. As he began to realize what he had done, and what he could have done, yet did not do, his shoulders and heart would bear some of the weight of that. It was a weight both I and my father understood. I wondered about the goodness that he had done, and could have done, had he just followed the same voice that had called his heart to serve the people. He had strayed so far and on that momentous day perhaps he knew that.

Grabbing a shower, my mind drifted to the many times he and I had talked. It also drifted to that day on the altar when he had apologized. That brief moment when I felt that he had actually got it. I remember thinking that day that that could be a turning point, but it wasn't. Well, at least not exactly turning in the direction that I had in mind. I was worried about all the survivors that had yet to meet with him. There was still a desire by many to sit down with him. Would they have an opportunity? Or would this be another opportunity missed, another survivor's hopes killed?

I got the usual round of calls from Bernie and Olan. I hadn't heard from Bob's office yet, but as soon as I said that to myself, my phone rang. It was Courtney telling me that there was a press conference at 10:00 a.m. They had rented a ballroom at the Back

Bay Hilton and wanted me there. I found out that Bernie, Paul, and Olan were called in, as well. I grilled Courtney, "Who called the press conference? Eric or Bob? Who was going? What was the tone?" The last thing I wanted was to be a part of a "dog and pony" show involving kicking an ex Cardinal. She told me that she didn't have the details yet and that they were still being worked out. She said she'd call later and fill me in.

My mind wandered to the last meeting and press conference. I was starting to realize why I had been so upset that day. It wasn't that I was worried about someone screaming at me. It was another breach of trust. I had placed my trust in Bob and Courtney. When I spoke to them about my abuse for the first time, I was trusting them. I had believed that they would stand up for me and do the right thing. It was about trusting someone again and it was about that trust being violated again. That's why it had bothered me so much. We had formed a relationship at a huge personal risk for me. That relationship was damaged, not because of something I had done, but because of something they had done. My God, for a moment in that meeting, I was waiting for someone to stand up and protect me. I was 12 years old again and my trust was again being tested. That evening they failed that test, and I was beginning to see it in those terms.

Therapy was working, though, because at least, I could see it in those terms. As I thought about it, I realized that, years ago, I would have climbed up over the table and grabbed that guy by the throat, not caring who was in the room. But I had developed enough insight, by that point, that I could see it differently. That outburst wasn't about me. It was about him. He had the problem, I didn't. Well, I didn't have a problem with him, although I did with everyone else in that room who didn't stand up and do the right thing. Yes, perhaps there really was something to this therapy.

I didn't know why all these thoughts were going through my head, my emotions were running rampant that morning. I was surprised that the events of that day would impact me like that, but my mind and emotions were racing with all kinds of thoughts and all kinds of feelings. I wasn't ready for it, I hadn't prepared for this, at all.

A few minutes later Bob called and said that he wanted to make sure that I was coming in. I told him that I wasn't sure about it but I was talking to Bernie and Olan. He said he didn't have time to talk but that I should be there and he would call me in a bit when he had more time. While talking to Bernie, he and I decided to head in together. We would have time to talk on the way in and could decide what we were going to do. Olan was working and decided not to go. He had had enough with the press, anyway. "Hey, didn't I say that I was taking some time off? You should too. This has been a long road. With him resigning today, we should be able to take a breather. If you guys want to head in, then you should, but I'm outta this one." In my head, thoughts rumbled. "You're the voice of reason. People will be looking for you to talk on this issue ...There are many survivors that look up to you and they will be looking to see how you handle this...Some people have seen you as sympathetic to the church and you need hold the line on this one..." There were many other thoughts going on as well. I really didn't know what to do. I still wasn't sure, but Bernie told me that Bob had called and said that we all needed to be there. I felt obligated, and I'm not one who enjoys feeling obligated to anyone.

I met Bernie at our usual meeting place and we headed in together. We started talking about what had happened that morning and about that fact that neither of us wanted to go into Boston again. We were both beat. Olan was right, it had been a long road. Christmas was around the corner and we all needed a break. Neither Bernie nor I had forgotten about the last press conference. It was still a sore subject for all of us. A few minutes later, Bob called. Over the drive into Boston, Bob and I had the most heated exchange we had ever had. I wasn't about to be led into a den of wolves again and I told him so. I wanted details, I wanted to be sure that this was not going to be a "Cardinal bashing" press conference, and I wanted to make sure that I would not be around the lose cannons that were around the last time. I didn't have the patience. I had no reserves to draw on. I wasn't budging on my questions and Bob wasn't giving any answers. He wasn't giving them because he didn't have them. They were playing this one spur of the moment and no one knew what was going on. I found no comfort in the truth in that answer. At times while driving and talking, Bernie would lean over and say, "Take it easy man, you're gonna have a heart attack." He was right, but I was still not budging. Bob couldn't tell me who was going to be there, nor could he guarantee me who would "NOT" be there. He didn't know who would be covering it or what the topics would be. Those answers just weren't good enough for me and I pressed on. The hotter that Bob got, the hotter that I got. Damn it all! Couldn't someone just tell me what was going on without expecting me to just be there and trust it was going to be okay? This wasn't a photo op for the press at any cost. These were people's real lives and real feelings. My father's tears from that morning had set me off that day.

As the conversation continued it was clear that I was asking questions he couldn't or wouldn't answer. In the end, he said, "Gary, I'm asking you to trust me. You need to be here, I can't stress that enough. I'm right on this one and you're dead wrong. This is going to happen with or without you. I want you here, but it's your call. I have to go." And he hung up. Bernie looked at me and said, "I've never heard you talk like that before. Wow, you do have a temper. I never thought you and Bob would argue like that." Neither did I. That morning Bernie was the voice of reason for me. "Listen if Bob said we should go, then let's go. If we don't agree with what's going on, screw it, we'll take off." My blood pressure was up there, but I agreed to go. "It's a good thing, 'cause we're almost there anyway," Bernie said, laughing. Looking around I realized that Bob and I had been on the phone for the entire time it had taken me to drive into Boston. I hadn't even realized it, but we were only a few minutes away.

We arrived at the hotel and made our way to the conference room. There were many, many people there that day. Some faces I recognized and some I didn't. Some were friendly and some were not. The press was everywhere. The conference room was huge. It was the typical room where a wedding reception would be held. Today it was more like a funeral, though. I saw the usual round of local reporters and talked off camera to most of them. I had no intentions of doing interviews today. I also noticed a huge batch of new reporters, as well. Apparently this was big news, much bigger than I had thought.

As the room began to fill up, Bernie and I lagged behind in the hall area. I hadn't seen anyone from the law office arriving yet except for Sandy Grossman, who flew in from Florida that morning. Sandy was the press liaison for the entire firm and works out of the corporate offices in Florida. That day's events must be important if Sandy had flown in. She caught my eye and pointed to the room and said, "Get in there." Bernie and I walked in and took a seat a few rows from the front. Paul Chimiataro met us there as well. Paul had called me in the morning and wanted to head in with us. It had just dawned on me that I told him I would call him back in five minutes, my favorite saying. I hadn't called him back. A few minutes later, Eric walked in and came over to us, "What are you guys doing here?" My first thoughts were, son of a bitch, not again. Don't tell me that we came in here for nothing. Then he said, "What are you doing here? You guys aren't sitting there. You're sitting there." He pointed to the stage. There were three rows of chairs next to the podium and he wanted us to sit front and center. I was surprised and I wasn't prepared. But the three of us got up and sat down exactly where he wanted us.

I was still concerned, though. I hadn't seen Bob or Jeff yet. The last time that had happened, the night didn't go well. My mind was racing. But this day was going to be different. The moment Eric took the podium and started speaking to the ranks of cameras and the rows of people, I could tell that this was going to be very different. I listened as Eric spoke like an eloquent statesmen. It was a side of Eric that I hadn't seen before. I saw and heard Eric, the human being, that day and not Eric, the attorney. It was an Eric that I would see more and more of as time went on. It was an Eric that I admired. As he spoke, my heart stopped racing and my emotions overtook me. Eric would introduce several survivors, some of whom I'd met and had grown very close to, and others, I had never met before. Out of the corner of my eye, I had also caught Bob and Jeff walking in. I felt better. Each survivor who spoke touched my heart that day and some brought me to tears. I was starting to realize that what had happened that day had more of an emotional effect than I had thought.

Thank God, I wasn't addressing the crowd that day. I was an emotional wreck. But just as that thought sifted through my mind, Eric was at the podium again, saying "And now I would like to introduce Gary Bergeron. Gary Bergeron is one of the founding members of Survivors of Joseph Birmingham, which is a support group for 54 men who were abused by one priest, Joseph Birmingham. He'd like to say a few words. My heart was in my mouth. I looked at him and then glanced at Bob who gave me this "oh shit" look. I slowly got up, dried my eyes and started to walk to the podium. Bernie and Paul got up with me. I wasn't sure what I was going to say, I hadn't prepare anything, but I walked to the podium and sucked in my breath for a minute. Suddenly I was okay and I felt a peace and a calm come over me. I don't know why, but my sister Terry came in my mind and oddly, I felt her. I just felt her there for a second and suddenly, I was smiling. No one could see my smile, but on the inside I was smiling and she was smiling back at me. For a brief second I could hear her voice in my head saying, as only Terry could say, " What are you being stupid for? You know what to do, just do it." I began to speak.

"I don't have anything prepared today, so I would like to ask you to bear with me. This has been an emotional day for many of us, me, included. I don't know what I am supposed to say at this moment in time." I suddenly glanced back over at Bob. "A year ago when I came forward and spoke to many of you at a press conference, I began by saying that I was there, not to only represent myself, but to also represent my brother Edward, who was also molested by Joe Birmingham. As I speak to you today, I would like to, again, say, that I am also here to represent my brother again. A year ago, at that first press conference, when again I didn't know what I was suppose to say, a man who has come to be my friend, Bob gave me this advice, talk from the heart. I'm going to try, so please bear with me. Over the past six months, I have had the opportunity to meet with Cardinal Law a half a dozen times. I took those opportunities each time I could. It wasn't because I had a fondness for Cardinal Law. It was because I felt then, as I feel now, that the only way anyone can understand the effects that this abuse has had on my life is to sit and talk with me, one-on-one. At each meeting I would stress one point and tell him one thing. Simply, do the right thing. When I met with him last July, I asked him to do the right thing. At every other meeting, I would ask him the same thing. And when I met with him last Wednesday for the last time, I asked him to do the right thing. This morning, Cardinal Law did the right thing."

"I have been asked by several of you if I felt happy today. This morning at 6 a.m., I got a phone call asking if I had heard that Cardinal Law had resigned. No, it wasn't from a member of the press, it was from my mother. She asked me to come upstairs. I went there to see my father in tears watching the news unfold about the Cardinal resigning. It brought me back to a time over 20 years ago when I watched my father crying the night that Richard Nixon resigned. My father didn't cry that night because of his love of Richard Nixon, he was crying because he was worried about what his resignation would do to the country. Today, as my father cried, it wasn't because of his love of Cardinal Law. My father was crying because of what this resignation would do to his Church. Do I feel happy today? How could I possibly feel happy about being a part of something that continues to bring my father so much pain?"

I went on talking briefly asking the incoming bishop to do the most important thing he could do, help heal the wounds of the survivors and their families whose pain runs so deep. I was about to finish up when my father's comment reminded me that this wasn't all about Cardinal Law. "For all of you who think that this is only about Cardinal Law, we have received thousands of pages of documents about priest, after priest, abusing child, after child. For every document with the name Cardinal Law on it, I have seen a hundred with the name (Bishop) John McCormack on it. Bishop John McCormack, I'm coming after you! I'll see you Monday morning." As I said that, I looked directly into the cameras and pointed my finger.

Many people didn't know what I had meant by that. But the following Monday, Bishop John McCormack was being deposed and I was going to be in that deposition. I knew what I meant, the attorneys knew what I meant, and John McCormack knew what it meant.

As I said those last words, the crowd erupted in applause that lasted several minutes. I wasn't the only one who knew about the negligence of John McCormack. Many people knew. I stepped away from the podium, looking at Bernie as the crowd continued to applaud. Bernie looked at me and whispered, "Thanks pal How am I supposed to follow something like that?" But he did, and he did just fine. Bernie got up and talked about his mother and father, going to Bishop McCormack, then Father McCormack, to complain about Birmingham. After Bernie, Paul got up and, with incredible dignity, talked about his family. He ended with, "Mom and dad, I love you." We were finished, and sat down. There were one or two more speakers that got up, including Bob. Several minutes later, the press conference was over. The first person to come over was Bob. I held out my hand and said, simply, "You were right, I was wrong. I'm glad I came in." He ignored my hand and hugged me. We both stood there hugging each other, tears streaming down our cheeks for several minutes. I think we both understood something that day. I would trust him, if he would trust me.

I walked out of that hotel room quickly. More than several people were asking for interviews, but I had to get outside for a few. As I headed to the men's room, I turned my cell phone back on, planning to call and check on my dad. Before I had a chance, it rang. It was Olan. "Boy, when you do it, you really do it big." I asked him what he meant. There was no way he could have seen that already. Laughing hard as hell, he said, "Man, talk about throwing down the gauntlet. I thought you said you were taking some time off. Man, you just took on Bishop McCormack. I hope you don't have plans for the next six months," he said, laughing. Olan knew what I didn't know and what no one had told me. I couldn't believe that they were playing that news clip already. "Playing the clip? You've got to be shitting me. Don't tell me you didn't know? Gary, that press conference was carried live, on every channel including CNN, for over 45 minutes. EVERYONE saw that."

I had no idea. I had never heard that anyone was carrying it live. I received calls the following week from all over the world. Not just press calls, but calls from many, many survivors. Bernie got calls from relatives in Scotland he had visited 20 years before. The whole world knew that I was taking on John McCormack. You know what? I didn't care. Olan was right, that statement did end up costing me months of time. That statement also did the trick. By 4:00 that afternoon the deposition was called off and the Archdiocese was asking for settlement talks. By the following week, I had received two phone calls from Bishop McCormack's personal assistant, apologizing for not getting back to me six months prior and asking for a meeting. Yes, I was glad that I went into town that day. For the record, Bob was right. I was wrong.

17.

The year 2003 began like no other in my life. The fallout from my now infamous "Bishop John McCormack, I'll see you Monday" comment was unbelievable. Comments went from "That bordered on a threat," to "Finally, someone had the balls to take on John McCormack," and everything in between. It was run and re-run and re-run again on television broadcasts and radio clips. In the last year I had learned about sound bites,." the 3 second statement that every newsperson wants on tape. They ask you for an interview, you bare your soul for the 10 minutes it takes to answer their question completely. They take that 10 minutes and condense it into a 5 second sound bite." I didn't like sound bites. Sexual abuse can't be condensed into a 5 or 10 second statement. My John McCormack statement was definitely "sound bite" material. I would continue to receive comments about it for months. It even made it on the "Top 10 News Moments" for 2002 on several networks, according to what some have told me. I had wanted to take some time off, I had needed to take some time off, but it didn't happen.

January started with the continued depositions of Cardinal Law and Bishop McCormack. The settlement talks came to their predictable halt and the depositions went forward. I had met with Bishop McCormack for several hours prior to the deposition. He had agreed to the personal meeting hours after we held a press conference in his hometown of Manchester, New Hampshire, just steps from his office. I have always said that the only way to understand the way someone thinks is to sit and talk with them. Bishop McCormack was no exception. I would describe him as a tall lanky man, soft spoken with boyish good looks. I would learn about him from his high school days to his days with Joe Birmingham and what I learned was this: Regardless of what the files say that he did or did not do, in John McCormack's mind, he did nothing wrong. This man actually truly believed that he did the best he could and it's that simple. He would tell me that he believed in Joe Birmingham and that he thought Birmingham had "cleaned up his act" and that therefore, there was no need to intervene. Every fiber of John McCormack believed what he was telling me. He was truly hurt that anyone would think that he could do anything that would help inflict harm on children. It was my choice that the meeting between McCormack and me took place before the depositions. The conversation he and I had was off the record. The conversation he would have at the deposition was on the record and I wanted to see how the two matched up.

The day of the depositions the firm had Cardinal Law in one room and Bishop McCormack in another, both being deposed at the same time. It was bizarre, to say the least, and at times that day, it bordered on the humorous.

The deposition of McCormack began with the attorneys for the arch diocese, Wilson Rogers III and his crew. Wilson Rogers Jr. was in the deposition room with Cardinal Law. I, along with Bernie, Olan, Paul, and Larry, sat in on the McCormack deposition. The defendants and their lawyers all sat on one side of the table, the rest of us and our attorneys were on the other. It began as usual. At times, Bishop McCormack would give his usual response, "I don't recall" and at times, he would squirm.

As with any deposition, the plaintiffs (us) in a deposition sat quietly listening to the questions and answers. We're not allowed to speak, but, at times, we would write a question on a card and slip it over to our attorneys and they could ask the question for us. I was all too familiar with the ground rules. I had sat through the depositions of Bishop Banks and Monsignor Jennings. For some of the guys, it was a new, and, at times, frustrating experience. The official present records every sound uttered in a deposition.

Every " umm," "ahhhh," or "uh huh" is recorded exactly as it sounds. More often than not, when asked a question, McCormack would nod his head and would be asked to verbally say his answer. After several hours of this, our attorneys asked a question regarding a "John Doe" who was a survivor. Although that person's name was not said out loud, McCormack needed to know who the person was so that he could answer the question. It was agreed that our attorneys would write the person's name on a piece of paper and slide it to McCormack. The court reporter needed the correct spelling of the name, even though that person was an official "John Doe." For deposition purposes their name would be recorded, but not released to the general public. When the court reporter asked for the correct spelling of that name, no one had it. Then Olan motioned that he had it on some documents that we had brought along.

We all went "off the record" for a minute, which meant that we could talk, and it wouldn't be recorded. We all agreed that Olan could produce the name and it would be accepted in written form for the record. Back "on the record," Olan wrote the person's name on a piece of paper and held it up for Bob and Courtney to see. Typically, in a deposition, there is no smiling, any niceties, compliments, or considerations shown. The mood is generally serious, often tense and occasionally adversarial.

As Olan held up the piece of paper he had written on, holding it up in front of Bob and Courtney to read, a look of shock and disbelief came across every face on the other side of the table. Olan and I instantly knew what had happened and completely burst out laughing. The night before that deposition, we had our usual SOJB support meeting, which at times gets a bit vocal. During that meeting, we jokingly had decided that when someone is talking at the meeting, we would let them finish before butting in. Olan at times can be, what he admits to as "longwinded," and I agree with him on this one. When I began to talk that Tuesday evening, I got up and said, "Now Olan, I would like to say something. I have the floor and I would appreciate it if you would listen and not talk for a change." Olan grinned and said, "Hold on a minute." With that, he wrote something on a piece of paper and held it up and said, " Okay, now I'll shut up and listen." What he had done was placed his hand on the paper, middle finger up, and traced it. When he said that he was ready to listen, he held up the paper tracing of his middle finger in my direction and said, "Just let me take some notes so that I get it right this time." I had burst out laughing, as did all the SOJB guys.

It was that same paper Olan had used to show Bob and Courtney the name, while he was inadvertently flashing the other side a middle finger. By the time we realized what had happened, it was too late. Realizing we were still on the record, I motioned for Olan to not try to explain, but Olan profusely apologized trying to clarify what had happened. I continued to motion to him to shut up, since we were still on record. Everyone on the other side of the table took it in stride when they realized what had happened, but Wilson Rogers III had to make a statement about it. "Well, I understand it may have been a mistake. I just want it on the record that I want to make sure it wasn't a subtle hint in my direction." Oops, I thought, he shouldn't have opened that door since I knew Olan was going to walk right through it. Part hoping that Olan would just let it go and part hoping that he wouldn't, I waited. "Wilson," Olan said, "You don't know me very well, but let me tell you this. If I wanted to send you a message, it wouldn't be in the form of a subtle hint. I would directly give you the message and you would know it was from me." There was silence and then a smile formed on McCormack's face. That story, as it happened, is now all part of the official deposition record.

There were other interesting things that happened that day, as well. We all broke for lunch at noon. Olan and I decided that the morning session was enough for us. We had a quick lunch with everyone and then walked into the other part of the offices. He went one way, I went the other. I was looking for someone. I went into the reception area and asked if Cardinal Law's deposition had broken for lunch, as well. I was told they had when Eric walked in. I asked him where Cardinal Law was having lunch. "Why? What are you going to do, just walk in on him?" My reply was that that was exactly what I was going to do. He pointed to a door, I knocked, opened the door a crack, stuck my head in, and said, "Hello." Cardinal Law was there, along with Fr. Connelly and Wilson Rogers Jr.

It had been a month since we had seen each other, but a lot had happened in that time. I wasn't sure what his response was going to be but it didn't matter. "Hello, Hello, come in, come in. It's good to see you, my friend," was his response. I held out my hand and he shook it. Then he grabbed and hugged me, It was a very strange experience. As this was happening, Fr. Connelly just looked on, smiled and said hello. Wilson Rogers Jr., on the other hand, looked like he was going to have a heart attack. He and I had never met but I knew who he was and, I'm sure, he knew who I was. He just sat there with a stunned look on his face, a sandwich between his teeth, lettuce on both sides of his mouth hanging out, not saying anything, not moving, just staring. I asked him, "How are you holding up?" He replied he was doing ok. Then he said, "When are we going to get this thing settled?" "Whenever you're ready," was my reply. We talked for 15 minutes or so and I said hold on a minute, I'll be right back. I headed out the doors and found Olan. Eric was watching this all unfold and just had a stunned look in his eyes. I think it's safe to say that never before had a plaintiff and a defendant, while in the process of being deposed, had casual conversations in their office. But then again, we weren't the norm, they would find that out over and over again.

Olan and I headed back into the room. Olan received the same greeting that I did. The Cardinal asked Olan the same question, "When are we going to get this thing settled?" However, Olan's reply was different. He said, "Well, Bernie, I'll tell you what. Why don't we close this door and between you, me, Gary, and Wilson, over there, if Fr. Connelly watched the door, this should take us about 15 minutes." Bernie Law laughed and said, " I'll give you whatever I have, but I don't have anything left anymore." We all laughed for a minute. Then the conversation turned serious again. "We all need an end to this. There's too much pain out there right now. Something has to happen and you can help, you know," I said to the Cardinal. "He's right, Bernie, it's time to do something and you're still a huge part of this," said Olan. "We're working on it, we really are. Would you boys like to join us for lunch?" "No thanks," we said. We still had things to do. "I would enjoy sitting and talking with you both again, when we all have time. I would enjoy that," he said. With that, we shook hands and looked at Wilson Rogers III, and said, "We'll see you again, Wilson." Wilson, just looked and stared, that sandwich still in his mouth, that lettuce still hanging out. Another meeting with the Cardinal didn't happen. Neither did lunch. It would become clear that Cardinal Law was out of the loop. There was a new man in charge and there was no doubt that the Archdiocese wanted a clear line between before Cardinal Law and after. There would, however be more meetings with Fr. John Connelly.

February would bring more meetings, more press coverage and more stress. The constant strain of what I was doing would start to become more evident in the weeks and months to come. That February Bishop McCormack agreed to a public meeting with the SOJB group and their families. This meeting was supposed to be similar to our meeting in November with Cardinal Law, hopefully bringing some healing to the survivors and their families, just as the meeting with Cardinal Law had. In the end, it couldn't have been any more different. In mid February, on a blistering cold evening in the same building used for Salem town meetings almost 200 years before, Bishop McCormack would come face to face with those impacted by his inaction of years past. It wasn't pretty.

As McCormack entered the hall that evening, he walked around greeting people and shaking hands like he was the mayor of Salem. I looked at Olan and said, "Oh my God, this guy doesn't have a clue." And I was right. Much like my personal meeting with him the month before, McCormack was still living in his perception of reality. Unlike the meeting with Cardinal Law, McCormack was definitely in enemy territory. Perhaps it was because Cardinal Law had been meeting with some of us for months, or perhaps it was because Cardinal Law came into Boston after most of us had been abused. More likely, it was because McCormack had made decisions that had effected nearly every survivor in that room. For whatever reason, the animosity was evident that evening. People were angry and emotional and they had a right to be. At times both Olan and I tried to keep control over the crowd, which, I feared, could get out of control. It was definitely up to Olan and I since Bernie was too close to the fire on this one.

There was a table set up in front where John McCormack would sit, along with Olan and me. Like the Cardinal Law meeting, this had been our idea. I had no problem sitting down next to them, up front and center. Facing the crowd that day, I opened up the meeting with one of my favorite quotes from Gandhi. "Forgiveness is not for the weak, for only the strong can truly forgive." I talked about behaving like human beings to one another that night. There was going to be tension, but there also had to be a level of communication, otherwise nothing would be accomplished. I knew that this was going to be a tougher crowd than the one in Dracut. I had never been more right.

Probably the most intense and poignant moment came when Gail Sweeney stood up and spoke. Gail had three brothers that were molested by Birmingham. One, Larry, I knew and had come to know well over the past year. One had committed suicide. Gail is a tiny girl with a huge heart and a voice that could carry for miles. In tears, she stood up and spoke. At times, she was almost screaming for McCormack to look at her when she was speaking. Most of the room wept as she spoke. Everyone was dead silent as she walked up and handed McCormack four bouquets of flowers and said to him, "I want you to go down to the cemetery where Birmingham is buried. I want you to put one of these bouquets on my brother's grave who is buried next to Birmingham. I want you to put one of these on Olan's father's grave who is buried next to Birmingham. I want you to put one of these on Gary's sister's grave who is also buried next to Birmingham and I want you to put the last one on Birmingham's grave. I want you to do it. Not someone else. You. I want you to do it so that you know where these people are buried and so that you know what we all have to go through just to visit our families gravesites." She was almost screaming at that point. I was sitting at a table with Olan and McCormack in the front of the room as she was standing up facing him, handing him each bouquet as she spoke. When she handed him the last bouquet of flowers, he looked at her and, in almost a whisper, said, "Yes, I will. I'm sorry." She looked at him face to face. This 5 foot tall girl and this 6 foot man, now face to face, took one of his hands in each of hers, and said, "What did you say? I can't hear you." He said, a little louder, "I'm sorry. Yes I will." Even louder, this time she screamed, **"WHAT DID YOU SAY THESE PEOPLE STILL CAN'T HEAR YOU ! "** He repeated it so that every person in the room could hear him.

That was how intense the meeting was. There were people that had called in from Florida who had complained about Birmingham molesting boys. There was a survivor that had even flown in from California for that meeting. At the end of that evening, McCormack would attempt to address everyone. This was not the same proud man that had walked in just a few hours before. He stood there, head bowed, speaking in barely a whisper, attempting to "try and understand the pain." His attempt didn't sit well. Especially with Bernie, who was the last person to speak.

I had gone with Bernie when he met with McCormack a few weeks earlier. Bernie had resisted going, but I knew that he needed to. I had hoped that some of the intense emotion that Bernie felt would be released in the private meeting. I was wrong. As Bernie spoke, his anger came through, but he closed that evening with a statement that was felt by lots of us. "John McCormack, you asked for forgiveness for everything you've done.

Well John, I'm not going to call you Bishop. I'm sorry, but no man deserves to be called Bishop after doing what you have done. You want forgiveness and you want us to heal? Then resign your post as Bishop. Then I welcome you to walk with us and heal. But that won't happen until you take responsibility for your actions and resign. Resign and then you can walk with us."

With that, the meeting came to a close. It had been almost three hours of intensity. Less than 10 minutes later, I walked a beaten Bishop McCormack to the door. When he asked me what I thought, I said, "I think it's going to take time to digest everything that was said tonight, but I can tell you one thing. You had better get those flowers to the cemetery." He looked at me and said he would and then practically ran out the door to his car. That night was painful for everyone.

For the next two days, we had severe snowstorms. That Saturday, I was in Virginia with my son and the phone rang. It was Fr. Arsenault, he was with the Bishop looking for the gravesites at the cemetery. After I gave him what directions I could, I hung up. I was thankful that he was doing what was asked. But I also chuckled to myself at the thought of a priest and a Bishop hip deep in snow, at the request of little powerful Gail Sweeney.

*****

Nine o'clock mass was finally over. I was the only altar boy serving with Fr. B. I went and got the candle snifter and put the candles out. Then I went to the sacristy to change out of my altar clothes. As soon as I put them on the hangers in the closet, Fr. B. called me and asked me to help him get out of his vestments. He went over to the electric box and, one by one, he switched off the lights. Click, click, click. Each switch made a loud noise in the big church. It was real quiet. While I was helping him take off his vestments, he was telling me how special I was. I was one of his favorite kids out of the whole school. I was so lucky that he liked me so much. As I helped him, he took his hands and put them on my shoulders. "I bet you like to wrestle, don't you? With all the boys in your family, you must be very good at it, huh?" He asked me if I'd like to wrestle him. I said that it would be fun, but I had to get back to school. "Don't worry about that," he said. We started to wrestle. I pushed him hard, but he didn't move much. He was so big. We were on the floor. His legs were wrapping around me. Then he was behind me. I was sweating as he started to kneel behind me. I wasn't having fun and it seemed like the harder I tried to get away, the more he was grunting and pushing against me. My pants were pulled down now. How did he do that, what's going on. I felt a sharp pain and tried to scream, but he had one of his big hairy hands on my mouth. "Shhhhhhhh," he said, "it's okay. You know you're one of my favorites."

When he said that it was time for me to go back to school, I knew he was done. I ran back to school. I ran as fast as I could. When I got there, I went into the big bathroom in the basement. No one else was there. I checked to make sure, looking under every stall door. My underpants felt wet. I looked down at them, and saw red. I was scared. I took off my underpants and threw them away. I couldn't let anyone at home see them.

*****

18.

     A year before I was working full time installing flooring, as well as, working on my property. By the following year, with my name and face on the front page of the New York Times, I had become an unofficial spokesperson for clergy abuse survivors. Was there an air of excitement? At times, yes. But more often than not, I felt drained. I would find myself thinking of my past abuse, more and more, and I had come to realize that depression was setting in. This was truly consuming my life and it would become blatantly clear that it was overflowing into my family's life, at times, as well. The abuse story was talked about and covered almost daily in the news. Each time a damaging story would appear in the news, my phone would ring. At times, I would feel like a social worker, and at times, it would strain the friendships I had formed along the way. It would also put pressure my family and my personal life, at times nearly to a breaking point. The daily phone calls from abuse survivors were emotionally draining and I was getting more and more of them each day. I didn't always know what to say to them, but I would listen. The toll, however, was high. Part of me felt guilty for feeling that way. Part of me maybe enjoyed the attention and at times, there was plenty of that. The biggest part of me was tired though and there seemed to be no end in sight. Each time I was in the press for something, I'd receive more and more phone calls. I began to understand the enormous cost that public officials pay. The pressure from survivors, survivors and advocacy groups increased almost daily. Each time I made a comment about anything related to the Church I would receive a share of thanks, and an equal would receive a share of thanks and an equal share of criticism. I was too hard on the Catholic Church, or I was too soft on the Catholic Church. Some thought I would never be satisfied with anything the Catholic Church did, others, I was spending too much time playing the professional role of victim, and still others, that I was the kiss ass of the Church for meeting with Church officials. Everyone had an opinion and everyone offered them to me, whether I wanted them or not.

They were delivered by phone, in emails or occasionally personally from people on the street. At times, I just wanted to move away again, just like I had done 21 times in the past. But my eyes had been opened and I realized that moving again wouldn't solve anything. I had opened this can of worms and I had to try and deal with it. The strain would show a bit more as each week went by. Financially, I was a mess. I hadn't worked in several months and the money that I had put aside from the sale of my building and my beloved Harley was just about gone. For the first time in many years I was broke and that added another twist to my life. I had made attempts to find work. I had contemplated going back into real estate sales. I still had my license but the reality of what I had become involved in became ever so clear when I sat and had a conversation with a friend of mine who owns an agency. She knew me well and said that he would welcome the opportunity of having me work out of that office. She also said however, that I needed to be realistic about my earning possibilities.

What was the likelihood of a homeowner entrusting the sale of their house to me, considering how public I had been about such a controversial issue? What was I willing to tell them if they said "You look so familiar. Don't I know you from somewhere?" I didn't have to tell them anything, she said, but she also knew me, and knew that I couldn't just not say anything. The reality was that as many people out there approved of what I had been doing, many still weren't comfortable discussing an uncomfortable topic, sexual abuse of children. What advantage would the seller of a home have in placing their listing with me? The simple answer was that my involvement in the issue had made my prospect of getting back into that field unrealistic. She didn't say it; she actually said that I was more than welcomed there, but our conversation made me realize reality. As they say, "reality bites," and sometimes it does.

For awhile, I would get by on the occasional subcontract installation, although they were getting scarce, as well. I was worried about money and I didn't like it. It wasn't about the luxuries; it was getting to be about the necessities. My main concern was not about supporting my life and lifestyle. It was about being able to afford basic things like child support, my biweekly trips to see my son, rent, etc. It was getting to the point that my rent was late and my home phone had been shut off.

I just didn't know what to do. Being so independent, like most survivors, I didn't share my financial situation with anyone except my girlfriend, who would watch me struggle to rub enough nickels together for a cup of coffee, at times. I just barely made it by each week. I started to notice things like the cost of parking each time I went into Boston - $ 29.00 in the parking garage. These were things that, a year ago, I wasn't worried about, but things that I thought about more and more. Needless to say, the tighter money became, the more apparent the stress was each day. As much as I tried to make off that it didn't bother me, it did. I was supposed to be the provider, I wasn't anymore.
 As the weeks turned into months, I would end up selling my truck to make ends meet and borrowing a car from someone. This definitely was consuming me. Yet as broke as I was, I just didn't have the drive nor the desire anymore; money didn't have that importance that it once had. I was changing, I just wasn't sure into what.

Sometimes I would mentally set a different course, like looking for a job. I would no sooner make that decision in my head when I'd be asked to get involved in another direction. I felt constantly pulled in opposite places.

Finances were one thing, personal relationships were another. And the toll on some of those was increasing, as well. My granddaughter was born in mid February. My daughter and I have always been extremely close. I was fortunate enough to be there at the birth, along with my parents. But in the few short months since her birth, I was spending less and less time with her and my granddaughter - and more and more time on the Church. That became painfully clear to me one day when my daughter, in tears, would say that she didn't know who I was anymore. "It's always the Church. Your family doesn't even see you anymore," she said, and she was right. I was either on my cell phone, sending email, in Boston with the attorneys or meeting with survivors. It was my daughter that made me realize how deeply I had been sliding. Realizing it was one thing. Climbing back up was a whole other matter. I had made a decision to get some normalcy back into my family life, but that was easier said than done. I had just decided to change my priorities when I was asked to take yet another direction.

I had met with the Attorney General Tom Reilly in January. Late the previous year, the attorney general had asked, via Bob, to talk with me but it had been put off by both of us because of time constraints. He had called a grand jury to investigate the Archdiocese and was still in the process of his investigation. We met for several hours one afternoon. Honestly, I wasn't sure what to expect, and I was apprehensive, as well as slightly nervous. That afternoon I told him my story, as well as that of my family's. I found him to be exceptionally compassionate and understanding. I also found him to be livid. He himself was Catholic and the outrage he felt was apparent during our entire conversation. It was probably the first time that someone with the power to do so said to me that he would do everything in his power to uncover the truth and prosecute to the fullest extent of the law. I believed him.

Shortly after meeting with the attorney general I was told about legislation that was being introduced. I was asked to testify at the statehouse on behalf of the hundreds of survivors. I was asked this right after I had just promised my family that I would make more time for them. I couldn't find it in me to say no. I was told my testimony could make thousands of children safe. I was also told that it would only be one afternoon, although in the end, I would be at the statehouse more than a dozen times testifying before the criminal justice committee, speaking to state senators and representatives and testifying before several other committees. If nothing else, I would do what I could to toughen laws that might protect future generations. My life seemed like it was anything but mine. Yet, I couldn't say no. I had gotten involved and just couldn't back out. We were so close to getting something accomplished and I had to see it through. So when an aide called and asked me to testify, I would go. At times, my father would join me, as well. nor was I the only survivor to speak. There were many others, as well. Hopefully, time will prove that we accomplished something.

The other direction that I literally took was the journey that took me to the Vatican. I had tossed around the idea of confronting the Vatican ever since I started reading the priest's files that were released. I had come across several documents direct from the Vatican and it had struck a chord with me. In particular, there was one directive that advised the Archdiocese to "avoid scandal." I remember that one distinctly because the day it was released to the public, I was visiting my father and walked into a local station, displaying that piece of paper on TV. I looked at my poor father and saw his eyes well up in tears again. "I can't fucking believe it. Even the Vatican knew and did nothing," he said. Before my eyes, I saw his faith diminishing. More documents and more pain. The Vatican came to my mind again in January and February, and again, it was because of my father.
One day in January, my mother came down to talk to me. My father hadn't been sleeping and when she had finally asked him about it, he said that all he could think about was "saving his soul." He reminded my mother of the conversation my parents had with Fr. Birmingham years before. Apparently Birmingham had stopped them both after Church one day to talk with them. He

had seen them in Church every Sunday, along with all of us. He asked my father why he hadn't been receiving communion. My father explained that he had been married before and divorced and that my mother and he had not been married in the Church. Fr. Birmingham told him that that was nonsense. They were good Catholics, sending their boys to Catholic school, attending mass, and Fr. Birmingham said that he could receive communion. My mother said that my father looked at him and said are you sure about this? Birmingham replied, yes. My father then said " Okay, Fr. B., but if you're wrong, then its on your soul, not mine." Fr. Birmingham's reply was, "No Eddie, nothing is on my soul. My conscience is clear. It's your soul to worry about, not mine."

Thirty years later, my father was worried about going to hell and saving his soul. After my mother told me the story, I went up to talk to my father. He said he couldn't help but get emotional about it and that it was all he could think about. I asked him if he would talk to Fr. Capone, his parish priest. "Why would I? Haven't you seen the papers today? Another priest raping kids and everyone knew, even the priest admitted it and wrote an apology, but Boston wouldn't let him send it. The letter was addressed and was still in his file. Why would I talk to Fr. Capone? They're all the same." My father has always kept me grounded in reality. This day was no exception. This is what my father - and people just like him - were going through. I asked him whom he would consider seeing and his answer stunned me - Cardinal Law. He said that at least he took a step by resigning. He would agree to meet with Cardinal Law but he wanted the Cardinal to hear his confession. I said I would take care of that. It seemed like an easy thing to do although I was stunned that he wanted to meet with Cardinal Law. Several times in the past I had asked him, but he declined saying that he was afraid of what he would say. However, now that Law had resigned, he wanted meet him and have him hear his confession. "You'd better tell him that now it's up to him to help me save my soul," he said.

Well if that's what he wanted, and if that's what would help him find peace after all this, then that is what I would set up. I wasn't overly concerned about it. A meeting had been set up with Law's temporary replacement, Bishop Lennon. It was a cordial meeting with him that lasted for about two hours. I didn't find him especially warm or outgoing, but he was cordial. He had also agreed to do three things that we had asked of him. 1) Set up a bi-weekly meeting to continue dialogue with us. 2) Send a personal representative to the mediation meetings that were ongoing. 3) Meet with SOJB and their families in a group setting. We had asked, and, he had agreed in theory to all three. After that meeting I had asked Fr. Connelly if he had a few minutes to talk and he agreed.

Fr. Connelly and I talked for 20 or so minutes. I explained what my father was going through and asked for me and my father to meet with Law. I also told him that there were several of us who were interested in going to the Vatican for a healing mission. Fr. Connelly looked at me and said, "Gary, those are the two easiest things that you've ever asked me for. I'm meeting with the Cardinal tomorrow and I ll talk to him. I'm sure neither of them will be a problem. I'll get back to you on Monday about it. No problem and don't worry."

And that was it, simple. Or so, I thought. Monday would come and go, and no call back from Fr. Connelly. Four weeks would go by and after phone calls, letters, and emails, I received nothing. No response. I was dumbstruck and I was bullshit. Here I was, again, asking them for help. Not money, not miracles, but a little spiritual help for my father. To simply have the Cardinal hear his confession, and I couldn't get a reply from anyone. After a month, I had had enough. Olan knew what was going on and I told him that I was about to turn up the thermostat on this. If I didn't get a response soon, I wasn't sure what I was going to do, but I had to do something. That evening, my phone rang, much to my surprise, it was Fr. Connelly apologizing for not getting back to me. I set up a meeting for the following Tuesday at noon. So Tuesday at noon, there I was again at the Cardinal's residency. Normally when I had been there in the past, meetings would last two hours, or so. There was always plenty to talk about. That particular Tuesday, however, would be different. I knew it the minute we sat down. It was only John and myself, same dining room, same building, but it was a different Fr. John Connelly. I found that out right away. Until this day, John had always been open and honest, or so I had thought. I never had to chase him to get an answer. That day was like a page out of a movie script, though.

"Gary, what's up? I know you've been calling me, what's going on?" What's going on? I asked him why he didn't get back to me like he said he would a month before. He didn't remember saying that he would get back to me then. I asked him about Cardinal Law and my father and he said that what I was asking for was unreasonable. I asked him about the Vatican and he said that I shouldn't be looking at Cardinal Law and the Vatican that way, that I shouldn't be selling my father a magic pill of healing. That meeting lasted less than 20 minutes. At one point I simply asked him to give me some kind of option on helping my father and he simply shrugged his shoulders, put his hand up, and said, "I don't know what to tell you." I just couldn't understand it. I didn't know why there was such a change in attitude, but there was. For the first time I looked into John's eyes and didn't see hope. I left there both angry and upset because I couldn't believe that I was giving them another chance to help heal the pain they caused and again they just slammed the door shut. It was like the first time I went to the chancery asking for help for myself and got nowhere. It was also just like when I went to the chancery asking for help for my brother Edward. Over the past summer, Ed had started drinking again and it became painfully clear that he needed some type of in house treatment facility. Like so many survivors that summer, he was reliving what had happened to him and the pain showed in everything that he did. In the beginning of the summer he had come up and stayed with me for a month. I could see Ed sliding further and further and I felt helpless. My parents knew what was going on, as well. Not only did I feel powerless trying to deal with Ed, but I watched my parents age in front of me. After being sober almost five years, I knew that if Ed started drinking, his problems would only multiply, and, multiply, they did. The renewed bond that grew between Ed and me when we both faced this issue together for the first time rapidly deteriorated. When he came to stay my only rule was that he would not drink in my home and he knew that. It got so bad during the month he was there that after he broke that rule for the third time, I asked him to leave. It broke my heart but I had to. I knew too well that enabling him by tolerating him drinking wouldn't help him. The last six months had been hard on him, being so far away without the support system that SOJB gave me. His pain was evident in everything he did. When Ed had fallen so deep that he called and talked about suicide for the first time, I knew I had to do something. I made call after call trying to get him into a program. He knew he needed one and so did I. Like many survivors not working in the typical mainstream job market, Ed had no insurance. I talked to social workers and to anyone that I thought may help. At one point, I turned again to the Archdiocese for help. I asked them to consider funding in-house treatment for Ed. He wasn't the only one out there in that position. We had received many calls from survivors that had been alcohol and drug free for years, but now had slid back into their destructive behaviors. Over 80 % of survivors currently are self-medicating. The thought of losing another brother and the thought of my parents burying one more child tore me up inside. I called the Archdiocese's Office of Healing and Ministry to ask for help. That day I was told that there was nothing they could do. "We not in a position to help right now. We can't afford to put someone in that kind of therapy." A week later, Ed layed down on his living room couch and took a bottle of sleeping pills. By the grace of God, his attempt at suicide failed. The Archdiocese also failed that week, and I'll never forget it.

Here I was, again asking them for help and once again, they failed. But this time though, I wouldn't wait for something to happen to my father. I would do more. That day is when I decided to get to the Vatican. I didn't know how I was going to get there or who I was going to meet, but it was becoming clearer than ever that between Fr. Connelly's behavior and Bishop Lennon's unresponsiveness, there was not going to be any decisive leadership coming from the Archdiocese in Boston. The Vatican was the last hope, for me - and for my father. I knew it was the one place that my father still considered holy. I also knew that the orders flowed from the top down. It was time to go to the top on this on. Maybe no one cared over there, maybe no one would listen. But maybe they would and I was willing to take that chance. It also seemed like it was the only chance we had left. I felt that if I, at least, made an attempt, I could ease my father's pain and maybe, heal some of my pain, as well. Someone in Rome needed to know first-hand what was going on in Boston.

I spoke to Olan and Bernie about my decision and they both supported it, adding that they would both be interested in going, as well. I also spoke to Ed about it and invited him, as well. Olan was concerned, however, that I may be "taking one for the team" by doing this, if I didn't go with the support of the Archdiocese. Mainly, he thought that the Archdiocese would take my decision about going as a threat and that unless I went with their help, I would be out of the loop. "The loop" was what we called the back channel that we had been working on for almost a year. We had been able to create and work a dialogue that had been somewhat successful in getting some things accomplished. By working in our own way, we had been able to get some needs of the survivors filled such as finally getting the Archdiocese to pay for in-house therapy. It had taken us months and months. We had worked hard at it for over a year because we felt there needed to be a clean line of communication - without the attorneys. It had worked, sometimes, better than others.

I told Olan that if I was going to draw a line, then this was the line for me. When the Church refused to help one of their own by declining to hear a confession, they crossed that line. Olan wasn't concerned about that back channel being closed, he was just concerned about me not being seen as a part of it. I was more bothered by the fact that Bishop Lennon was doing nothing that he had agreed to in January. There were no biweekly updates, the Archdiocese still refused to meet and talk with the mediators and these were the mediators that they had hired. It was becoming ever more clear to me that Bishop Lennon was there to simply stall for time. He had come in and stated that helping the survivors would be his first priority and yet his attorneys were throwing up every legal blockade in their bag. There was no dialogue of healing going on, yet there was plenty of blame and pain shed on the survivors. Alhough I saw Olan make attempt after attempt to get Lennon involved, Lennon as I saw it, simply chose not to.

I began writing letters to any Church official that I thought was in a position to help, including Bishop Lennon, to whom I wrote four letters. He never responded. I wrote to the US ambassador to the Vatican, the Vatican's ambassador to the US, to Cardinals and Bishops, both here and in Rome. Out of two dozen letters I wrote explaining who I was and what the trip was about, I received two responses, one from our ambassador to the Vatican and one from a monsignor in the Vatican. No one else bothered to reply. As the weeks went by, I started to realize that what I was trying to do, mainly meet with The Pope or one of his delegates, was going to be harder than I thought. Harder, but not impossible. Whenever someone talked about my plans, words like crazy, unrealistic and naive were used. The more skeptical a response I received, the harder I pushed. In hindsight, had I known what was ahead of me, I would have called myself crazy, as well. Aside from the logistics of going, there was the finance issue. I was broke, plain and simple. But, I decided, somehow I'd find a way. I had mentioned to my father that I was planning to go to the Vatican, but I didn't mention anything in detail and I didn't mention bringing him along. I figured I'd wait and see what the response was before I got his hopes up. The day after I talked to him about it, I was in the back yard and he stuck his head out the door and said, "Hey, you know I have my passport, in case you were worried." He was joking about coming with me, yet he didn't even know that I had every intention of asking him.

When I did finally talk to my father and asked him to come with us, he thought I was joking. But when he realized I was serious, for the first time since the pain of our abuse was exposed, I could see a glimmer of hope in his eyes. Throughout the years of my father's life, throughout the tragedy of burying his youngest and his oldest child, throughout the loss of his job late in life, my father had always leaned on his faith. It was that faith that was broken when my brother and I came forward and it was that faith that I wanted to help restore. Over and over again, he'd ask if I thought we'd get in andI simply said, "Of course." My answer would never change. I was trying to convince him, but I wasn't convinced myself. As the weeks went by I would wonder whether I had taken just a bit more than I could chew.

Eventually I spoke publicly in interviews about my plans to visit the Vatican, partly because I knew the value of the press and realized that I was going to need all the help I could get. Although I still remembered the story of the scorpion and the water buffalo.

I had already floated a date to leave for the Vatican, March 15th, which was almost a year to the day when I had come forward for the first time. Though with war with Iraq looming, I was pressured repeatedly to change the time frame. In the end, I stuck to that date. There had to be a personal connection made in Rome just as I had done with Cardinal Law, McCormack, and Lennon. I actually was surprised that no one had made the attempt before, it simply seemed like the logical step that had been missed.

Bernie was all for going. The more he thought of it, the more sense it made. Usually I'm not a detailed-oriented kind of guy, but neither was Bernie. As Olan struggled with his decision about whether to go or not to go, nailing the details of the trip would fall on me. It was more that I didn't trust anyone else to make them. Bernie wasn't really worried about travel arrangements, flights or hotel rooms weren't a high priority on his list. If it had just been he and I going, they probably wouldn't have been high on my list either. It was a different story, though, with my father.

I couldn't tell him the standard, "We'll worry about it when we get there." He would ask me things like, "Where will we be staying? What airlines are we flying? How will we get around?" I added the title "travel agent" to my other job descriptions, which had grown extensively over the past year. In the past year, in addition to carpenter, I had added, survivor, spokesperson, diplomat, referee, lobbyist, advocate and, at times, politician, to the list.

One evening Victoria Block, from Channel 7 called to ask about the Vatican trip. Throughout the year, she had called me more times just to see how my family and I were doing, than to ask for an interview. After a year of dealing with the press, I realized that's a rarity. On that particular day, she told me she had been at the Vatican the week before Law had resigned and we talked about who to see, where to go, where to stay, etc. In the course of the conversation, she asked how my father was doing. Vicky was one of the few people that knew about my father being a survivor. She asked if I would talk to her on camera about my decision to go to the Vatican. She also said that if my father wanted to, he could sit with me since it may be an important thing for him just to be there with me. I told her that I wasn't sure of that, but I'd ask him. I knew that Vicky was my dad's favorite reporter. He had said it before, I'm sure partly because of the way she had handled herself, and partly because of the way she had been covering this story. I told him about the interview and about Vicky's invitation. To my complete surprise, he said yes. I told him his being there could mean a lot to survivors whose parents were not as supportive as mine had been.

He said that although he'd sit with me, not to expect him to say anything because he was too emotional. As the camera crew was setting up, my dad came down. As Vicky introduced herself, he said, "I'm a 77-year-old man. Probably too senile to be here, but I'm here to support my son. If you ask me anything about this, I'll probably break down and won't be able to answer." Vicky said that he was wrong, " You're definitely not senile." Everyone laughed.

In the end, my father did speak that day and the story that Vicky did was one of the most compelling pieces that I had ever seen her do. My dad talked about his faith, his pain, his children and the Vatican. After it ran, I received letters from several people thanking us for talking. Families, men, women, all ages related that day to my father. The following day, my father received three phone calls from men thanking him for coming forward. They were men he knew as children who called to let him know that he was not alone. The same priest too abused them more than 60 years ago. My father realized that day, that he wasn't alone either, and I know he found comfort in that. Thank you Vicky.

As March 15th drew closer, I was getting more tense by the day. About the only thing I had ready was my passport. Other than that I had two responses from the letters I'd written. It seemed like we were going on a trip of hope. I hoped to get there, I hoped to get in, and I hoped not to make us all look like fools. I didn't know how we were going to pay for any of it. Sometimes there is truth to that saying, "Catholics don't pray for miracles, we just count on them." One evening while speaking at a Voice of the Faithful meeting, someone came up and asked if they could help fund this trip for us. There is a God, I thought to myself. It was the first time I considered it. There were many times when I had been a guest speaker for them over the previous year. At the end of every meeting, people would come up and offer me money. Pray, pay and obey. That used to be the Catholic mantra. Each and every time I would decline, usually asking them to give it to Catholic Charities, instead. That particular night though, I simply said, "Thank you for your offer. I'm not in a position to decline any help in that department. Thank you." This woman was on the board of VOTF and I knew that she had the power to help and that they had the funds, as well. Temporarily, I breathed a sigh of relief.
It was only temporary, though. Several weeks later I got a call the day before I was to be the guest speaker at a main meeting of

VOTF and their board members. In that call I was told that they had changed their plans for having me speak. Instead, I was asked to "submit a written proposal regarding your request for our funding of your trip." Unfortunately a group which had formed in direct response to this scandal, whose number one goal was support of the survivors, and whose number one critique of the Archdiocese was the structure of its hierarchy, had become a hierarchy, too. They didn't understand that I was not going to the Vatican to represent them. There was no way that I was going there presenting anyone else's agenda and there was no way that I was going to submit any written proposal for funding. I hadn't asked, they had offered. I realized that the Archdiocese looked at VOTF as a threat and I'm sure the Vatican would look at anyone with ties to them in the same manner. For all the goodness that they stood for, they were still in a state of flux, as far as I was concerned. I had always appreciated their support, both spoken and unspoken. I can vividly remember the first time I addressed them a year earlier. The last thing I said was, "You have come together and together you have strength. Don't spend time worrying about who's sitting where. Don't become the hierarchy that you so detest. Keep it simple and you will accomplish much." It seemed to me that Olan ran headlong into the same situation, as well. He had been actively trying to get an 800-hotline set up so survivors could call and get information. He had spent months on it working to get it up and running - and funded. It was his baby and I agreed 100% with him on it. Survivors that were calling us for help should have received much more help than we could have possibly have offered. We were doing the best we could, but we knew we couldn't continue. It wasn't healthy for us and we certainly weren't professionals. At times I felt like the marriage counselor who was giving out marriage advice who was twice divorced. Olan had tried to get the Archdiocese to provide and fund it with no results. VOTF had said that they would love to help. In the end, I remember Olan saying that he received a call asking for a written proposal outlining the objectives. I asked him what he was going to do. "What am I going to do? It's already done. I took a piece of construction paper and a Crayola crayon and wrote, "WE WANT MONEY FOR A VICTIM HOT LINE," across it and sent it. There, now they have my written request." I wasn't sure if he actually did it, or not, but I felt like doing the same thing. Like I had said, keep it simple.

There would be no donation from VOTF. There would, however, be other help. As word got out about the trip, checks started coming to my house. Individual members of VOTF who had heard through the email network about my trip were sending us their own money. Two parishes, Saint Anselm's in Sudbury and another in Marblehead, even took up collections at their parish meetings. Some were as small as a check for $5.00, but that five dollars meant as much to me as any of the others. In the end, we received almost two thousand dollars in donations from Catholics around the area. It wasn't enough to get us there, but it was a thankful start. A few installations jobs came up, as well, here and there. Somehow it just worked out.

With less than four weeks left, tickets and passports in hand, our funding was limited, at best. Very few knew about the trip, only Olan, Bernie and myself. At this point, it was down to three of us. My brother Ed decided that he wasn't going. He just didn't feel that the time was right for him and I fully understood it. Olan had been fighting with himself about going for months. His thoughts were that we should be invited there and not storm the gates. As much as he tried to get the Archdiocese of Boston involved, they refused. As it would turn out, fate would help make the decision for Olan. Three weeks before we were to leave, Olan landed in the hospital with heart trouble. We talked for quite a while about whether or not to put the trip off. Everyone thought I should. Our country was invading Iraq and the climate wasn't friendly toward Americans. After a long conversation I said, "What do you think?" Olan said, "You know you made that decision long ago. Gary, you go and you make sure you make as much noise as you can over there. It's not important whether or not the Pope sees you. What's important is that you go and try. We've knocked on lots of doors this past year, go knock on some more."

He was right, and that's exactly what we did. On Saturday afternoon, at 3:00 with nothing but a hotel reservation, plane ticket and passport in hand, Bernie, my father and myself left for the Vatican. There's a saying that "God watches out for fools." Well, as I left that day, I silently prayed that God had on his glasses, because these fools were heading to Rome. From the start of the trip, things didn't look like they were going to be going well. We left from Logan at 3 in the afternoon on Saturday and arrived in Italy at 7 in the morning the following Sunday. It was the longest flight any of us had been on. At times I would look over to see my father, eyes closed, saying the rosary with his prayer beads in hand. Nothing like putting a little pressure on. Arriving in Italy that morning, we found out that the hotel we were booked with was oversold. They had canceled our reservations and hadn't notified us. There was nothing they could do about it and that's just the way it was done there, we were told. We had an arrangement with someone that was doing a documentary from the United States. They had sent a videographer from Rome to meet with us and stay with us for the week to video some of our trip for them. I was told that he was going to meet us at the airport. At least someone who knew the language would be able to help us find another room, or so I thought.

After over an hour of waiting, with no one showing up, whatever hope I still held onto, began to fade. Talk about three guys looking like fish out of water. The first thing that greeted us when we got off the plane were security men and women holding submachine guns. After the second hour, I felt a pit in my stomach. Sitting, walking, killing time, and all the time surrounded by people speaking Italian who seemed as though they were constantly looking at us. Finally, I looked at Bernie and my dad, and said, "Hey I just figured out what they are all saying." Bernie looked at me and with a serious look and said, "Well what are they saying?" I said, "Hey, look at the stupid Americans. It looks like another hotel room got canceled." As soon as I finished, the three of us roared in laughter. We were all exhausted but the laughter broke the tension, and then things seemed not so bad.

We ended up booking a hotel through the tourism desk at the airport which also took care of the transportation. An hour or so later, we arrived in the heart of Rome in a cab driven by someone who spoke no English at all. Our new hotel rooms were less than five minutes walking distance from the Vatican. Sometimes fate deals a good hand. As the taxi driver dropped us off, he got the bags out of the back and then scurried back to the driver's door. I yelled, asking him where the hotel was and, as he drove away, he pointed. The only problem was that he was pointing nowhere that looked like a hotel. So, as the taxi cab drove off, the three of us, bags in hand, stood in the middle of the road, looking like, again, three fish out of water.

Bernie had this puzzled expression on his face. "Hey, what's going on? That's not right. Where's the hotel? What are we going to do?" He fired off 20 questions in 20 seconds. I jokingly told him that we had just been scammed by the oldest scam in the world. We just gave our money to someone for a hotel who scammed us, putting us in a taxi and telling the driver to "get rid of 'em." My dad started to roar with laughter, and when Bernie realized that I was kidding, all three of us joined in. We were laughing so hard at times we were like three school kids playing a prank on each other. You could tell we were tired, but our sense of humor carried us that day. It would carry us that week, as well, especially when we needed it the most.

Moments later, a man came out of the café across the street and told us in broken English that he would check us in, in a little while. "As soon as I finish eating," he said. He walked away, us still standing in the road, and laughter soon followed. After checking in and unpacking, we should have rested. Instead we all headed down to the Vatican. I have to say, that as unimpressed as I was with the city of Rome, I was in awe of the beauty and history of the Vatican. Walking down the cobblestone road leading to St. Peter's Square was an incredible experience. Each time we walked that road, and we walked it plenty, I was overcome by the thought that we were actually there in Rome at the Vatican. We had lots of doors to knock on that week, yet, on Sunday, we found that the Vatican itself is closed. Closed on Sunday. We walked around St. Peter's Square and headed into the Cathedral. It was truly awe-inspiring. Seeing the architecture, statues and hundreds of people walking around in silent reverence was a spiritual experience. It is truly a beautiful place, yet for all its opulence and glory, we were there on a mission and Bernie and I began to realize exactly what we were up against. The Vatican is a sovereign nation. It is ruled by the Pope and is, literally, a country within a country. Not only did it seem like an independent country to me, it seemed like another planet. I had a hard time that day and continue to have a hard time justifying the statues and buildings as being tributes to Christ, who was a simple man in its purest form. I still have an internal fight when I look back at the opulence and wealth that surrounded us that day. I wonder what Jesus Christ would say if he walked the earth and saw wealth at the Vatican, all present under the pretext of his name. I thought he said, feed the poor, clothe the naked, shelter the homeless. I don't think he said, "Build a luxurious temple in my name." Later that week when we finally got a chance to break free from our door knocking, we would tour the Vatican Museum. Again I would find myself asking those same questions. I had a very difficult time enjoying the millions of dollars in artwork when I had to pass paupers on my way in the door. How far the Church seemed to have strayed from its mission.

Walking around at St. Peters', we found our way to the tomb of Saint Peter. Silently the three of us knelt, each praying in our own way. My father would break the silence of that moment only by saying, "Well, I prayed to St. Peter to help us this week. If anyone can open the door for us, he can. It's up to him now." It was only after that that I learned that Saint Peter is also known as the Keeper of the Keys to the Gate of Heaven. It would be a week that we began with hope, endured through frustration, yet ended in hope as well. The following day, we were invited to the foreign press association for an interview about our trip. Arriving there, we were surprised to find ourselves in a large press conference. We were not prepared for something of this magnitude. It reminded me of the first press conference I was talked into doing almost exactly a year before. It lasted for over an hour and was covered by press from almost every country you could think of. It seemed like the war wasn't the only thing that other countries were interested in. Afterwards many reporters told us that we were the first people to ever publicly talk about this issue in Rome. I was stunned. The "Catholic Abuse Scandal" as it had come to be known in the USA was covered almost daily in the USA, yet in Rome, it had never been talked about. I was realizing more and more the challenge we were assuming by being there. We also finally met up with the video guys. Finally there was someone who could translate for us. That day we were also fortunate to meet John Allen. John is the Vatican correspondent for the Catholic Reporter, which is the largest Catholic news magazine. John sat with us that day and, over cappuccino, spent several hours talking with us and giving us direction. We were very fortunate to have found this unlikely ally. His help that day, and through the entire week, was invaluable. He told us how the Vatican worked with regards to getting appointments, getting around and getting noticed. It wasn't going to be easy, he assured us. It was probably going to be nearly impossible to get anyone to meet with us. He realized our resolve, however, and offered any assistance he could.

So, with the press conference behind us, and John Allen's advice, our next stop was the Vatican. I had received a reply letter from a monsignor who had told us where we could, at least, get inside the Vatican and who we needed to see. In his letter he talked about the "big brass doors" as being the entrance. Walking into St. Peter's Square, we found the doors. They were 12 feet tall and they were brass. They were also manned by the Swiss Guard who did not let people through without an appointment. My letter in hand, the three of us simply walked up, showed him the letter that told me to see "the Prefecture of the Papal Household." He looked at the letter, on official Vatican stationery, spoke to his supervisor, and we walked in. We were inside. As we walked inside those Big Brass Doors, the three of us glanced at each other, not knowing what to do next. We went up a huge set of stairs to the second floor and into the office of Bishop Harvey, the Prefecture of the Papal Household. We had already been told that the probability of meeting with Harvey was nil, but we were, at least, in his office. A priest who misunderstood why we were there greeted us. He disappeared for a moment and returned with three tickets for the Papal audience. Bernie stared to explain the real reason we were there, but before he could go any further, I kindly thanked the priest for the tickets and took them before he really did know why we were there. With the tickets safely in my pocket, Bernie explained who we were, and why we were there. We had brought a letter explaining all of that and handed it to him for Bishop Harvey. After he read it, he looked stunned. It dawned on him, finally, what we were about. He explained that Bishop Harvey wasn't there at the moment but that he would forward the letter to him and asked us to return later in the day.

Education. That is the one word to describe what we received that first day. It was like your first day in school. When you realize who your friends would be and who to stay away from. You learn what time the bell rings, and what it means. We were on a crash course that week and that Monday we learned quite a bit. For instance, when they tell you to come back later in the day, it means come back before 2:00, because you can't get in after 2:00. Everyone's gone and the big brass doors, though open, are really closed. Lesson learned. We also learned that when someone in authority asks where you are staying, you don't say "in a hotel." You do say which hotel, which room number, and what phone number. That's because when you are seeking an appointment, you leave your contact information and they decide when and if they are going to get back to you. That's how it's done. Another tough lesson learned. Over the course of the next several days, we would repeat our efforts to see bishops and cardinals over and over again. It was frustrating, and at times, we felt beat up pretty badly. Each time it seemed like we were getting nowhere, we'd get lucky. Each day we would make some kind of personal contact. Tuesday our plan was to find the contact who replied to my letter. It seemed simple enough, however, it was anything but simple. When we went to the Vatican that day, I asked a Swiss guard where was the office of Monsignor "Jones" (not his real name) I showed him his letter and the guard's reply was that the address didn't exist. I showed that letter to a dozen people and no one knew where the address was or who Monsignor "Jones" was. We also tried to phone our mystery monsignor and found out how difficult the phone system was. We tried from 7:00 in the morning until 11:00 in the morning with no luck. Finally, while looking through the folder, I found the return address on the envelope. It was from his home address. Grabbing a taxi and a driver that knew where the address was located, off we went. We arrived at something that looked like a compound, gated and guarded. Speaking to the guard through the fence, we explained who we were there to see. "He no home, He no home," was the response we got. He got the monsignor on the phone, though, and handed it to me. I explained who we were and asked him if he would be willing to meet with us. He said that he would be more than happy to but that he was at his office and he needed to leave by noon. It was 11:30 and it had taken us almost 30 minutes to get where we were. I put the taxi driver on the phone, and through hand signals said step on it. None of us, but the driver, knew where we were going. We just sat back and held on as the driver navigated the streets like a crazy man. The longer he drove, the more I looked at my watch. I was the only one who knew that the monsignor had to leave by noon. I didn't dare tell my father how little time we had to get there. As the taxi drove on, I watched as we got closer and closer to the Vatican. I was horrified when the taxi driver returned to the taxi stand where we had originally started. All I kept thinking was that he had gotten confused about where we wanted to go. It was almost 11:50 and we were running out of time. Suddenly, he pulled up just feet from where we had gotten in, rolled down his window, and pointed to a building. We had just spend almost 5 hours looking for a building that no one could find, but was right next to the taxi stand where we began an hour before.

Running now, with my 77-year-old father keeping up, it was five minutes before noon, but we had found our monsignor. He was a priest formerly from the Boston area. I had received his name and contact information from my father's parish priest Fr. Al Capone, who had been helpful over the past year. We sat in his office and talked for the next hour and a half (he missed his noon appointment) talked. He knew who we were, he had been following the news daily from Boston. He would learn more about us that day and, in turn, we would learn much from him, as well. It was this monsignor who had told us about the reality of Cardinal Law's resignation and about how the Vatican viewed the situation in the USA. The Vatican did see it as an overblown, media-hyped situation. It was a "United States Catholic" problem. As we all listened it became clear how hard it was going to be to get through. When we talked about Bishop McCormack, he said that it was up to the everyday people in the pews to do something about him. The Vatican was not going to get involved in replacing him, not unless the uproar was loud enough for them to hear from the states. "The Bishops are in place to deal with the daily issues of running their Archdiocese, the Vatican will not get involved." He went on to kill the rumor about Cardinal Law handing his in his resignation in the spring and it being refused. "It didn't happen that way, it's simply not true. That's not how it's done in this system. If he had handed it in, it would have been accepted. The truth is more like he was summoned for his resignation, and he asked for more time." The monsignor gave us other contacts, as well. I'm not sure if it was because he felt a connection to Boston, or because he realized that we weren't the "zealots" often seen picketing with bullhorns in front of churches. Whatever the reason, he helped that day. When I asked about the possibility of meeting the Pope, aside from the inside contact he told us we needed, he said, "Gary, I can see what it will mean for your father to meet with Our Holy Father. Honestly, you have your tickets to the audience tomorrow. Get there early, by 7:00 a.m. It's going to be very hot tomorrow and, as good as your father looks for his age, he's elderly. Ask one of the guides to put him in a wheelchair. There's an area where wheelchairs are put and it's on the top platform near the Holy Father. Sometimes the wheelchairs are wheeled to the Holy Father and he meets with each one. I know it's only a possibility, but I'm telling you what to do, without telling you what to do."

I got his message loud and clear, but also knew that we weren't there to get a handshake and a blessing. I did appreciate all that we had learned that day. Monsignor "Jones" helped us more than anyone that day

Leaving his office, in better spirits than we arrived, we climbed into another taxi and headed back to the Big Brass Doors. We made another attempt at seeing Bishop Harvey, The Prefecture. Again, we were able to get inside with our lucky letter. This time as we walked up the huge marble staircase to the second level, we stopped and took a few pictures. Heading back into Harvey's office, we had a different reception. Perhaps word was getting out. It was the same priest sitting at the desk, this time, however, he gave us different information. Just like the monsignor, he told us to fax or drop off a letter with our request. Though it took us hours to find a fax machine, and hours to get through, we faxed our request. We also made yet another trip and dropped off the letter. From there we headed to the US embassy.

With another lucky letter in hand, we were standing outside the US embassy. I had written Ambassador Nicholson a letter about our trip and he was kind enough to reply. Many people, including Bob Sherman, said that while we were there, we should drop by. "Just walk in. You're a citizen of the US and go in and tell them what you're trying to do." Well, perhaps it was because the US was at war with Iraq, or perhaps it's always like it was that day, but you don't just walk in. There were guards around the embassy, submachine guns and all. Not Marines, much to the surprise of my ex-marine father.

We spoke to the guard at the gate and waited. Thirty minutes later an assistant came out and said that there must be a misunderstanding. Ambassador Nicholson wasn't there and she didn't know of any appointment. As she was talking, I thought it strange that we were on one side of the gate and she was on the other. When I gave her a copy of both letters, she left for a moment and then the Guards let us in. After handing over our passports and going through security, we were let into a large room. We were able to meet that day with the assistant ambassador and his assistant. They were both very sympathetic to our plight and offered whatever assistance they could. They did tell us though that we had a tough road ahead of us. "It took over three months for the Vatican to meet with the new ambassador when he arrived. I'm not sure what we can do, but we've forwarded your request on to the Vatican and we're supporting what you are doing as much as we can. I'm not sure what else we can do." There was a silence that followed. It was the silence of us realizing that if it took over three months for the ambassador to meet with the Pope, what chance do we have?

It was at that moment my father said, "If our own government says they can't help us, I'm not sure what else we can do. We're the greatest country in the world. We have to stop this abuse somehow." The room went silent again and then Bernie looked and said, "There must be something else you can do." We left that meeting with just a bit more information, more people to contact. We spent the rest of the afternoon making, or trying to make phone calls and send more faxes. That in itself is a tough task in Rome. You never realize how much you really take for granted when you live in the US. Placing a phone call, finding an internet connection, sending a fax, or simply getting a copy made are things we take for granted. It's a totally different story in Italy. Our phones in the hotel weren't working. Each day we would ask and each day they would say that they would be fixed. We ended up stopping people on the street with cell phones and paying them to use their phones. In the letters we faxed and dropped off at the

Vatican, we left the phone number of the little café next to the hotel. Then there was the 6-hour time difference. When we needed something done in Boston, by the time we found out what we needed, which was usually around noon, it was only 6:00 a.m. Boston time. By the time Boston would get back to us, it was after 9:00 a.m. Boston time, which was after our 2:00 p.m. Vatican deadline. If we needed done from the Boston side, it had to be done by 2:00 p.m. Boston time because the café closed at 8:00 p.m. Rome time. After that, our phone link was gone. Without a phone in our hotel rooms, we were pretty much useless. Just more obstacles which we encountered daily. There were a few people in Boston who knew of our trip that had offered help. One of those people was Ray Flynn, the former mayor of Boston and himself, the former US ambassador to the Vatican.

Bernie had been in contact with him and he was pulling for us. He had made a few calls to his contacts and was continuing to do what he could. These kind of connections were most valuable. Although no one outwardly offered any help after hearing from us, it seemed that everyone would offer help after meeting with us. Each day we would make an attempt to meet someone. Each time we did, we had another advocate for what we were trying to do. Each day I was proving what I had been saying for months. To understand who we were and to understand the abuse and its effects, it had to be handled face to face, not through a letter, or a newspaper article. If we could only get through to someone, that was our hope. Our knuckles grew raw from our persistent knocking on doors. We took it all in stride though, and we didn't give up.

After seeing my father safely to our hotel room Tuesday evening, Bernie and I headed out for a walk. Though my father was tired, Bernie and I hadn't adjusted to the time difference and we found ourselves a bit restless. The area we were staying in was a mix of "resi`dentia's" or residential condominiums and retail stores. As safe as we were told the area was, we were still a bit concerned. There was graffiti on almost every single building we walked passed, including our own hotel. "Assonate Americans" was written in huge two foot letters across our hotel. We continued to walk past clothing stores, ice cream stands and the numerous cafés which cover Rome. At one point we walked by a piano store. A little known fact about Bernie is that he plays the piano. I had heard him play on a few occasions. The first time was in Salem when he sat down and, much to my surprise, started to play "Lean on Me." As we both stood there looking through the glass at rows of beautiful pianos, I coaxed Bernie into going inside to see if they would let him play.

We walked in spoke to a saleswoman. I watched as Bernie tried to explain that he "was an American visiting and would like to try out a piano, to see if it was the one" he wanted. I watched in amazement as Bernie sat in front of an absolutely gorgeous Rosewood piano and noticed that it had a $ 265,000.00 price tag on it. As only Bernie could do, he gingerly began playing "Lean on Me." Several minutes later when he got to the chorus, he, not so softly, started singing "Lean on me, when you're not strong, when you need strength and you can't carry on." I thought he sounded great. Unfortunately, the store owner didn't agree with me. Suddenly a man came running out, yelling and waving his hands. In mixed Italian and English, as he frantically waved his hand, he said, "This is a no disco pub. NO, NO, NO. You no play disco music here. You leave, you leave a NOW!" I watched as Bernie tried to talk to him, but it was no use. Bernie got up, walked over to the man and said, "Well sir, I am a wealthy American who was considering buying this piano. People pay thousands of dollars just to see me in concert. You have insulted me now. And I am no longer interested in buying this piano. I am leaving and don't try to talk me out of it." We walked outside and, as soon as we were out of sight of the store manager, we both burst out laughing. With that episode behind us, we headed in the direction of our hotel and ended "Bernie and Gary's Excellent Adventure," at least for the evening.

Wednesday morning we arrived at St Peter's Square at 7:00 a.m.

Both Bernie and I were determined that, at the very least, we were going to get my father close enough to see the Pope. At the gates opened, and the tickets were taken, Bernie dashed off. I walked with my father, now starting to slow down a bit. The last three days were starting to take their toll on him. He had kept right up with us even though we had put in long days. On that day, I could see my father was slowing down a bit. I was hoping that it wasn't because we weren't getting enough accomplished. His eyes lit up when he saw that Bernie had gotten front row seats, though. It was a good thing we had gotten there that early. Within the hour, that square filled up and there wasn't a seat or standing area to be found. So there, on Wednesday morning, we waited. As we would wait, one wheelchair after another would appear. As they started to go by, I looked at my father and he said to me, "Don't even think about it. Those poor people need them to get around. You're not going to put me in one of them before I have to be in one." The three of us had another laugh. Several hours later, with over 75 people in wheelchairs up on stage, and with thousands of people around us, choir music playing, out came The Holy Father, riding in the back of his Popemobile .

My father's face radiated. As the Holy Father was driven by, he was only feet from us. It wasn't good enough for Bernie and I, but for my father, I know it was. I was surprised by the Pope's frailty that day. Yet as frail as he was from disease, he spoke that day in seven languages and I could see that his mind seemed as sharp, as ever. To be there that day with my father, with the square filled with thousands of people chanting, singing and at times in prayer, is a moment frozen in time in my mind. For my father, it was not the "magic pill" that Fr. Connelly spoken of. It was about his faith and his belief that the Pope was a holy man. It was what my father believed in that was important, not what others believed in. You can call it faith or call it a magic pill, or call it whatever you want, but it was healing for my father, and perhaps just a bit for Bernie and me, as well.

As we watched the ceremony ending, and as the VIP sections

would get up to personally greet the Pope, Bernie whispered to me, "Well we're safe with the wheelchair thing anyway, with all those people in them, he's not going to meet them all." He had no sooner said that than a wheelchair was slowly wheeled in front of the Pope. Then one by one each wheelchair was wheeled for a personal greeting. Bernie and I looked at each other, as my father placed his hand on my arm and said, "Don't worry, I wouldn't have done it even if I'd known. Those poor people need those wheelchairs, I don't." I don't think I've had ever seen my father in a prouder moment in my life.

We left the audience and headed back to the Big Brass Doors. This time, Bernie went up to the Swiss guards and tried to drop off another letter, but they wouldn't let him in. My father and I sat in the square and watched Bernie. For almost 30 minutes he would stand there, trying to convince the guards to let him in. We watched his arms flailing trying to use hand signals to get in. He sure tried, but it didn't happen that day. We ended up trying to meet with others that day. Cardinal Ratzinger was one of them. I had sent him several letters, to which he didn't respond. Ratzinger is in charge of the Congregation for the Doctrine of the Faith, which the Pope had named to deal with this issue. We stopped by his offices and dropped of another request for a meeting, to which he never responded, either. The other stop we made that day was at Monsignor Roche. This was our second trip there. We had stopped by on Monday and had met with a wonderful nun, Sister Catherine. She talked with us and promised to hand deliver our letter to him. That Wednesday afternoon, when we arrived, Sr. Catherine was gone. We explained who we were and were asked to wait in the courtyard. A priest approached, walking slowly past us. He said good afternoon and I asked, " I don't suppose you're Monsignor Roche are you?" He replied that he was and stopped. Without asking who we were, he asked if we had seen the grounds. An odd question, I thought, but I said no and he proceeded to give us a grand tour. For 30 minutes we walked and he talked about the olive trees, the birds, the architecture, the coffee and he just went on and on. As his tour wound down, he looked and asked us who we were. When we told him, it was as if we said we were the devil incarnate. He told us that he couldn't help us with anything. "That's not my department. You'll have to ask someone else, all I do is give out tickets here and I don't know what letter you're talking about. You name it, he had an excuse for it. My father just sat and watched, shaking his head. We'd get no help from this guy, it was apparent, and we headed out. Wednesday was winding down. We were leaving early Friday morning, we only Thursday left. We were all getting tired. It felt like we had walked all over Italy and had been beaten up badly, at times. Why was it so difficult to find someone who was willing to listen, and also engage us? What were they so scared of? It only deepened our determination the next day. We got up Thursday and flooded the Vatican with faxes. Every contact phone number and fax number we had received a fax or a phone call from us that morning. And we headed back to the Big Brass Doors again.

This time we decided that perhaps just two of us would be better off trying to get in. I would sit outside as Bernie and my father went in. I watched as Bernie held a box of pastries, and my father held the golden letter, as it had become to be known, approaching the Swiss Guards. In they went. I sat for over two hours that morning. As they came out, my father was smiling, but Bernie wasn't. Their story of their "two hour tour" was worth the wait. Apparently while they waited outside Harvey's office, someone approached them and asked what they were waiting for. The pastries they brought were for the priest who had given us the tickets earlier that week. But Bernie looked at the man asking him and said, "We're here to meet with Bishop Harvey. We have an appointment to deliver this to him and meet with him." The man looked puzzled but led them into another area. There they waited again until a priest that we had all met days earlier walked by. Bernie told my father not to look up and made off like they were in a deep discussion, hoping that the priest didn't recognize them. The priest did a double take though, and their little gig was up. Several minutes later, someone came up and told them that Harvey was unavailable and that he would personally see that their "delivery" was made. As they got up to leave, Bernie decided to knock on a few more doors. Apparently they "accidentally got lost." I could just picture them, walking around opening one door after another, at one point walking into a meeting where they saw "this guy had on all kinds of medals on his chest and a woman in a gown." That couple actually was the Dutch and Duchess of a small country I'd never heard of. Eventually word got around about the "two Americans" lost in the Vatican, and they were politely escorted out the two Brass Doors. As they walked out, I watched the same two Swiss guards who had been stationed by the doors all week turn and speak to them for a few minutes. They had asked Bernie and my father, "So, how far did you guys get today?"

Sometimes you're the windshield, sometimes you're the bug. I'm not sure which was which that day, but they definitely got noticed, as only Bernie and my father could do.

We spent our last afternoon in the Vatican Museum. Several hours of touring the halls took their toll on us. It was beautiful, it was opulent, but it wasn't anything that I could really appreciate. We headed back to our little café, to check our messages. Today there was one. A note was left, which simply said, "The Vatican called, please call back," and there was a number. It's the kind of note we had been waiting for all week. Bernie was the one who returned the call. While he was calling back, I was on another phone calling John Allen. I was trying to get as much information as I could about who it was that had called. When John found out who it was, he said that he would meet us so we could talk at length. My first thought was that they where just sending someone just to appease up. Apparently, I was wrong. By John's account, and his opinion was one we held in high esteem, the person who was coming to see us wasn't just anyone.

I cannot give out details about what happened that evening without divulging details I promised I would not. I'm not really sure which button we had pushed over the previous several days to get a response. No information was volunteered that evening. I also don't know how the information finally flowed to our direction. No information was volunteered about that, either. All I do know is somehow someone got the message - and I was thankful. The video crew that had been following some of our journey that week was there when we got our message. They pleaded with us to let them set up a camera to record the meeting. We declined. That evening, after days of frustration, we finally had an opportunity to meet with someone who had some influence. What followed was an extremely intense meeting that lasted slightly over two hours. It was an open meeting where dialogue flowed both ways. As far as the details, we all agreed to keep certain things private, but the article below was John's account.

Persistent Sex Abuse Victims Get Message From Pope
By JOHN L. ALLEN JR.

At any given time, Rome is swimming with people who believe they have some urgent reason to see the pope. Motives run from the kooky (wanting to brief John Paul on the latest Masonic plot to subvert the Church) to the charming (a Boy Scout troop wants to give the pope an honorary merit badge). I once happened to be standing at the bronze door of the apostolic palace waiting for an appointment, and in a span of no more than twenty minutes five different parties showed up to make their case for being received by the Holy Father.

For most of these folks, the closest they'll ever get to the pope is a Swiss Guard explaining how to get tickets to the Wednesday general audience. Especially these days, John Paul has neither the time nor the physical capacity to meet everyone who wants a piece of his attention.

Thus when Americans Gary Bergeron, his 78-year-old father Joseph, and their friend Bernie McDaid, all from the Boston area, arrived in Rome on March 23 to seek a private meeting with John Paul II, they faced long odds. And in fact, they flew back to Boston the morning of March 28 without any face time with the pontiff.
They took home, however, something that the vast majority of seekers never get: a personal message from the pope, carried to their hotel by one of his senior aides, communicated over the course of a private meeting that stretched over more than an hour.

What makes the Bergerons and McDaid different? All three say they were sexually abused at the hands of Catholic priests, and they came to Rome to try to make the pope understand the nightmare they and the American Catholic Church have lived through.

Gary Bergeron and McDaid are in their early forties, and say they were abused by the same Boston-area priest, Fr. Joseph Birmingham, when they were altar boys. Only after Gary disclosed this experience to his father did Joseph reveal that he, too, had been abused, also when he was an altar boy. The pain of that revelation seems not to have dulled, during a March 24 press conference at Rome's Foreign Press Club, the elder Bergeron did not speak, but wept quietly.
"I would like five minutes to explain what is really going on," Gary Bergeron said that day of his request to see the pope.

In search of those five minutes, the three men spent the better part of a week knocking on doors, making phone calls, and sending faxes. They visited the apostolic palace each morning, to the point that they developed a joking relationship with the Swiss Guards, who would ask them: "How far did you get today?"

All of this activity was complicated by the fact that the tiny hotel they selected on the Via Gracchi, a 10-minute walk from the Vatican, was having problems with its phone system. Hence the three had to go to a coffee bar across the street to make or receive phone calls.

By way of summing up their efforts, Bergeron told me they tried six times to get in touch with Bishop James Harvey, an American who heads the papal household. They left three messages and sent a fax to Bishop Stanislaw Dziwisz, the pope's personal secretary. They left two messages for Cardinal Joseph Ratzinger, the Vatican's top doctrinal official, and two other messages for another official in Ratzinger's office. They also sent two letters to Fr. Ciro Benedettini, the deputy director of the Vatican press office.

The result? Nothing. No response.

To be fair, Bergeron told me, the people at the American embassy to the Vatican were helpful, and one English-speaking Vatican official did take an interest in their situation, apologizing that he couldn't do more to help. Yet by mid-afternoon Thursday, facing a return flight home and with little to show, the three men were feeling stymied by what Bergeron jokingly called "a Roman hex."

Then the phone at the coffee bar rang. It was Msgr. James Green, newly appointed as the head of the English desk in the Secretariat of State. It's an important job with access to the pope, previous occupants include the current head of the papal household, the secretary of the Council for Promoting Christian Unity, and the Archbishop of St. Louis.

"We understand you want something from us,"

McDaid said Green told him. Green declined comment on the story. McDaid said he briefly explained why they wanted to see the pope. Green was cautious, but offered to come see them that evening at 6:30. McDaid said Green was concerned that there not be any lawyers, McDaid assured him they would be alone.

As a footnote, Vatican officials at Green's level don't just hop into cars and go see the Boy Scouts and the conspiracy theorists clamoring to see the pope. His willingness to meet the three men signaled above-average interest.
When Green arrived, along with a second American priest, he opened the meeting with an "Our Father." At the end of the session, Joseph Bergeron, who describes himself as a very devout Catholic, asked for a blessing. The group also prayed the "Hail Mary." Green passed out rosaries.

In the end, Bergeron told me, the meeting was "very intense, very emotional, very good." Green, Bergeron said, wanted to know what they made of the U.S. Bishops' new sex abuse norms, their views about Bishop Richard Lennon (the interim replacement for Cardinal Bernard Law), and in general about the climate in Boston and the American Church. "Everything was on the table," Bergeron said.

The most unexpected development came when Green told the men he had a "direct message" for them from John Paul II. "The Holy Father realizes the seriousness of this problem, and is doing all he can," Bergeron said Green told them, saying they were free to share the message with other victims. "He will continue to do all he can to heal the Church and to pray for the victims. He will see that this doesn't happen again."

Bergeron said Green then told them that the pope had also directed him to bring back messages from the three men that very night. Joseph Bergeron went first. "The Holy Father needs to make sure that this never, ever, ever happens to another child," he told Green.

McDaid followed. "The Holy Father needs to heal the Church, not just the survivors but the Church itself. He needs to realize how the Church in the United States is hurting." Gary Bergeron concluded. "The Holy Father needs to put a face with the problem, meaning he needs to meet with us," he said. "If not me, meet with my father. If not him, then some survivor that he can associate with the problem. Only then will he understand the depth of the wound."

Bergeron said Green seemed "adamant" that they were unlikely to get a meeting with the pope. Yet Bergeron told him they planned to be back in Rome on July 29, his father's birthday, and would come knocking on the door again. "Maintain your courage," Bergeron says Green told them.

We had finally gotten something accomplished, though we fell short of our plans to meet with the Pope. We were also committed to a return trip. We all slept well that evening. As we awoke the next morning, there was a package left for me. It was a note with package containing several sets of rosaries. The note read, "Gary, these rosaries from the Holy Father are a momento of your visit."

With that, we headed back to the airport, and we headed home.

Mission accomplished, partly. So, the three musketeers, or the three stooges, depending on who's opinion you follow, made it from Boston to the Vatican, and home safely. At the very least, we were able to open a direct link for dialogue with the Vatican. I wasn't sure how much weight our trip would have on the upcoming days. But since that trip, I have not hesitated to write to those that we met when something is not as it should be at the Archdiocese of Boston. I would find myself writing and faxing more and more letters in the weeks following our return, as things in Boston were not going well.

19.

Returning to Boston, the only good news was that Olan was out of the hospital and recovering well from his surgery. He would be in and out of the hospital several more times over the next few months, however, I could continue to see the stress affecting all of us. Bernie was in the middle of moving out of his house and separating from his partner of 27 years. Olan was having trouble with several medical problems and I was dog-tired. I had lost a little weight and came down with bronchitis. Our bodies were telling us "enough already." Part-time diplomats, part-time advocates, part-time social workers and part-time referees -it was all taking its toll on us. Over a year had passed and thus far, there was still no end in sight. Legally, we had given the Archdiocese a 90-day extension, which was ending without anything being accomplished. For our attorneys, there was only one case that was not part of the stand down.

The Ford case was proceeding with litigation. Tactically, it was a good idea. I understood that there still needed to be someone on the outside applying legal pressure. Without it, the Archdiocese would just drag their feet. We would find out that even with that case, they would drag their feet as well. While Bishop Lennon promised to ease the litigation and focus on mediation and spiritual healing, time and time again, just the opposite would happen. In the months since he had taken oven, the situation had backtracked and things like the deposition of therapists were going on. Personally, I didn't have an issue with my therapist being deposed, considering I was suing the Archdiocese. If they wanted to depose my therapist, then that was fine with me. Perhaps then they could understand what my life had been like and what damage was caused because of this abuse. Maybe if they spoke to a professional, one that I selected from their list, they would understand and start to believe. In the early spring, I had stopped going to my therapist. I had missed several appointments, which, as a rule, therapists frown on. I planned to go back, just not then. I still didn't have an issue with her being deposed. She had enough information on my life and me.

I did believe, however, that by deposing a therapist, Lennon was going back on his word. The reality of his decision was that when word got out about this, the majority of survivors simply stopped going to therapy. This was horrendous. For many survivors, their therapists were the only people that they talked to. Their therapists were their lifelines and that lifeline was gone. Practically speaking, this meant that Olan, Bernie and myself would be receiving more and more phone calls. Whenever someone was in "crisis" mode, one of our phones would ring. If they didn't get Olan, they'd call me. If they didn't get me, they'd call Bernie. It also resulted in phone calls from other survivors whom we hadn't heard of before. We started getting calls from survivors who were represented by attorneys other than our own. More often than not, those phone calls would turn into morning coffee with them. And very often, those morning coffees would happen several times a week. One of the things that our firm had done was hire a full time licensed social worker, Diane Nealon, who became part of the Greenberg team in the spring of 2002. In Catholic terms, she was a godsend. I am not aware of any other firm that hired someone with similar qualifications to help their clients. It was one of the most applauded decisions that our firm had made. Applauded especially by Olan, Bernie and myself. She was able to handle an incredible load of the phone calls and support questions. Whenever we had a problem that was over our head - and there were plenty of them - we called Diane. Unfortunately many of the survivors that we were hearing from were not represented by our firm and did not have that support mechanism in place. While I was talking to my legal team more than several times a week, some of the survivors I would meet had only talked to their attorneys on one or two rare occasions. I was shocked when I found out that attorneys representing hundreds of survivors had almost no contact with their clients, let alone offered a support person like Diane. Bishop Lennon's decision about deposing the therapists had an incredibly damaging effect on many men and women.

The other legal maneuver that Lennon played out was the First Amendment right in which attorneys for the Archdiocese presented pleadings in court that all of the cases against the Archdiocese be dismissed based on the First Amendment rights of separation of church and state. As each month passed it became more and more apparent that Lennon was not the type of leader that was going to lead us anywhere, except further away from an ending to this.

Spiritually, as far as I was concerned, there was nothing coming from the Archdiocese, as well. Lennon had instituted a set of "healing ceremonies" throughout the Archdiocese. At the first one, less than 80 people showed up. When Lennon asked for delegates from each parish come to mass on Ash Wednesday at the Cathedral, less than 100 showed up, and that included 70 priests. How could a man suggest healing the people one week and be pushing damaging legal tactics the next week? They just didn't get it. I had given up on Lennon. After the responses I received in January and after watching the legal maneuvering for the previous four or five months, I had no confidence in him, whatsoever. Olan, the eternal optimist, continued to push for solutions. I was definitely odd man out at the Archdiocese. I didn't mind it, not at all. I knew that Lennon was not there to stay. In one of the meetings at the Vatican, we were told point blank, "Don't worry, Lennon will be replaced by Labor Day." Well for me, Labor Day wouldn't come fast enough. Even though Lennon had agreed to meet with the mediators in a mediation session, it hadn't happened. It was nonsensical that the Archdiocese had hired a mediation team to help mediate and then refused to meet with them. In other words, for the entire 90-day stand down period, there was never a time when anyone from the Archdiocese attended a mediation session. It was utterly ridiculous. Even the mediators said that they had never ever been involved in something so ludicrous. The 90-day stand down was coming to an end and absolutely nothing was accomplished. As that date drew closer and closer, it seemed like further litigation just had to happen. Each day there would be a round of phone calls. There were continued pleas with Lennon's office to work with the mediators. "It doesn't matter what you have, just put something on the table, even if it's a $1.28 put something on the table here so that another 90 days wasn't wasted."

I continued to work the Vatican, Bernie continued to work the parish meetings at local churches. Several weeks before the stand down was over, I sent over a letter to Rome along with 20 articles condemning the Archdiocese that had been printed in the news within the previous week. One week before the stand down was over, I faxed several contacts at the Vatican, including Monsignor Green, with a letter informing them of the climate in Boston. I told them about getting no resolution and I also told them something else. In the Birmingham lawsuit, the first thing filed at the end of the 90-day stand down would be a court order requesting all documents relating to sexual abuse between the Archdiocese of Boston and the Vatican. This motion had been filed in January but had been held off because of the 90-day stand down. No one knew what was in those files. One thing was for certain though, if the Boston Archdiocese didn't bother to examine what the files contained of the 150+ priests that they had turned over, then the Vatican didn't know what was in their files either. I was sure that they didn't want to find out. I was also sure that they didn't want anyone else finding out either.

Lennon had been given an option. On Friday, three days before the stand down ended, he was told that we would agree to an additional 30-day stand down under the following conditions: 1)

That he publicly ask for the stand down himself. 2.) That he or someone with his authority attend the mediation. 3) That they make some type of offer to settle the cases against them, regardless of the amount. On Monday morning, Lennon had agreed to all three terms. We all had another 30 days. It was also agreed that there would be weekly mediation meetings for that month and that several survivors would be at those meetings representing the more than 500 men and women who had filed suit. The three men that were asked to attend were Olan, Bernie, and myself. I fully realized what a precarious position we were being placed in. Not only were the three representatives who had been selected all from the same law firm, but the same priest, Birmingham, also victimized them. These mediations were held under extremely strict confidence. I didn't have an issue with that. I can only imagine what the friendly advocacy groups would say if they knew who was attending.

We had held off war, for at least another 30 days, but just barely. The four meetings that were planned ended up being only two meetings. The first one was basically a posturing meeting which Olan did not attend. It was the first time in a year and a half when all parties were represented in a room at one time. The Archdiocese and their attorneys, survivors and their attorneys, and the mediators were present. It seemed endlessly fruitless. Our attorneys would ask a probing question and Rogers would walk around in circle after circle not answering it. Then another question, and another, and then another circle and another. I had no patience for this. I started asking direct questions and tempers started to flare. I didn't care. I wasn't there to be a diplomat. I was there feeling the weight of 500 people on my shoulders. "You keep saying that you're waiting for the insurance companies to kick in. Well, to be blunt, I don't care about the insurance companies. I wasn't molested by the insurance companies, nor were the 500 people we are all here representing. I don't want to hear about the insurance companies. Tell me what YOU are prepared to do. What's your back up plan?" There was silence. "Come on, you have to have a plan in case the insurance companies back out of this. What's the back up plan? What are YOU prepared to do?" They didn't have an answer. The fact is they weren't prepared to do anything. They were stalling for time. That's all they did was kill another two hours of time. Before the meeting ended, I said to Rogers and to Fr. Connelly as well, "I realize that this was just a meet and greet, but you guys have 28 days. You don't want to meet next week, which means the next time we meet you'll only have 14 days left. I hope by then you can come in here with something more than promises. It's been a year and a half you've got 28 days left to do something."

Tick tock went the clock. Each day would go by, and there would be more phone calls, but no action. There would be more meetings with Fr. John and there would be more faxing to the Vatican. Nothing seemed to move them, though. The stress level at all our homes was at an all time high. My salvation was my weekend visits with my son. If not for them, I'm not sure how I would have kept my sanity. If not for him, I'm not sure I would have stuck it out so long. But every other weekend, I would get that reminder from him. It was like a voice in my head, saying, "Don't let it happen to me." Sometimes I thought it was Evan's voice. Other times it seemed like my voice, but my voice 30 years ago. Whatever it was, I wasn't backing away now. I just kept plugging. At times, we looked at each other and talked about how crazy we were for taking this on. "Life was so much easier in that fog, huh?" one of us would inevitably say. Olan had been, more or less demoted, in his job, I was unemployed, and Bernie was now out of his home and in an apartment. What had we gotten ourselves into? Thankfully, most of the time, we were so busy we didn't have time to ask that question very often. It seemed like every time one of us would talk about taking some time off, we'd get yet another call asking for help getting someone into rehab, asking for an interview, listening to a new voice talk about their abuse.

For me, those were the hardest. I remember how hard it was for me to make that first call. Talking into the phone, leaving a message to Bob Sherman's voice mail for the first time, that was hard enough. I was still getting almost daily calls from survivors of abuse, who were telling their story for the first time. It wasn't just me, Bernie and Olan got their share, as well. For me, these calls were the most draining. Each time, whether it was a new person, or someone I knew who wasn't in therapy, I was emotionally drained. I couldn't keep doing this, but I didn't have it in me to say no to them. Sometimes I didn't want to be the spokesperson anymore, I just wanted to be me. I was beginning to wonder, more times than I care to think about, who the real me was.

Our next mediation meeting went no better than the first. They were talking about insurance companies and we kept talking about real people with real lives. They still had no back up plan. All they had was this "trust me" answer that they used again and again. The second meeting was even shorter than the first. The only concrete thing that I got from that meeting was a promise. It came from Wilson Rogers, Jr., straight from his mouth and directed to me. I even asked the mediator to explain it to me twice, so I was sure I got it correctly. The last thing that was said at that meeting was this, "To answer your question, I'm telling you that regardless of what the insurance companies come up with, we hope to have a reasonable offer by the 27th, which I realize is the last day. But I'm telling you this, that regardless of what the insurance companies come up with, we will have an offer to present to you on the 27th. I'm telling you this. I hope you understand it. We will present whatever we can to you on the 27th. You have to trust me. I'm working on this as hard as possible and we will present an offer on the 27th."

Now I'm not sure about anyone else, but I thought he said that on the 27th of June he was going to present an offer, regardless of what it was. Hmmmmmmm, funny. Everyone else thought he'd said the same thing. We were hopeful, but we were careful, as well. A week later, Bishop Lennon would publicly say during television interviews that there would be an offer within the week.

The 27th would come and even as Olan worked the powers that be at the chancery as hard as ever, no offer came through. Nothing. It came and went, and the only thing that happened was Bishop Lennon released a written statement saying that they were unable to reach an agreement with their insurance companies. That weekend was one of the longest two days in quite a while. Litigation was about to start up. The following Monday morning, over 150 pages of requests for depositions were about to be delivered to the Archdiocese. But the warm winds of Rome, the winds we had felt in March at the Vatican, were finally about find their way to Boston.

On Tuesday, July 1st, Sean O'Malley, Bishop of Palm Beach, was named as the permanent replacement to Cardinal Law, replacing interim apolostalic administrator Bishop Lennon. Somebody had finally made a decision. It was about time. Rumors about his appointment had started Monday, the day before. Our friend John Allen had broken the story. I was working around the house that day when my cell phone started to ring. I was being asked my opinion of someone I had no opinion of. That Tuesday I was feeling all kinds of emotions. I was relieved that someone had finally been named. I was also furious about the previous five months of rhetoric that we had been going through. I was also feeling hopeful. By all accounts, Bishop O'Malley was the right man for the job. Even Eric, who hadn't spoken favorably about any Catholic official in a long time, was extremely pleased with this choice. "He's the one man that can get this job done," was Eric's first statement about O'Malley. I was a bit more reserved and said publicly that I was "cautiously optimistic" about this choice. I was waiting to see what actions he would take before I heaped on praise. As I watched him during his first public outing, I was struck by the difference between the styles of the past and the style of the present. Gone was the grandiose style of pomp and circumstance of his predecessor. He wore the simple brown cloak of his denomination similar to St. Francis of Assisi. I was optimistic about his humble style and that humility seemed to radiate. By appearance this was a different man for the job, but I had learned too much information in the last 18 months to believe anything on face value.

Suddenly, it was if I was the bad cop in the press. Everyone was praising this choice and in interview after interview I held out judgment. O'Malley would waste no time in beginning to prove himself, though. During his first visit to Boston that week, he would meet with a group of survivors. Although I wasn't present at that meeting, I was impressed by those who did attend. Olan, Bernie and Tom Blanchette were there. The Ford family was also invited, as were others. This was a fair group of survivors and I was sure that they represented all survivors more than adequately that day.

Bishop O'Malley's soon added his own personal attorney into the mix. This was also another step in the right direction. There was definitely no love lost between survivors, their attorneys, and the Rogers law firm who had represented the Archdiocese for over 30 years. I believed, and had said publicly, that the Rogers firm was part of the problem. They could never be part of the solution. They weren't out yet, but it was clear that O'Malley was going to make choices with which we were starting to agree. This was a wonderful change from the status quo. As O'Malley prepared for his future as the Archbishop of Boston, I was preparing for the grand jury report from our attorney general Tom Reilly. I was also preparing for our return trip to Rome that was less than a month away. Since the announcement of a new Archbishop, I had thought about putting off the trip until the fall. My father was actually the one to suggest it to me. "Why don't you meet with him first and give him a chance." I thought about it hard and long. On one hand it didn't matter who the new Bishop was. The dialogue that we established needed to be maintained. I still felt strongly about someone needing to make that personal connection with the Pope. It was about putting a face on the tragedy that the Church had caused. I also still felt that with all the challenges that the Pope had incurred in his lifetime, it would truly be a tragedy if, like Cardinal Law, this became his legacy. In the end, the decision was left again to fate. A week before I finalized the details of our return trip, I received a phone call. It was from the Archdiocese asking if my father and I would like to attend the installation of Bishop O'Malley. Again, walking a tight rope, I realized that whatever I did now, I could be criticized, either way. If I didn't go, it would seem as if the Archdiocese was reaching out and I was not accepting. If I did accept, it would seem as though I was playing patsy to the Church again.

Before I decided on that question, the Attorney General's report would come out. Tom Reilly, the Attorney General of Massachusetts, had convened a grand jury that had been looking into the sexual abuse of children by the Archdiocese of Boston. The grand jury had been investigating for over 14 months and the long-awaited report was going to be published. I had met with Tom in mid-January. Not under a subpoena. He had requested a meeting. I had pretty much realized that there would no be any indictments because of the way the laws of the past were written. I had expected as much to be said by Tom. I also knew that this would not please many survivors. I was not among them. I fully realized that his job was not to bend the law, but to uphold it. It was equal justice under the law, equal for all. The same law that others wanted to be "creatively interpreted" to go after the leaders at fault, could have been "creatively interpreted" to go after anyone else. That's not what I wanted. Equal justice under the law also meant equal protection under the law. Justice is a double-edged sword and I accept that. Was I disappointed that there would be no charges? Yes, but I accepted it under the same scales of justice that would protect all of us. I also believed that even though it seemed that the cardinals, bishops and priests were going to escape the criminal court system, they were not going to escape the civil court system. Nor were they going to escape the court of public opinion.

I was prepared for the lack of indictments by the grand jury. I was not prepared for the press conference that Tom Reilly held. Sitting alone on my couch that day, I watched a public official, for the first time tell it like it was. I watched and listened as Tom spoke about the crime of sexual abuse of children at the hands of the Archdiocese of Boston. It was the first time any public official had ever stood up and spoke with exacting details. I listened and heard the anger and compassion, which I had felt for so long, coming from someone else, and that someone was the attorney general. The 75+-page report detailed the actions and inactions of priests, bishops, cardinals and the Archdiocese, in general. It was one of the most emotional days I had had in the last year and a half.

Maybe it was that I wanted affirmation that I was doing the right thing. Maybe it was that someone was just finally standing up and saying, "This is wrong." Words that I had been waiting to hear for a very long time. Whatever the reason, his statements and that report, resonated deep inside me, and it moved me. It moved many of us. The report outlined the horrendous behavior of not only Joseph Birmingham, but also those who allowed him years of unobstructed access to children. It talked of Cardinal Law, Bishop McCormack, Bishop Banks, Bishop Dailey, and many others. It was published by the state, it had weight, and I finally felt as though someone had listened.

Between the attorney general's report and the invitation to the installation of Bishop O'Malley, I would again find myself, like many survivors between a rock and a hard place. I had been there before. This time, however, it seemed just a little tighter fit. Publicly, I supported the report, which didn't sit well with some of the advocacy groups. I would applaud his decision to follow the letter and intent of the law and I would also applaud his decision to publish the report. Others would publicly say, "He should have found a way to get somebody in jail." However, there was no way he could have justifiably done that. As I thought would happen, I was criticized for not being hard enough about Reilly's report. I had never worried about what people thought when I had come forward over a year before, I wasn't concerned then. Did the criticism hurt? At times, yes. Would I be criticized again? I didn't anticipate how my personal decision to go to the installation would outrage so many but I would soon find out.

The email opinions about those invited to the installation of Bishop O'Malley started as soon as it was made public. The vast majority of the emails I received, some anonymous, were against going. Not only was I asked not to go, but also I was told that I shouldn't go. There were literally hundreds of emails about it. I had decided that I was going to attend for many reasons. Some were deeply spiritual for me. Regardless of what had happened over the last 30 years of my life, I still wanted to believe that someone had finally arrived representing the Archdiocese who would do the right thing. Maybe it was called hope and maybe it was hopeless. I just wanted to believe in it, I just had to believe in it. I wasn't sure if Bishop O'Malley was the real deal. I had no idea if he was the man that could lead our community into a better place and bring about the healing that was so desperately needed. I didn't know if he could do all that and more, but what if he was the man? Out of all the Church officials I had met over the previous 16 months, Bishop O'Malley was the first official to ask me to come to Church. That may not seem like anything to some people, but it was a huge thing for me. I was going and my parents were coming with me, as well. It would be the first time in decades that I would walk into a mass with my parents. Over the previous 16 months, I had tried to be as fair as possible regarding decisions that the Archdiocese had made. I tried to do that both privately and publicly. In the press I tried to be as fair as I could. Some may or may not believe that. When I talked publicly about mistakes the Archdiocese would continue to make, I was viewed as someone who wasn't happy with anything. When I publicly thanked them for doing the right thing, I was too soft on the Church. There was no pleasing everyone. All I could do was try to be true to what I set out to do. Bob would say it was "speaking from your heart." Catholics call it "following your conscience." My heart was telling me to go. It was an extremely unpopular decision. It seemed like the hate mail that I had received when I first started meeting with Cardinal Law was being sent again. The only thing different was the date on the email.

I had made my decision and I felt good about it. My parents were so pleased about going. Like me, they still wanted to believe. I guess, as a parent, the one thing that you can't afford to lose is hope. If you lose hope, you give away your child's future. We would all go that day. I had crossed picket lines in the months before and had survived. This day would be no different. An olive branch was finally being extended by the Archdiocese and I was not going to turn my back on it, regardless of how many times I felt that they turned their back on my family. The installation of the new bishop was about hope, hope in my children's future, in my parents healing, and in finding some peace in my soul, as well.

If Bishop O'Malley was not going to do the right thing, I would be knocking at the chancery door, just as before. I would give him this day though. I would give him an opportunity before I would pass judgment. I would also be there to be the same "presence," as Olan called it, that we had been whenever we met and talked with the Archdiocese. As with Law, McCormack, and the rest, you could be on the outside of the Church doors and when they are closed, no one inside hears you. Or you could sit inside, in their home, where they have to look at you, and they can't ignore you. I had long discussions about my decision to go with lots of people. I wasn't sure about the legal aspect of it and how my decision would affect the others survivors, how the public would react, and what effect that might have, as well. Bob and I had a long talk about it, too. Both he and Eric said that it was a personal decision. Some of their clients who had received invitations were going, some were not. Independently, they supported both decisions. Bob ended up saying, "Gary, you know what this will mean for your father to go. You know what your heart is saying, just follow it. Forget about everything else having to do with it, follow your heart, and call me when it's over." I was going.

Along with my parents, Julie, my girlfriend of the past three years, would be going with me. It would be the first time that she had ever attended any event surrounding anything having to do with the Church. That had been my decision, not hers. This day was something different, I just had that kind of feeling. I'm not sure if it's because I had never wanted to share the ugliness of it with her, or because it was such a personal and deep issue that I was dealing with. Perhaps it was because I felt as though there may be a corner that was being turned and finally a positive step was about to be taken.

That Wednesday, my father and I headed in early. My mother and Julie would meet us there later on. I chose to head in early so that I could be sure that my parents had a decent seat. It was open seating and I knew that more tickets than seats had been extended. I hadn't slept the night before, anxiety had taken over. I was looking forward to going, yet I was still worried about my parents dealing with the ceremony, as well as having to cross the picket lines and pass by protestors as well. I knew that there would be plenty of protestors out that day but I was also told that it would be a quiet and respectful protest. Regardless, I was concerned about how my parents would handle it all.

Arriving at 8:00 a.m., the protestors were already in full force. With three hours to go, my dad and I had grabbed coffee and walked around a bit. By 9:00, the sidewalk was filling up with people in line. Protestors and news cameras were milling around, as well. Bernie and his mother were there, as were public officials. At times there were literally hundreds of priests, bishops, and nuns. It was a strange feeling standing in front of a Church with all these "Catholics" around me. All the while the protestors were chanting and screaming, holding their signs and using their bullhorns. I wasn't so sure about a respectful and peaceful protest anymore.

As the doors opened, people headed in, my father and Bernie's mother, among them. I had made sure that my father was settled and then headed outside to wait for my mother and Julie. If standing outside with my father was strange, standing alone was even stranger. I was not planning on doing any interviews at this point so I was standing away from the cameras. As far as I was concerned, I was just a guy in a suit standing in front of a Church smoking a cigarette. One by one, people started to come up to me, shake my hand and thank me for what I had done. There were survivors whom I didn't know. There were priests, and even bishops coming my way. It was the strangest thing that had happened to me in a long time. I didn't know what to do or say. I wanted to head inside and avoid it all together but I knew that my mother was on her way and I couldn't leave. They just kept coming and coming. In hindsight, it would help me get through the rest of the day. A day that didn't go so well.

Perhaps it was my suit, or perhaps the priests and bishops talking to me that set them off. I don't know what it was. At some point the protestors turned to my direction and I heard some yelling, "Bergeron, you, hypocrite." I just turned away. It had happened before, no biggie. It wasn't over though. At one point, my father came out to get some air, and as I walked with him, another chant of "Bergeron, yea, you know who you are, you hypocrite." But this time, we were spit at. For an instant, just an instant, I was about to lose all control. I felt that rage that I hadn't felt in a long, long time. It wasn't the fact that I was spit at, it wasn't even the fact that cameras were there taping it all, it was the fact that my father was there with me. It was just an instant, and then the rage was gone. I just looked at the man in the eye who had spit at me and I felt sorry for him. I walked away. I wasn't the only one that day to receive the badge of spit. Unfortunately, it happened to other survivors, as well. So much pain and so much healing to do. At one point, I watched Bishop Lennon standing on the stairs. I walked up and extended my hand. He looked at me, a bit stunned, and said, " I remember you, but I can't remember your name." I looked at him and said, "I'm Gary Bergeron and I just wanted to say hello." I held his grip for a second too long and watched as he stumbled to say something. He tried and I just said, "I just wanted to say hello." Watching him turn red, I walked away. Several months before, when I had met with Fr. John Connelly regarding my father and the Vatican, I had given Fr. John something to give to Bishop Lennon. That day in January, as the meeting had quickly wound up, I pulled out a set of framed pictures. It was a simple clear frame with pictures of my son, my daughter, and my granddaughter. I gave them to Fr. John and simply said, "John, will you please hand this to the Bishop and tell him that everything I've done this past year and everything I will do about this, I do to protect these kids. I'll never do anything to embarrass them and I'll never stop until I feel that I've done everything I can to make sure that this never happens to them or any other child. Please give Bishop Lennon that message." Apparently Bishop Lennon forgot.

If history does have a habit of repeating itself, then this is definitely the repeat of Watergate. Different institution, but the same players. In my mind, Cardinal Law will be remembered as the Richard Nixon of the Church. He didn't do anything that his predecessors hadn't done, yet he didn't stop doing what they had done either. In my mind, Bishop Lennon will be remembered as Gerald Ford. The, at times, stumbling assistant brought in to steady the boat until a leader is found. Like Ford, Lennon did nothing to rock the boat, nothing to steer the boat, just kept it afloat.

As Julie and my mother arrived, we walked in, sat, and watched the procession start. Holy Cross Cathedral was sweltering that day. It was filled to capacity with over 2,500 people there. This was not how I remembered the Cathedral the last time I was there. When Olan and I were there the previous fall to confront Cardinal Law, it was nearly empty. Today was different. Every single seat was occupied and there were several hundred people standing. With the choir singing, the long ceremony began. Hundreds of priests, bishops and cardinals walked two abreast down that aisle. Several of them stopped at my pew, shook my hand, and thanked me for coming. It was a touching moment. As the choir continued singing and the sun beamed into the brilliant stain glass windows of the cathedral, Bishop Sean O'Malley, the new Archbishop of Boston, walked down the aisle. The church erupted in applause that was loud and long. Everyone was ready for a change. Everyone was ready for a new leader. Everyone welcomed him. Everyone, including, me.

As the mass started, I kept an eye on my father. I knew my mother was going to be okay, since she was always the rock. It was my father I was concerned about. I knew that this was going to be as emotional for him, as it was for me. I was 41, he had just turned 78 the day before. He looked tired, but seemed to be doing okay with the heat. As the ceremony went on, I waited to hear what Bishop O'Malley had to say in his sermon. It seemed like an eternity but I can tell you that this was one time I felt as though it was worth waiting for.

As Bishop O'Malley started to speak, the realization started to sink in that O'Malley was not Cardinal Law. As he would speak, I witnessed a humility and sense of compassion I had searched for such a long time. Yes, these were just words, but they were just words with feelings. I heard him speak of "the crime of sexual abuse of children." I had never heard the word crime spoken by a Church leader before. He talked about healing, about protection, about feeding the hungry and clothing the naked. He would talk about healing the sick and healing the abused. He would beg for forgiveness and plead for people to come back to their Church. You could feel the spirit of hope throughout the church that day.

It was the first time in so long I felt the sense of community which had been missing from my life for so long. It didn't mean that the pain was gone, or that everything was going to be okay from then on, but it did make me feel good to be there, listening to those words with my family and friends. Time and time again, applause would erupt as he talked. He would laugh at himself, and the people would laugh with him. Maybe, just maybe, the right person was among us that day. It was much to soon to know, it was only one moment in time, but I was optimistic, for the first time in years.

Shortly after the sermon ended, I saw my father waver out of the corner of my eye. The heat had gotten to him and he was about to pass out. I grabbed his arm and we both walked to the back of the Church, heading outside. As we walked, my father stumbled several times and all I could think about was him collapsing in the middle of the isle. The further he walked, the more weight he put on me. We did make it, without him collapsing, but just barely. I got him outside and he sat on the steps. He was pale white, and in an instant I realized how tough this had been on him. I saw a mighty man and an elderly man at the same time. As the paramedic rushed over, loosening his tie, he kept saying, "I'm okay, I'm okay, I just needed some air." With two paramedics working on him, putting heart monitors on him, and giving him water, my father looked up and said, " I don't want to miss communion." The paramedics looked at me, and didn't know what to say. They got water into him, but said that he needed to get checked, I knew that there was no way that was going to happen. He said that he needed some cool air, or something to eat and he'd be okay. Looking over, I saw the line of camera trucks and realized that they had to be air-conditioned. I walked my father across the street, to the chanting and screaming of the protestors. And so, with the ceremony going on, my father sat inside the air-conditioned news truck of Channel 5, ate a donut, drank some water and rested. After several minutes, the camera man stuck his head out and said, "He said he wants to receive communion. Ummm, what do you want me to do?" My dad and I walked back across the street and sat down on the steps again. Helping him up so that he could receive communion, I spent five minutes convincing him that even though he had a donut, at his age it was okay and he could receive. I watched out of the corner of my eye as several priests overheard my reasoning. I told my father that he could ask one of them if he didn't believe me. They all just looked at us and finally one nodded. With that, I helped my father, took his arm in mine, and walked him back down the aisle in the cathedral so that he wouldn't miss communion. Then I walked him back outside where we waited until the installation was over.

As the church emptied the reporters over took the sidewalk. Though I had not planned on doing any interviews that day, as I watched the protestors ranting and raving, I changed my mind. "Today, I may have heard a leader of the Archdiocese for the first time speak from his heart. If he continues to speak from his heart, and listen to his heart, and lead with his heart, we may find ourselves in a better place in time." Suddenly with my family watching and a reporter asking what I thought of O'Malley's sermon, a female protestor came running over, screaming. She was totally out of control screaming about the Church and the survivors, although truthfully, I couldn't understand all of what she was screaming about. I looked back at the camera for a minute and simply said, "I think the new Archbishop has a lot of work ahead of him."

I looked back at my father who was obviously feeling better. That day, I was feeling better, as well. We would all go to the chancery grounds that day for the reception. It was truly a different kind of experience. It had been a long time since I was among so many priests, bishops, nuns, and just plain Catholics and on that day, they were smiling. We would also meet the new bishop that day, face to face. We didn't feel uncomfortable, we didn't have the door closed on us. On that day, the door was opened wide. As I introduced Bishop O'Malley to my mother and father, I watched both my parents fill up with emotion, as did I, as our hands reached out to the other.

Later that evening, Bob called me and asked me how the day went. "I had a good day today, Bob," I replied. "Tell me," he said. "Well, do you want me to start with the spitting, or my father fainting, or the screaming woman?" I said, with a little chuckle. "Well, Gary, without evening knowing the story, any time you can say you had a good day after mentioning spitting, fainting, and screaming, it makes me wonder what your days are like when it's not a good day." We both laughed, and then I said, "Bob, with all that happened, today was a good day." It was a good day. Maybe the Church turned a corner that day. Maybe, just maybe, we all did.

The fallout continued regarding my decision on going inside the church that Wednesday, as opposed to staying outside. I kind of expected that it would. Here we were, almost a year and a half later, after all the things that survivors had struggled with and after all of the combined efforts of the advocacy groups, as well. For all intents and purposes, individually and collectively, we had challenged one of the biggest establishments in the world, yet some were so caught up in the heat of the battle, that they failed to respect the rights of others.

There were some who believed it was inappropriate to tell a survivor he was out of bounds. "You have to let him be angry, he's a victim," was the usual reply. That didn't sit well with me. Everyone gets angry at one time or another, but everyone doesn't make an ass of themselves, and everyone doesn't spit on people. They were supposed to be advocates. I didn't know what they were advocating that Wednesday. What I had set out to do when I first came forward was what guided me each day. Find out the truth, protect my children and heal. It was always that plain to me. Everything else that came along, I dealt with using that as a guideline. We had found out the truth, and were continuing to do so. By coming forward, we began to educate the public about sexual abuse of children and in doing so were able to get legislation enacted. My healing would come day by day and it was up to me to decide that path.

Wednesday was a step on that path. Over the long months that passed, I also realized what was, and what was not, a part of real healing. Anger, compensation, forgiveness and justice were all a part of healing. Vengeance was not. It wasn't when I started the journey, it certainly isn't at that point, either. For some though, the fact that I walked in those church doors wasn't about my healing. It was about their anger with the church. While some protestors spit and others screamed and taunted everyone in their sight, others with them stood by. No one had the courage to stand up and simply say, "You're wrong in doing that," Thirty years ago, a priest by the name of Joseph Birmingham abused me. He would go on to abuse many other children while his fellow priests looked on and did nothing. To them it was okay, he was a priest.

A few days after the installation ceremony, Bob called and asked how I was doing. Although I had developed a pretty thick skin, he knew what had happened at the installation had bothered me. He was right, it bothered me deeply. Not because it was directed at me, but because it had happened with the whole world watching. Bob and I talked for a long time that day. He reminded me of everything that had been accomplished during the previous 18 months. Many things had changed and slowly we were not only changing the future, we were protecting it as well. At some point he said to me, "Gary, that spit is a badge of honor. I want you to know that you're in good company. You're not the only one who got spit on when trying to bring about change. I want you to remember that men like Martin Luther King were spit on. So was Gandhi and, if you remember, they spit on Jesus Christ, as well." I knew he was saying that to make me feel better. "Bob, I want you to remember that those three men you just mentioned were all killed. If that's your idea of a pep talk, call me later." I still had a lot of living to do.

The day following his installation, Bishop O'Malley removed Wilson Rogers as lead attorney for the Archdiocese. The Thursday following his installation he announced that he would not be living at the palatial residence at the chancery. He decided that he would be residing in the rectory of the Holy Cross Cathedral, which is in a middle class residential neighborhood. That same Thursday he announced that he would be saying mass the following Saturday at Saint Michael's Church in Lowell. Coming to Lowell was something that we had asked both Cardinal Law and Bishop Lennon to do. Bishop O'Malley had decided to come without our asking. On Friday, less than 10 days after his installation, an initial settlement offer of $55 million dollars was presented by Bishop O'Malley to resolve the cases that had been filed against the Archdiocese. One step at a time, the new Archbishop was taking appropriate steps in the right direction. The dollar numbers weren't impressive to me. What was impressive is that there was no talk of insurance companies. What was also impressive was that he had accomplished more in 10 days than his two predecessors had accomplished in the previous 20 months.

I had a harder decision about attending the mass at Saint Michael's than I did about going to his installation. Part of me said that I should not go and let the community of Saint Michael's enjoy their day. I didn't want to be the focal point of the day. I was high profile enough as it was. I also was concerned that if I didn't go, it would be seen as a snub to the new Archbishop, as well as my father's parish pastor Fr. Capone, who had offered assistance to me and my family on more than several occasions during the past year and a half. That Friday evening, Olan called and told me that he was trying to put together a small private gathering for the Lowell Birmingham survivors after the mass. He was feverishly trying to get Bishop O'Malley to attend, as well. He had less than 24 hours to put it together and there were many concerns that were being worked out.

On Saturday, at 4:00 p.m. I, along with my parents, my sister Cathy and Julie, sat in a packed Saint Michael's Church to watch Bishop O'Malley celebrate mass. It was an extremely emotional time for me. I watched as the new Archbishop of Boston stood upon a church altar just feet from the sanctuary where I was abused as a child. I was filled with mixed emotions. The demons of the past and the hopes of the future were all present that day. As difficult as it was, I was glad I went. Perhaps it was that day, that I began to realize that Joe Birmingham no longer had that hold on me that had haunted my life. He was still there, but he was no longer looking down on me. I was looking down on him. I was not filled with shame anymore. I was starting to realize that it was shame on him.

As mass ended, I skirted the reception line, exited by the side entrance and walked behind Bishop O'Malley to greet Fr. Capone. I was just about to walk to my car when I realized that there were dozens of cameras pointed in my direction. I immediately realized what the effects of my simple action could be construed as. I had sidestepped the receiving line because I knew I would be meeting the Bishop privately later that evening. The cameras didn't know that and could very well consider my actions otherwise. Suddenly the headline "Lowell Victim Turns Back on O'Malley" popped in my head. I turned around, headed back in line. I was the last person to greet him and with a simple handshake, he said, "Hello again, nice to see you." I replied "Thank you for coming here. I look forward to seeing you a bit later on." It was that moment that the cameras were waiting for. They took their pictures and I walked to my car.

What has happened to too many men and women had been happening for decades and it may take decades to clean up, as well. After mass that evening, in the small living room of a modest home of a residential neighborhood, 15 people, including Archbishop O'Malley, sat and simply talked for almost three hours. That evening, five survivors and their parents talked about their pain of the past, their frustrations with the present, and their hopes for the future. We cried, we talked, and we hoped.

The Following day, Sunday, August 10, 2003 at a small ceremony in Saint Michael's Church in Lowell, surrounded by family and friends, my granddaughter Kyleigh was baptized into the Catholic faith. It was a day of hope.

20.

"You have to decide whether it's time to be a rock star or a diplomat," Bob Sherman said to Bernie and I when we were deciding on how to handle the trip to Rome several months before. Bernie had been talking about allowing a local news team to come with us and follow us around that week. It would certainly play well on television, but would it help or hinder what we were trying to do?

Bob's response was to ask us what our goal was. What was the end result that we wanted? It wasn't about being rock stars. It was about getting something accomplished. With the installation of the new Archbishop behind us and with the settlement negotiations going forward, I thought that we would be able to step back for a bit and let the mediation progress, but as the days turned into weeks, his statement would come into play and our diplomatic roles would increase almost hourly. The value of our dialogue with the Archdiocese, as well as the back channel that I had to the Vatican, took on new meaning as they were both used more and more. In some ways, Olan, Bernie and myself each had established our own channels of communication. Collectively we worked well together but we were also individuals who had our own methods. You probably couldn't find three individuals who were more different. There was a bond that was created over the previous year and a half, yet there was also a guarded trust we each used in every aspect of out lives. By the third week in August, each of those back channels would be used to the brink of exhaustion.

There was a new sheriff in town and his name was Sean O'Malley. It was clear that he was calling the shots now. He had brought in his own legal team and the mediation talks were happening almost daily. There were almost 50 attorneys involved now representing over 550 men and women with claims against the Boston Archdiocese. It's hard enough to get two lawyers to agree to what day it is, let alone 50. In early August, it was agreed that an executive committee of seven attorneys would be set up to represent the attorneys and negotiate on behalf of the plaintiffs. It was a plan that seemed reasonable.

As the days progressed, however, I could see the battle lines being drawn - even between members of the executive committee. Egos loomed. I would get daily updates on the progress of the mediation and I would listen as one day I would hear how great the mediation session would be and how close they were on coming to an agreement and the next day it would seem as though they were miles apart. After two weeks of going back and forth, I made a decision to work whatever channel I could. I didn't ask, I just worked them. The realization that this could linger on for months loomed in my mind. If there wasn't pressure from every side, even if the executive committee didn't know where the pressure was coming from, survivors would find themselves facing another year without any closure in sight.

There was no master plan. I just wanted to make sure that whatever the presented offer was, it included an option for every one of the plaintiffs to settle, regardless of what their claim was. There were some survivors that had a problem with the statute of limitations, there were others that had a problem with damages, and there were some that had claims that were conceivably weaker than others. For instance, some of the Birmingham survivors had a problem with notice, in other words the Archdiocese simply didn't know about Birmingham's abuse in the early years. My theory was that instead of some survivors getting nothing because of this, let's level the playing field a bit. I wanted a basic way of allowing all the claims to be acknowledged in the process. I knew that it was going to be a tough sell, but I felt it was worth fighting for. It meant that whatever the total amount that was going to be offered, everyone would have an option of being compensated. It also meant that some of the stronger cases would receive lesser amounts, but some of the weaker cases would not be dismissed.

It was almost impossible to get the attorneys to consider this when some days they were not even talking to each other. I worked it just the same The three of us all held our conversations with our contacts very protectively. There was no secret plan. We were each doing whatever we felt we could do to continue to push the football a little further down the field. There was no game plan though. At times it felt like we were like a football team with 3 quarterbacks, no coach, and no game book.

I had never explained to Bernie or Olan or Bob, for that matter, what my connection was. While I was in Rome, one of the officials I had met talked with me and we continued to exchange emails. We both realized that it would be the quickest way to get unfiltered messages across. We had both agreed to keep the dialogue open and to use it when it was necessary, straight forward and unfiltered. I hadn't told anyone about it and was even paranoid at times about it. There were several times when I brought a bit of information to Bob or Olan and when they would ask me how I knew it, my reply was, "Trust me, I just know."

After several emails went back and forth, and the information we both had sent was accurate, there was a mutual trust that began to grow. I had set up a separate email address which I used just for this channel. No one had access and no one else knew about it. It wasn't that I didn't trust anyone, it was just that I had to keep it in the background. This email account was simply put in the name of Fr. Smith. The only person who knew who Fr. Smith was, was my Vatican contact. I had suggested the name in humor, but my contact actually liked the idea, just in case someone from his end ever found his emails.

By the second week in August, the mediation sessions were overheating. The Archdiocese had put an offer on the table of $65 million dollars. The attorneys said that they wouldn't accept anything less than $90 million and they said it publicly. The problem now was that there was mounting pressure not to move off this $90 million dollar amount. There were problems getting the executive committee to agree how to disburse it, there were problems getting extended therapy and there were even problems about how it would be worded. They were at a standstill. Neither side was giving any ground on any issue. I had been pushing for a meeting between all the parties. I wanted Bishop O'Malley to sit down with his attorneys and I wanted each of the attorneys on the executive committee to bring one or two clients with them as well. I had asked for this several times and each time, I was told the timing wasn't right yet. I thought differently, but no one would agree. Then something happened which shocked all of us.

On Saturday August 23, former priest John Geoghan, who was in prison serving time for molesting children, was murdered. It was also a wake up call that everyone needed. On Tuesday of the following week, everyone agreed that there would be a meeting on Saturday and that the attorneys, the bishop and 12 survivors would all be there. Details would be worked out but everyone agreed that it was time. The details were the problem. I don't know who else was asked to be there, but I was asked by Bob, and I know that Olan and Bernie was asked as well. It was going to be a private meeting without press. On Wednesday, I got a call from a news reporter asking about the meeting. It hadn't even been 24 hours and someone had already leaked it to the media. We had known for months that there was a leak in the system. We all had our idea on where the leak was, but no one could prove it.

Everyone had been accused of leaking stories, even me. It even got to the point where false stories would be put out to flush out the leak. This time, proving it wasn't going to be a problem. We found out that one particular attorney on the exec committee talked to the media about it and had additionally promised "up to the minute" briefings. It seemed incredibly stupid, not to mention counter productive. Someone was trying to make this a dog and pony show and I wanted no part of it.

There was a power struggle going on in the executive committee. It was happening on a daily basis and it was happening at the cost of the survivors. I was on the phone all day long, trying to work things out. At the same time, this attorney was creating problems hourly. It was typical of the "Victory at any cost" mentality that some attorneys were publicly showing.

The next day, Thursday, August 28. It was becoming clear that one particular attorney on the executive committee realized that there was another line of communication which was at work. He was furious about it, but didn't know where it was coming from, nor who it was. I was told that he was pointing in our direction, but couldn't prove anything. At one point during mediation on that particular day, there was a physical fight between him and one of our attorneys.

By mid-afternoon, I had a decision to make, and I called Bob. He was on the same track and we all agreed to back out of the Saturday meeting. If it was going to be a circus, then I was not attending. We were playing a hand of poker and the stakes were incredibly high. Greenberg Traurig represented over half of the survivors in litigation and I believed that without our team there, the Archdiocese would back out, and this attorney would be left standing there alone with his TV cameras. It was a gamble but, it was a gamble that worked. The next morning the Archdiocese issued a statement saying that the meeting was canceled.

Though the meeting on Saturday was canceled, another round of negotiations were planned for Saturday afternoon. By Saturday evening, all sides were incredibly close. There was still a multi million dollar gap, but the framework and details had been hammered out. The Archdiocese agreed to waive the issues of notice and statute of limitations which meant that, in essence, they were accepting every claim on face value. There would be no one left out because of those issues. They had also agreed that they would continue to pay for therapy for every person. This in itself, was a huge step. We were making progress, but we weren't there yet. Another round of talks were scheduled for Sunday evening and Archbishop O'Malley had agreed to sit in on them. Another huge step.

That evening I sat down and "Fr. Smith" sent his usual email update to my Vatican contact. His reply was a request to keep him informed and he was pleased, but not surprised that O'Malley had agreed to be there Sunday evening. We exchanged a few emails regarding the importance of the coming week. There was a bishops' conference starting on the following Wednesday. I mentioned that it would be to their advantage if this was put to rest by then. When he asked what the sticking points were, from our end, I let him know and he said that they would be working on from his end, as well. I only hoped that he would continue to follow through. We were getting so close. With the tensions so high between the attorneys, I continued to work almost hourly to make sure that everyone kept an eye on the ball. The bruised egos from the fiasco of the canceled survivor meeting that morning didn't help any.

After tossing and turning all night I woke that Sunday morning. I knew that the meeting wasn't until later that afternoon, I was definitely on edge. It was crunch time. I called Olan and Bernie for updates, and at that point, neither had much to say. Whatever information they had was kept close to the vest. Everything seemed on target though, and relatively quiet. That didn't last long, however. By mid morning, I was pale and pacing the floor. I had checked my email and in the separate account that I only used for my Vatican contact, I found five emails from news reporters addressed to "Fr. Smith." I was literally drenched in sweat. Somehow, they had gotten a hold of an email that I had just sent to my Vatican contact and all five were asking "Fr. Smith" questions about it.

I started going crazy trying to figure out what was happening. I had no idea what was going on and was in a panic. How could someone possibly have hacked into an account that no one ever knew about? I ignored the emails from all of them and got ahold of my Vatican contact. With the 6-hour time difference between here and Rome, he was surprised to hear from me at that hour. I told him that I was having a problem with my email. I didn't go into details, but I did ask him to check his email account. His reply was that everything seemed okay. He was a bit nervous because of the phone call , but I told him not to worry and that I was just double-checking everything because we seemed close to getting this done.

I didn't know what was going on and I didn't share what had happened with anyone. My other personal email account was fine. Although there were no survivors allowed in the meeting that previous night, I would receive an occasional message from Bob via my email. He always carried his wireless pager with him, and if I kept my message short, he would reply via his pager. I'm sure that at times it may have seemed like a pain for him to be receiving emails on that pager. I know how close we were to getting the legal end of this behind us though, I was tired and my patience was thin. I kept sending, he kept replying. Though he never asked me questions about my contact, information I received which I thought would be helpful I passed on.

There was still my email problem. On the next morning, Monday, September 8, I found more messages in my Vatican mailbox. A half a dozen reporters had emailed "Fr. Smith" sending a message saying more or less "thanks for the joke." There was one email that concerned me. That reporter sent several emails asking for more and more information. His name was Eric Convey from the Boston Herald. His emails helped me figure out what had happened. His questions made me realize that they had only received one email from "Fr. Smith", with no information as to whom had sent it or to whom I had sent it. Luckily the email that they had received was one that hadn't given out too much detail.

After contacting a friend of mine who was extremely computer literate, I found out that somehow there was a virus on my computer at home which had taken email addresses out of one of my address book and automatically sent out that particular email. It was the email address book that I had only used for press contact when we issued press releases. I wasn't sure who had, or who had not received it.

If that was the only email that went out, there was a chance that the Vatican connection was saved. That day, I went to the public library in Lowell, sat down and created another email address which I forwarded to my Vatican contact with instructions to use it. I also continued to ignore the email from that persistent reporter, though his emails were much more telling than the one that he inadvertently received from "Fr. Smith".

The most interesting email that "Fr. Smith Received was this one.

```
Dear Father Smith :

I have a bet to make: I know who you are.

If I'm right, I find myself in a reportial di-
lemma out of which you can help me to our mu-
tual benefit.

If you are who I think you are, then I don't
want to make trouble for you. It's your busi-
ness to be anybody's source you want. I like
you. I'd even go so far as to consider us
friends. And if I'm right, then I'll drop the
matter of your identity never to be brought up
again.
```

Who are you? Well...I know where you went for recreation Sunday night. I know where you went for drinks Tuesday night. I know where -- and how you spend your weekends.

If you are who I think you are, then just say the word to me in person very soon. Say, "Eric, pls. drop the e-mail matter." And the e-mail matter will be dropped never to be raised again. Your secret will be safe.

I also hope that if you are who I think you are, you'll appreciate that I've written this message so cryptically (on the off chance I'm wrong) to protect you from an unfair accusation.

If you are who I think you are and you DON'T warn me off, then I have to let you know I plan to vigorously pursue the e-mail matter because it's: 1) Important to the settlement issue and 2) Important for another reason having to do with church politics that I'll not broach in an e-mail. I'll be chasing the story only because I'll have assumed -- having not heard from you -- that you are not the true Fr. Smith.

And in fairness I want to let you know that your e-mail left an electronic trail that my brother, a researcher in computer science at an Ivy League university, was able to sniff out for me.

Please understand, I am sending this e-mail precisely because I do not want to give you a hard time if you are who I think you are. In fact, out of friendship and respect I'm willing to give up a good story if you are who I think you are. This really is not intended as a hassle or chop-busting. Now if you're not who I think you are -- and you should have a sense of that by now -- let the games begin!

Yours Truly,

```
Eric Convey
aka "one of those 'smart' reporters"
```

Between that email, and a few others he sent, I had a clearer picture of exactly who his contact was, and where the leak had been coming from all along. At one point in the day I received an email from the server letting me know that there had been an erroneous email request. Someone had tried to get the password to that account. Several times that day, I continually changed the password on that account. When Eric talked about continuing to write a news story about the email, I engaged him in a bit of banter in the hopes of redirecting him and putting him off. I knew that later on in the evening another round of mediation talks were going on and I had to keep this from blowing wide open. The banter between Fr. Smith and Eric of the Herald continued, and another disaster was averted.

For me, that day was one of the longest days of the previous two years. By 6:00 that evening, I continued to pace the floor although I was feeling that the email problem was under control. Every now and then I'd get an email from Bob. Finally my girlfriend Julie walked in the room and said, "Will you just go out? I can't sit here and watch you pace the floor for another five hours. Go bring Olan a coffee." That was all the coaxing I needed. Arriving at Olan's, coffee in hand, I walked up his stairs and poked my head in the door. He was sitting at his computer and laughed out loud. "You couldn't take it anymore?" he said. "No, Julie threw me out," I said, laughing.

For the next two and a half hours we watched the clock tick by. Occasionally I'd check my email and a reply would be sent. At one point when the email received said something like "We're still 10 apart" and email was sent that said "tell O'Malley that the cross can also mean a plus sign." So it went, back and forth. Finally at 8:00 that Monday evening, the last email received from Bob, simply said, "It's done."

Several minutes later Olan's phone rang, it was Bob. Two minutes after that, my cell phone rang, It dawned on me that Bob had no idea that Olan and I were there together. "Gary, I want you to know that this is over. In less than two years, you have been able to change an institution that hasn't changed in over two thousand years. Congratulations, I want you to take some time and think about what you guys have accomplished over the last two years. It's over." The flood gates opened and the tears rolled. I hung up the phone, and called my brother Edward.

As I drove home that night, I was numb. I knew the next day would be hectic and I was wondering what happens next. By the time I got home, my cell phone started ringing. As I picked up the phone, I realized that I should have just turned it off. After the first reporters called me asking if I had heard anything. I said no. I knew that we were sitting on an incredible story. I knew that they all knew something was going on. I also knew that everything had to be keep under wraps till the next day so that the agreement could be sanctioned by Judge Sweeney. My phone rang again, and I for the first time in months, I turned it off. I stopped in on my parents and told them it was over, then I went to bed.

The next morning the rumors started hitting the news stations. Call after call came in and I kept silent. At 10:00 a.m., I got a call from Bob's office. They were going to be in court at 1:00 p.m. that day and Bob wanted Olan, Bernie and myself to walk the agreement with them from the law office to the courthouse. Olan and I planned on going in together and Bernie was going to meet us there. I called Olan and said we needed to leave a little earlier. When he asked why, I said, "Before we head into Boston, we have one stop to make."

After picking up Olan, I stopped at a public garden and picked a few flowers and then drove into Saint Mary's Cemetery. Eighteen months before I had knelt in the same spot and whispered a silent promise. I had also asked them to give me strength in what I was about to do. As I knelt down and kissed their gravestone, I silently said, "You didn't let me down. I hope I didn't let you down either. We made a difference." I placed the flowers down, got back in the car, looked at Olan, and said, "Now, I'm ready."

Driving into Boston that day was one of the most memorable moments of my life. We didn't talk much that morning, we both just reflected.

Arriving in Boston, I was surprised. All along I had thought that all of the attorneys on the executive committee would have had some of their clients with them on that day. It was an important day and everyone had worked so hard to get to there. As incredible as it may seem, our attorney Bob was the only one who thought enough to call some of his clients in to be there that day.

Walking though a sea of cameras, we worked our way past them up to the courthouse steps and into the courtroom. We were stunned to find out that it was going to be a closed hearing. We were not going to be allowed to sit in. As we were all shown into a private waiting area, I looked at Olan and Bernie and realized that they were as upset as I was. This was simply not right. We sat with Courtney and Diane in a second floor office area. There was tension in that room that was overflowing. We weren't just upset, we were fuming. As Olan, Bernie and I began pacing back and forth, Courtney sent Bob an email via his pager. It hadn't dawned on me that the same little wireless pager that Bob had used the night before, could be used now. When I did realize it, I began typing my own messages.

After a half hour of pacing and waiting I looked at Olan and we both knew what we were each thinking. At exactly the same moment we both headed for the door. Diane Nealon, who was waiting with us, looked surprised and asked us where we were going. "We're getting into that courtroom, they're either going to let us in, or they're going to have to physically throw us out. This is bullshit." As Olan, Bernie and I headed down the stairway to the courtroom, Bob was heading in our direction. "Where do you think you guys are heading? I thought you wanted to be in the courtroom." he said with a smile on his face. Apparently he had gotten our messages. He knew us well enough to know where we were going. He had spoken to Judge Sweeney and she had agreed to open the courtroom and agreed to have the hearing made public. We all walked down the stairs and into the courtroom.

There were what seemed like hundreds of cameras piled into the courtroom that day, all of them recording history. As we walked in and searched through the throngs of cameras and reporters for a place to sit, the only row that wasn't filled with reporters was the back row. We sat, we watched, and we listened as the Honorable Judge Constance Sweeney looked over the settlement. A butcher, a painter and a carpenter looked on as the $85 million dollar settlement was approved.

Leaving the courtroom and walking to a small park, the attorneys began to address the press which had been gathering since early that morning. As the attorneys began to speak to the huge number of reporters, I watched and my mind drifted. Visions of the past 18 months drifted in and out of my head. I began to think about everything that had happened and about all the lives that had touched us. Thoughts of all the Birmingham survivors whom I hadn't known two years before, the endless meetings with survivors, bishops and cardinals. I thought about Cardinal Law resigning, our trip to the Vatican, my family and all the lives that had intersected with mine. Over the last 18 months, so much had changed. The cameras continued filming and picture after picture was being taken. Everything that we had set out to do seemed to point to this exact moment in time. I had never known what the term surreal meant. I had heard it lots of times, but never quite understood it until that moment. It truly was surreal. I thought of men like Jamie Hogan who should have been with us that day. I also thought of Dave Lyko who had been with me at that first news conference which seemed like an eternity ago. He couldn't be there that day because his life was in chaos. Like so many survivors who came forward publicly, the strain had been too much. So many people had worked so hard and so many lives had been so harshly exposed during that past 18 months. I thought of all the sacrifices that had been made and of the tremendous cost everyone had paid. Marriages and relationships had broken up, jobs had been lost and the financial strains were mounting. I never realized that so many people would pay such a high cost simply for telling the truth. I thought of Olan, Bernie and myself, three working guys who followed their hearts. We had done it day after day, week after week, and month after month. We had started out 18 months ago with a promise to fight the good fight for the right reason. In 18 months we never wavered from that promise. I glanced over to Olan and Bernie and my eyes began to well up. Three ordinary guys who tried to make a difference. As my emotions began to overflow, Bob got up before the rows and rows of microphones and cameras and introduced the three of us. Then he asked us to speak.

" …What is important to remember is the first line of this document. This is not a settlement, it is called a memorandum of understanding. Let today stand as a message and an example to society that the way in which we all view the sexual abuse of children must change……"
…….**Olan Horne.**

"….When we all came forward two years ago, it was about protecting the children. Today, we're one step closer to making that happen….."
…...**Bernie McDaid.**

"…..This document means one thing to me and many of the men I represent here today. From this day forward, in the eyes of you people here, and in the eyes of the Archdiocese of Boston, I am no longer an alleged survivor. I am recognized, I am a survivor…. For the past 18 months the Archdiocese of Boston has been an example of everything, everything that is wrong. If the Boston Archdiocese uses this document and continues to take the steps it began taking several months ago, the Archdiocese of Boston has an opportunity and an obligation to become everything, everything that is right. …" …...**Gary Bergeron**

It was not a settlement, it was a "memorandum of understanding." Olan was right, there was a difference. The details were as unique as the name of the document. Each of the 554 survivors who had filed suit had an opportunity to take part or "opt in" to the agreement within 60 days. There had been an established range of between $ 80,000 and $ 300,000 set for each claimant. The actual amount was to be determined by an independent mediator. In addition to the monetary award, each claimant was able to receive therapy for the rest of their lives, regardless of whether they opted in or not. I had pushed for another provision, and although it was included, I received quite a bit of backlash for it. I wanted to make sure that each survivor had the opportunity to have a representative from the Archdiocese present in their mediations. And I wanted to be sure that each survivor could have their mediation recorded. These were options, not obligations. My hope was the same as it had been a year earlier when we began meeting with cardinals, bishops, and priests. I wanted them to sit through these mediations and, hopefully, begin to grasp what we had all been living through.

If you change the way a person feels about something, you can change the way they think about something, and then you can change what they do...

My reason for wanting the language in the agreement about allowing each survivor to have their mediation on record was in hopes of having an official record of these mediations which could then be given to the Vatican to be made part of Vatican record - and permanent history.

It was not the ideal solution. As Bob said that day, "This is not the ideal solution. The ideal solution would be to give these men and women back their childhood and their innocence." There were all kinds of opinions about the agreement. Some said it wasn't enough money. Others said that there needed to be stronger wording about the Church's guilt. I, personally, struggled for weeks about opting in. I was careful each time I was publicly asked about it because I knew that after the last 18 months, there were people who may have been basing their decision of opting in or out on my decision. Whenever I was asked, I made the same statement. I would decide what I would do after I spoke to my family.

My problem with the terms was that I realized that there was a finite amount which was going to be distributed. If each individual amount was based on two hours of individual mediation, then to me, that meant that for every dollar I received, someone else would receive one dollar less. That may not make sense to some, but that's exactly how it felt to me. The thought of having to tell my story again, even though I had become quite public about it, nauseated me. The difference this time, was that I was going to have to do it for money. I struggled with this for weeks. I knew that I could have opted out. I knew that our relationship with all the players had grown such that we could have asked for a separate settlement aside from the larger pool of survivors. I also knew that if I didn't opt in, I would probably have a large pool of survivors following me. What was right for me may not have been what was right for others.

Of the 554 survivors who had the option of opting in, less than 10 opted out. At 9:00 p.m., on the last possible day, I opted in to the official "memorandum of understanding."

As the individual mediations started, I was asked to sit in on several of them. The first one was Paul Chimitaro. There was also my brother Edward's. There was also a man who had signed on as a "John Doe," not a Birmingham survivor, and not even someone who our attorneys represented. Each of the three mediations were as different as the men themselves. Some had brought parents, some had asked for church representatives, some had asked me to speak on their behalf. They were emotionally-draining, they were heart-breaking, they were painful and they were unforgettable.

On Saturday, December 13, 2003, the last of the 554 cases filed against the Archdiocese of Boston were individually arbitrated. The last cases arbitrated on that day were those of Olan, Bernie and me. I had asked Bob about having Paul Finn, the chief arbitrator be my mediator. I wanted to meet the actual person who would put a value on my life. I wanted to know if he was just a guy doing a job, or if he really got what this was about.

Olan's case was mediated first. Mine was second. I had asked that Deacon Rizzutto be present from the Archdiocese. Deacon Rizzutto was the person who was in charge of the new child protection programs which were being created. I had also brought my parents, my daughter and my girlfriend Julie with me. I wanted to give them all an opportunity to speak, if they wanted to. Bernie was the last to be done. In my mediation, Bob, Courtney and Diane also sat in. I can't imagine a more emotionally-draining, yet emotionally-cleansing day in my life. I also can't imagine anyone other that Paul Finn being there. Paul was the leading arbitrator for clergy abuse cases. His company, Commonwealth Mediation, had mediated more cases of clergy abuse than any other in the country. He's a straightforward kind of guy, with a sense of compassion and an even more important sense of timely humor. At one point in my mediation, I told the story of my first marriage.

I got married the first time when I was in my early 20s. I had dropped by an old girlfriend's apartment late one night, extremely drunk. I asked her to marry me. We left that evening and got on a plane and flew to Las Vegas and were married. I woke up sober and married and called my parents to let them know that I was married, I was okay, and that I would be home that evening. It's a funny story other than one thing. When I got home, I had to call up my best friend Ron and asked him to do me a favor. I asked him to move my girlfriend out of my house. I was living with one woman and had married another. I had told that story several times in years before. I would always end up roaring with laughter. This time, I had tears in my eyes. This time I realized what I had done.

No one had heard that story before. I had not even told Bob or Courtney. At that point, Paul looked up at me, took his glasses off and said, "Gary, I've been mediating these kinds of cases for over 20 years. I have mediated more cases than any other person in the country. I have to tell you, that is the most fucked up story I have every heard. You're telling me that you told your therapist that she had a year to fix you? Do me a favor, I don't know what you're planning on doing when this is over, but please do me a favor and stay in therapy." Everyone in the room, including me, went from tears to rip roaring laughter. Paul is the only person I can think of that could have said something like that, at such an intense moment, and get away with it. Emotions ran the gambit that day and we all needed that moment of laughter.

Other mediations that I had been asked to attend which were done by other attorneys generally lasted anywhere from an hour to an hour and a half. I was asked by one survivor to attend his mediation who was represented by another law firm. That mediation lasted less than 45 minutes. The mediations for Olan, Bernie and myself started at 9:00 a.m., and ended at 6:00 p.m. that evening.

As I stood in the parking lot that evening, walking to the cars, I watched as Bob walked over to Courtney to say goodbye. I thought for a moment about the draining day we all had just gone through. As I thought about the day, I watched as Bob broke down and sobbed on Courtney's shoulder. It had been almost two years. There was no longer a question in my mind that day. Bob got it, he really began to understand all of it. He understood what we had been talking about. Not only did he understand it but he had just lived it for over eight solid hours. It was an unforgettable day.

It seemed fitting to me that of the 554 survivors, we were the last three men to be mediated. It also seemed fitting that it happened on December 13, 2003. It had been exactly one year to the day of the resignation of the Archbishop of Boston, Cardinal Bernard Law.

On Sunday December 14, 2003, the day following my mediation, I received a phone call from Bob. He had called me that Sunday morning and asked me if I would introduce him to someone that he had heard so much about.

That afternoon I went to St. Mary's cemetery in Tewksbury Massachusetts and visited the grave of my sister Terry. With me that day, was Bob Sherman.

That day, the two of us also visited the grave of Joseph Birmingham.

Epilogue.

There are many parts of this story that have been too personal to tell and there are many names that have been intentionally left out. Whenever I quoted a victim/survivor in this book without using their name, it was done because I wanted to respect their privacy. Some of the details have been altered to enable me to do just that. I have only used survivors by name who have spoken publicly about their abuse or have been quoted by name in the press. That includes my brother Edward. I have not gotten into details about Ed because he is fighting his own personal battle. Edward, like all other survivors, has his own demons to deal with and I couldn't do justice to his story. Publicly speaking out on this issue is a personal choice. I made that choice for myself, I can not make that choice for others.

Over all, the general public's response has, thankfully, been supportive. People that I know, and more often people who know me, usually deal with this issue in one of four ways. Some of them have chosen to deal with it using humor, usually because it's too uncomfortable for them to talk about. "Is it too late for me to join the law suit? I was an altar boy too and I think someone may have touched me." Though I didn't find their humor funny, I would smile and just say that they shouldn't wish that on themselves. Others would deal with it by not dealing with it at all. With some friends of mine, it has never been brought up, no mention of it, not once. Others, though, have wanted to talk about it. I've had deep discussions with people. Their usual response has been, "Good luck, you're doing the right thing." Finally, the last group represents those who have asked me, "Isn't this just about the money?" Or, "Did you get the money yet?"

My joining a lawsuit had nothing to do with money.

It had everything to do with everything else. Being a part of this lawsuit enabled all of us to bring the Archdiocese to the table. Without it, this would have been kept as the "dirty hidden secret of the Church." It would have also been kept as the "Dirty little secret of our minds."

When I met with Cardinal Law, one of things I said was that I intended to keep the issues separate. I told him, "Let's suppose that you were the vice president of a large trucking company that delivered goods all over New England. You had general managers and personal managers that handled the drivers. Over the last 30 years, some of your drivers were known to drive recklessly and caused repeated car accidents. It was widely known throughout your business that this was acceptable. Your managers would just change the routes of these drivers in the hopes that they never had another accident. Eventually, one of these drivers got into an accident so severe, that the person he hit had serious damage.

The person was damaged to the point that he couldn't work. He couldn't care for his family. That person, as a human being, should get an apology from the driver. The driver should, as a human being, feel obligated to accept responsibility. That human responsibility should extend from the driver, to the manager that perpetuated the danger by moving him from route to route and to you, because you knew of the situation, you hired the managers, you chose not to make safety an issue. The person who was injured also deserves compensation for himself and for the family he provides for. In my mind, you Cardinal Law, are that vice president, and the item you were supposed to be delivering was the word of God. Now, regardless of what the attorneys do, you have a moral responsibility to do the right thing, morally and spiritually. You should be doing the human thing here."

That is exactly how I thought of it then, and that is how I think of it now. Nothing has changed in my mind. I have been asked what kind of money I was expecting. I never actually gave it much thought. Money has never been important to me. A check at the end of this did nothing to help heal my soul. A check did not restore my father's faith. A check will never change the place where my sister and brother are buried.

It's not about the money, it never was. It was about change, it was about children, it was about the truth, and it was about time. For the record, many people have asked me if I received extra compensation because I was in the public so much. I did not. Nor did I receive the maximum award.

My "award" was simply a symbolic amount. Nor did I receive any special discount in the fees which I paid my law firm, they earned every penny they were paid. People continue to ask. It was never about the money.

This is not over for me, nor it is over for the thousands of other survivors. Some are beginning to heal, some will never heal and some are no longer here. I find strength in my family and in the friends that I have found along the journey that I started in March of 2002. If every cloud does have a silver lining, then the silver lining that surrounded the cloud that I had lived with is the incredible group of men that I have met along the way and who surround me now. Without their support and help, I would not be the person I am today. Though the Tuesday night support meeting of SOJB has disbanded, individuals from SOJB continue to help and support many survivors.

I continue to struggle on a daily basis with the demons that have been caused by those early years of abuse. I am not alone in that struggle. Today, though, I know what I'm dealing with. Something has definitely changed in me. The road was never easy, but now at least it's a bit easier. Now, I know what the goal is. I'm back on the road I was detoured from years ago at the hands of an abusive priest named Joseph Birmingham.

I have a family that's always been supportive of my decisions and supportive of me. I have been in a relationship with a wonderful caring woman who never knew about this part of my past until in 2002. Julie accepted this unknown part of me and supported me along the way. I couldn't have asked for more, I know it has not been easy. It was her suggestion that I write this book. She, like so many other women in so many other men's lives, didn't know. Nobody knew. Nobody knew because we never told them. They know now.

I have come to realize many things in these past few years. I have also come to learn many things. Things not only things about myself.

The men, who wore the Roman collar and used it to as a source of power, were just men. The men, who allowed it to happen for so many years, were just men as well. The power that lay in the collar was not as much put there by God as much as it was put there by us. Society gave them power and that power almost came at the expense of their future, almost at the expense of their children, almost. As incredible as that power became society learned that no institution is as powerful as one simple word called "Truth."

Men are men, whether we call them priests, bishops, presidents, lawyers or carpenters. The first time that I met with my attorneys, I put them on a pedestal. Now, after taking the time to know them, I've learned that they are just men, as well. All men make mistakes. All men including me. Some learn by theirs and some live by theirs. I recently received a phone call from a survivor who was asking questions about the legal process which they were about to begin. My one word of advice was for them not to look to any attorney for justice. There is no justice for what sexually-abused children go through. I believe that no one can give you justice when what you're really looking for is peace. Peace is something that you have to find in yourself. The rest will come. Though there is no way to turn back the clock, there is an opportunity to level the playing field with an attorney. Believe me though, it's a battle. In this kind of battle there are always wounded. My attorneys were my sword, shield and armor over the last two years. I was the one in the battle, though. I've learned the easiest way to battle the ugliest of truths was with integrity. I've also come to realize that even though we are all just men, nothing is impossible, as long as you are willing to do what is necessary. You don't have to walk over people to do that. You can do what is necessary while extending a hand and helping people. One person can make a difference. Minds can be changed.

There are still good days and bad days in my life. The bad days are when something happens that reminds me of the past that I wanted to forget. It can be as simple as the smell of certain burning candles that put me back in time to the altar boy lighting the candles before a mass. I tend to shrug those off, but not without acknowledging that they are real feelings. The difference is now I deal with those feelings. The bad days are when I ask myself if we really made a difference and if the last few years were worth it. I have had time to reflect and realize that I would never put anyone through what I put myself through in the last few years. I also know that I would do it all over again, without batting an eye, if there was any chance that the kids would be safer. The kids are safer.

Earlier in this book I wrote about a newspaper reporter and radio talk show host who used the term "pedophile lottery," to which I took offense. In early 2004, I received a phone call from his radio producer who asked if I would be willing to sit and do a live 30-minute radio interview with him, face to face, in his studio. Everyone who knew the story said that I would be crazy to agree. Naturally, I ignored everyone's advice and accepted. I partially thought that he must have forgotten about it. I also partially believed that I was about to go toe to toe with him. That 30-minute program ended up going live on air for two hours. As those two hours passed, it was apparent that minds had been changed. Minds which included that reporters. Those two hours proved to be the answer to the question I continue to ask myself. The answer is yes, we did make a difference.

The good days are when I receive a letter, or a stranger stops me and thanks me for coming forward. It still happens in the grocery store, at the bank, and in the airport. More times than I care to think about, someone will come up to me and say, "Don't I know you from somewhere? You look so familiar to me. I'm sure I've seen your face somewhere." I usually smile and simply say, "I must just have that kind of face."

The toll which the last two years has taken on me was incredibly high. Friendships were formed, but friendships were also lost because of this. Lives were saved, and lives were lost as well.

New programs need to be developed for survivors of this type of abuse. I've talked about some of the effects which this abuse has on survivors. One of those effects is called self medication. That's the politically correct way to describe someone who is using alcohol, drugs, love, sex or any other kind of dependency or addiction to mask the pain in their lives. Buried beneath those addictions is the pain that they are trying to hide. Those addictions are simply being used to numb the pain.

I was recently at an event where I had two men independently come up to me and reveal that they were each sexually abused as a child. They both said it while there were other people in the room. One man was a pillar in the community, the other was not. One man was sober, the other was not. Later in the evening a woman came up to me and told me how proud she was of one man, and then went on to tell me not to waste my time dealing with the other man. "He's just a drug addict and a drunk. He's just a waste of time." I witnessed another harsh lesson telling me that there is a lot of educating which needs to be done.

The normal roads of therapeutic advice for addictions is the 12 step program. I know many, many people who have been helped by this incredible program. For lots of clergy abuse survivors there's a slight problem with these programs. The 12 step programs are based on 12 steps to guide a person in recovery. The second step of this program talks about "coming to believe in a higher power". The third step talks about "making a decision to turn our lives over to God, as we understand him". For some survivors of clergy abuse, the last time they asked for help from God, as they understood him, was when they were abused. They have a different view of God than others and they have a huge problem with this kind of thinking. I know that the basis for these two steps are not necessarily God in the Catholic sense, but the years of blaming god must be addressed long before this kind of program can be helpful. I remember reading about the 12 steps and thinking "You want me to turn my life over to WHO ?.

Childhood sexual abuse is not a Catholic problem, It's a societal problem. It just doesn't happen in the Catholic Church, it just doesn't happen in Boston, and it just doesn't happen in the United States. As a society, we must all do more to address this issue. The sexual abuse scandal of the catholic church has enabled a door to begin to open. Society must be brave enough to walk through it. It's not popular, it's not pretty and it may even seem dark. Once the door is open though, light will enter and darkness will fade.

One of the questions I've been asked most often is "How do you feel now about the catholic church, do you still believe.? My spiritual life is probably stronger now, than it has ever been. I do differentiate spirituality with religion, be it organized religion or any religion. I have felt a deeper sense of faith over the last few years. It has grown to become more of a faith in mankind though than in religion. I can believe in a religion that was founded on the principals of a god who preached of feeding the hungry, sheltering the homeless and healing the sick. I cannot believe in a religion which was founded on those principals and yet sits on millions of dollars while people are still hungry, still homeless and still ill. There is something fundamentally wrong with that.

As far as how I feel about the catholic religion? I'd like to answer that with the following story. Earlier in this book I wrote about our trip to the Vatican. One of my fathers most prized possessions from that trip was the set of rosaries which was left us the day we left Rome.

My father had those rosaries in his car and from time to time I would see them hanging from his rearview mirror. Just like he did 30 years ago, I know that he would say the rosary from time to time when he was driving. Several weeks ago I was in his car with him and I noticed that they were gone and I asked him about them. My father plays cards in the morning with friends he's known for years. On a good day, he wins a dollar or two. On a bad day, he looses 75 cents. It's that kind of card game. One day a younger member of the club who had been extremely ill, came in. My father asked him how he was doing and the friend told him that his last operation didn't go well and that he had run out of options. My father got up from the table, went out to the car and came back in with the rosary. He handed it to his friend and said "Here, I got these from the Vatican, I want you to pray and I want you to use these."

My hope for the catholic church is that one day, they will be deserving of a faith so strong, and a faith so pure.

The end of this story is not yet written. This book only scratches the surface for me, and for others as well. The life I knew for over 30 years was not real, it is not the life I live today. Today my eyes are open. My heart and soul are beginning to open. The day I came forward, I began to heal. I continue to heal today.

I can assure you of this though, I'll continue to tell my story and I'll continue to have hope. I have to. I owe that to my children, my family, and most importantly, I owe that to myself.

Peace.

A report released by the Roman Catholic Church in 2004 states that as of today, over 4,550 priests in the United States have had over 11,000 allegations of abuse levied against them since 1950. Since 1985, more than 150 priests have been convicted of criminal charges relating to sexual abuse of children. In Massachusetts, alone, within in the last two years, the files of over 230 priests have been turned over to the authorities for investigation because of the sexual abuse of children

In the Spring of 2004, Boston's new archbishop Sean O'Malley published a list which announced the closings of more than 60 church parishes throughout the Boston archdiocese.

On that list was Saint Anselm's in Sudbury.

Olan Horne is now an independent arbitrator working with other clergy survivor cases across the United States to better the process of mediation.

Bernie McDaid works as an independent mediator and continues to work in his painting business.

Gary Bergeron is the executive director of The **T.R.U.S.T.** Foundation, *Treatment, Recovery & Understanding Sexual Trauma*, a non-profit foundation he established to help adult survivors of sexual abuse. It was established in April of 2004, exactly two years after he publicly came forward.

Cardinal Bernard Law, former Archbishop of Boston, was appointed as the Archpriest of St. Mary Major Basilica in Rome by Pope John Paul II on May 27th, 2004.

Bishop Robert J. Banks submitted his resignation to the Vatican and it was accepted by Pope John Paul II on November 10, 2003. His resignation was accepted as part of normal retirement.

Bishop John B. McCormack continues serving as the Bishop of Manchester, New Hampshire.

Statistics you should know.

It is estimated that there are 60 million adult survivors of childhood sexual abuse in America today.

Source: Forward, 1993

Composition of substantiated child abuse victims in 2000: 879,000 Victims 10% of those victims who were sexually abused, or 87,900 Victims.

Source: US Dept of Health and Human Services, Administration for Children & Families, National Clearinghouse on Child Abuse and Neglect, 2000

The typical child sex offender molests an average of 117 children, most of who do not report the offense. Girls are sexually abused three times more often than boys; Boys have greater risk of emotional neglect & serious injury than girls.

Source: National Institute of Mental Health, 1998

About 22% of the child sex offenders reported having been sexually abused themselves during childhood.

Source: Bureau of Justice Statistics

When sexually abused boys are not treated, society must later deal with the resulting problems, including crime, suicide, drug use and more sexual abuse. The suicide rate among sexually abused boys was up to 14 times higher.

Source: Finkelhor et al.,1990

If you would like to support The T.R.U.S.T. Foundation
Please contact:

The T.R.U.S.T. Foundation, Inc.
175 Central Street Suite 222
Lowell MA 01854

Or visit us on the world wide web at:

www.thetrustfoundation.com

The T.R.U.S.T. Foundation, Inc.
Treatment, Recovery & Understanding Sexual Trauma

"Healing Today's Generation, Protecting Tomorrows"

Resources

Alcoholics Anonymous
A.A. World Services, Inc.,
Box 459, Grand Central Station,
New York, NY 10163
Tel. (212) 870-3400.

www.aa.org/

NARCOTICS ANONYMOUS
World Service Office in Los Angeles
PO Box 9999
Van Nuys, California 91409 USA
Telephone (818) 773-9999

www.na.org/

Sexaholics Anonymous International Central Office
P.O. Box 3565
Brentwood, TN 37024
E-mail: saico@sa.org
Toll-free: (866) 424-8777

www.sa.org/

Survivors Network of those Abused by Priests
SNAP
7234 Arsenal Street
St. Louis, MO 63143
(314) 566-9790

www.snapnetwork.org/

Rape, Abuse & Incest National Network
RAINN
National 24 Hour Sexual Assault Hotline 1-800-656-HOPE

www.rainn.org/

The Survivors of Fr. Joseph Birmingham

Our Lady of Fatima, Sudbury, Massachusetts   1961-1966
Stephen Blanchette
Donald Blanchette
Edward Davin
George Costanza
John Doe 2
John Doe 4
Thomas Blanchette
James Davin
Michael McCabe
John Doe 1
John Doe 3
Jane Doe 1

Saint James, Salem, Massachusetts   1967-1970
James Hogan
Bernie McDaid
Laurent Bedard
Stevan Gauthier
James Murphy
John Doe 6
John Doe 8
John Doe 10
John Doe 12
John Morris
Robert Abraham
Robert Courtney
Russell Bergeron
John Doe 5
John Doe 7
John Doe 9
John Doe 11
John Doe 13

Saint Michael's, Lowell, Massachusetts   1970-1977
Gary Bergeron
Edward Bergeron
Mark Janeczko
Larry Sweeney
Charles Fitzpatrick
William Zielinski
Michael Barros
Richard Smith
John Doe 15
John Doe 17 Deceased
Rick Boumil Deceased
Roger Hamilton
Davie Lyko
Olan Horne
Lawrence Finn
Daniel Finnegan
William Smith
Norman Gendron
John Doe 14
John Doe 16
John Doe 18 Deceased

Saint Columbkille's, Brighton, Massachusetts   1977-1985
John Doe 19
John Doe 20

Saint Ann's, Gloucester, Massachusetts   1985-1987
Paul Ciaramitaro
Joseph Favalora
Heath Vachon